2ND EDITION
REGRESSION
BASICS

To Cathy, Jacob (who made it into the first edition) and Zoe (new to this edition), with love and appreciation.

2ND EDITION
REGRESSION
BASICS

Leo H. Kahane
California State University, East Bay

S SAGE Publications
Los Angeles • London • New Delhi • Singapore

For information:

Sage Publications, Inc.
2455 Teller Road
Thousand Oaks,
    California 91320
E-mail: order@sagepub.com

Sage Publications India Pvt. Ltd.
B 1/I 1 Mohan Cooperative
    Industrial Area
Mathura Road, New Delhi 110 044
India

Sage Publications Ltd.
1 Oliver's Yard
55 City Road
London EC1Y 1SP
United Kingdom

Sage Publications Asia-Pacific Pte. Ltd.
33 Pekin Street #02–01
Far East Square
Singapore 048763

Printed in the United States of America

Library of Congress Cataloging-in-Publication Data

Kahane, Leo H.
Regression basics / Leo H. Kahane.—2nd ed.
    p. cm.
Includes bibliographical references and index.
ISBN 978-1-4129-5126-5 (pbk.)
    1. Regression analysis. I. Title.

QA278.2.K34 2008
519.5'36—dc22   2007020636

Printed on acid-free paper.

07   08   09   10   11   10 9 8 7 6 5 4 3 2 1

Acquiring Editors:	Lisa Cuevas Shaw and Vicki Knight
Associate Editors:	Margo Crouppen and Sean Connelly
Editorial Assistant:	Lauren Habib
Production Editor:	Sarah K. Quesenberry
Copy Editor:	Liann Lech
Proofreader:	Jenifer Kooiman
Typesetter:	C&M Digitals (P) Ltd.
Indexer:	Sheila Bodell
Marketing Manager:	Stephanie Adams
Cover Designer:	Gail Buschman

Table of Contents

Preface

The motivations for writing this second edition of *Regression Basics* are the same as they were for the first edition of the book: to provide the reader with a basic, intuitive understanding of statistical regression and to illustrate how these tools can be used to study a broad scope of topics. Furthermore, it has been my experience as a teacher that students unfamiliar with the topic of regression analysis often find it difficult to pick up a standard textbook on regression analysis and begin reading it with comprehension. Thus, this book is designed to serve as a companion to more comprehensive books used in courses on regression analysis.[1] Finally, as is noted in the preface to the first edition, the prevalence and power of personal computers has brought to the fingertips of many people (some unknowingly) the ability to conduct regression analysis. However, the proper use and understanding of this powerful research tool is essential if individuals employing it want to produce meaningful results. To repeat a phrase of a colleague of mine, personal computers have done to regression analysis what microwave ovens have done to cooking: Nearly everyone has a microwave, and by popping a frozen Chicken Cordon Bleu dinner into the oven, people think they are gourmet chefs.[2] Hopefully, after reading this book, the reader will have a better understanding of what regression analysis is and how it can be creatively applied to a great variety of research questions.

As with the first edition, the techniques used in regression analysis are illustrated with a variety of examples drawn from multiple fields. An introductory-level understanding of statistics is the only prerequisite for the materials presented in this book.

---

[1] Regression analysis is the core subject in a field of study that economists call **econometrics**. In various points throughout this book, the reader is referred to books on econometrics for further information.

[2] The phrase is attributed to friend and colleague Andy Abere.

New to the Second Edition

There are several additions to this edition of the book. First, two new interesting examples have been added to the text. The first uses British data to study the factors determining regional crime rates across England and Wales. The second draws from the field of education and explores the factors affecting the performance of first-year college students. These new examples are designed to further demonstrate how regression analysis can be applied to a wide range of topics.

In addition, these new examples allow us to explore several topics new to this edition. For instance, we will begin by studying crime rates in the 42 police force areas in Britain for the year 2004.[3] Later, in Chapter 6, we will add 8 additional years' worth of data, giving us a total of nine observations for each police force area (that is, a total of $42 \times 9 = 378$ observations). This type of data set, where we have multiple observations across time for the same police force area, is an example of what is termed a **panel data set**. Panel data sets, because of their richness, are becoming more commonly used in empirical research, and for that reason, a very basic introduction on how to get the most out of panel data is provided.

In the case of the college student performance example, this example gives the reader experience in working with a rather large data set (it contains 1,200 observations). We also use this data set to see how interaction effects can be used to not only consider group effects (e.g., males vs. females), but subgroup effects as well (e.g., female athletes vs. those not female athletes) in regression analysis.

Also included in this edition is a brief discussion in Chapter 7 of the important topic of **omitted variable bias**. Finally, many of the data that appeared in the first edition's examples have been updated to include more recent figures.

The organization of this book is similar to the first edition as we start with the simplest (two-variable linear) model and work toward the more complex (multivariate) regression model in later chapters. In all chapters, the discussion will use the examples mentioned above to illustrate and motivate the ideas at hand. The data for these examples, with the exception of two examples (due to space limitations), are provided in Appendix A at the back

---

[3] The British government collects data for 42 regions called "police force areas" in England and Wales.

of this book.[4] In addition, two other examples, one that studies the factors determining a person's salary and another that studies the variables affecting automobile prices, are presented as problems in the back of each chapter. The data for these examples are also provided in Appendix A, and all data sets are available online.[5] It is *highly recommended* that the reader use the data provided in the appendix to replicate the results found in the text.[6] In doing so, the reader can have tangible, hands-on experience in *performing* linear regression analysis. Indeed, this is the ultimate goal of this book: to equip the reader with the knowledge and ability to perform and interpret the results of basic linear regression analysis. As noted, there are problems at the end of Chapters 1 through 7, and the solutions to these problems are provided in Appendix D. The reader is encouraged to work through these problems as they should help the reader have a better understanding of the concepts presented in this book. Finally, throughout the book there are words or terms that are in bolded text. These are key terms whose definition appears in the glossary at the back of this book.

Acknowledgments

I wish to thank Lisa Cuevas, Sean Connelly, Margo Crouppen, and Sarah Quesenberry for their support for this new edition. I would also like to thank Chris Aberson, Humboldt State University; Michel Dupagne, School of Communication, University of Miami; C. Y. Joanne Peng, Indiana University at Bloomington; Thomas W. Pierce, Radford University; Laura A. Wilson, School of Public Affairs, University of Baltimore; and the reviewers of the first edition, whose input and suggestions have led to numerous improvements to the text. Funding for this project, provided by the College of Business and Economics at California State University, East Bay, is also greatly appreciated.

---

[4] The data for the college student performance example and the panel data set for British crime are both too large to include in Appendix A. They are available online (see footnote 5).

[5] The data can be found (as ASCII files) at the following Web site: http://www.cbe .csueastbay.edu/~lkahane/

[6] There are many computer software programs capable of performing regression analysis. The analyses performed in this book were carried out with Microsoft Excel and/or SPSS.

1

An Introduction to the Linear Regression Model

The basic goal of regression analysis is to use data to analyze relationships. Thus, the starting point for any regression analysis is to have something to analyze. That is, we begin with some idea or hypothesis we want to test and we then gather data and analyze these data to see if our idea is verified. The purpose of this chapter is to provide the reader with several examples of the kind of research that can be done with regression analysis techniques. These examples, which are woven throughout this book, were chosen in such a way as to illustrate to the reader how regression analysis methods can be used to understand relationships across a broad range of subjects. Once we understand the basic notion of regression analysis, we then proceed to Chapter 2, where the more technical aspects of regression analysis are discussed.

Baseball Salaries

Suppose we are interested in exploring the factors that determine one's salary. There are many such factors, one of which would be the experience an individual has in his or her profession. That is, for most professions, the longer a person has been on the job, the greater is his or her salary. The logic behind this relationship is that workers learn with experience and become more productive over time. As such, employers reward workers for their increased productivity that comes with experience. But how large is the reward in relation to increased experience? That is, as a person gains another year of work experience, by how much can he or she expect his or her salary to increase from one year to the next? One method of trying to understand this relationship between salary and experience is to collect data on individuals within a profession and use a graph to visualize the relationship between the two. As an example, let's consider the occupation of professional baseball players.

Salaries earned by Major League Baseball (MLB) players have been the subject of great discussion in the media largely because in recent years, players have earned enormous amounts of money for playing the game. We may consider, then, how a player's salary is related to his experience in MLB.[1] Data on players' salaries have become public information these days, as a number of media sources publish the earnings of players as well as other information about them, such as years of MLB experience.[2] Suppose we collected a sample of data on player salary and experience and plotted these

Figure 1.1

---

[1] There has been, in fact, a great deal of empirical research done on this topic; see, for example, Scully (1974) and Zimbalist (1992).

[2] For example, data on player salaries are published annually by a number of newspapers (e.g., *USA Today*) and are also available online at various Internet sites, including Sean Lahman's "Baseball Archive," which is located at www.baseball1.com. Information on player experience and performance can also be found at this Web site and is published annually in various other sources, including Thorn and Palmer's *Total Baseball* (1997).

pairs of numbers on a graph with a player's salary on the vertical, or Y, axis and the corresponding years of experience on the horizontal, or X, axis. Figure 1.1 shows an example of how this graph may look.

Viewing Figure 1.1, we can observe that the collection of dots, each of which represents an individual player's salary and his associated experience, tend to rise as we move out along the X axis. As a means of trying to represent the general behavior of these dots, a line has been run through them that shows their general tendency to rise. As the line suggests, as a player's experience (X) increases, his pay (Y) tends to increase as well. This would seem to support our hypothesis that workers (players) are rewarded with greater salaries as their experience (years of playing in MLB) increases.

By adding a line to our Figure 1.1, we were able to capture the general relationship between salary and experience. But in doing so, it also implies a more specific assumption about the behavior of Y with respect to X. This assumption, known as the linear regression model assumption, forms the basis for regression analysis and is explained below.

Linear Regression Model Assumption

The easiest way to understand the linear regression model assumption is to illustrate it with an example. Returning to our case of baseball, suppose instead of just a sample of data, we collect data for *all* MLB players. Having such a large collection of data, we could then order our data such that players are grouped according to the number of years of MLB experience, which was our X variable for this example. Thus, all players with, say, 1 year of experience would be grouped together. All players with 2 years of experience would be in another group, and so on. We could record the salary of each player in each group, and then use this information to calculate the average salary for each group as well. This procedure is illustrated graphically in Figure 1.2a.

Viewing Figure 1.2a, we can consider players with 1 year of MLB experience who have their salary plotted on the graph above the value shown as 1 on the X axis. Notice that some players in this group have higher salaries than others, perhaps because of differences in other skills (this point is expanded on later). If we calculated the average salary of players in this group, its value would lie somewhere in the middle of these plotted points, such as the point shown with a heavier dot. Thus, this heavy dot represents the mean or average salary of players with 1 year of experience. We can carry out this same exercise for players with 2 years of MLB experience. These individuals have their salary plotted above the value of 2 on the X axis. As in the previous case, some players in this group will have higher salaries than others, and the average

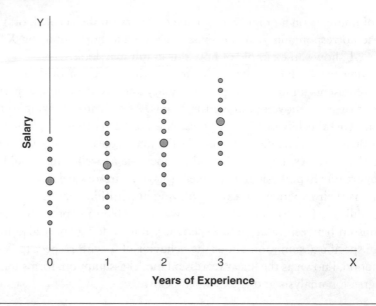

Figure 1.2a

salary for all players with 2 years of MLB experience is shown by the heavy dot above 2 on the X axis. This same kind of analysis can be done for players with 3 years of MLB experience, and the heavy dot above the value of 3 on the X axis represents the mean salary for all players in this group.

This procedure can, in fact, be done for all values of X, MLB experience, in each case calculating the mean value for salary (Y) for given values of experience (X). Given this graph, we have the following assumption: *The linear regression model assumes that the mean values of Y, for given values of X, are a linear function of X.* Or, in terms of our graph, the heavy dots (which are the mean values of Y for given values of X) lie on a line. (It should be noted that in some cases, the relationship between the mean values of Y and X may be *non*linear. Examples of nonlinear relationships are discussed in Chapter 5.) This assumption is shown graphically in Figure 1.2b, which takes Figure 1.2a and adds a line connecting the heavy dots.

This assumption can also be expressed somewhat more formally by using the following mathematical expression:

$$E(Y \mid X_i) = \alpha + \beta X_i. \tag{1.1}$$

The E in Equation 1.1 stands for "expected value" or mean, and the vertical line, $\mid$, can be read as "for given values" of X_i. (The subscript i is used

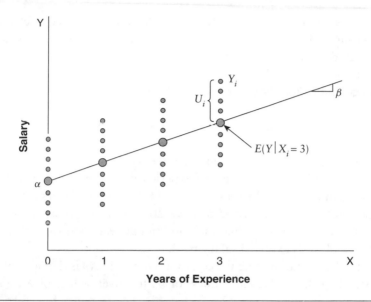

Figure 1.2b

to keep track of different values that X can take on.) The expression on the right of the equal sign, $\alpha + \beta X_i$, is simply the equation to a line. Or, putting it all together, Equation 1.1 can be read as: "the expected value of Y for given values of X_i is equal to a linear function of X_i." As for terminology, the variable Y is called the **dependent variable** because its value is said to depend on the value that X_i, which is called the **independent variable**, takes on.[3] The symbols α and β in Equation 1.1 are constants and are referred to as the intercept and slope terms, respectively (it is common in regression analysis to use Greek letters such as these). The intercept term α tells us what the expected value of Y (in our case, salary) would be for individuals who have no experience (i.e., new, or rookie, MLB players). That is, if a player has no experience, then his value for X_i is zero. Plugging in zero for X_i in Equation 1.1, we have

$$E(Y \mid X_i = 0) = \alpha + \beta(0) = \alpha. \tag{1.1a}$$

This is shown in Figure 1.2(b), where a line representing Equation 1.1 intersects the vertical axis.

---

[3] The independent variables are also sometimes referred to as "predictors" or "explanatory variables."

The slope term β in Equation 1.1 tells us how Y is expected to change for each one-unit increase in X_i. Or, in the case of MLB salaries, how salaries are expected to change for each additional year of experience. To see this, consider a player with 1 year of MLB experience. His value of X_i then is 1, and plugging this into Equation 1.1 yields

$$E(Y \mid X_i = 1) = \alpha + \beta(1) = \alpha + \beta. \qquad (1.1b)$$

Comparing Equations 1.1a and 1.1b, we see that the difference between the two is that players with 1 year of experience are expected to have β more in salary than players with no experience. In the case of players with 2 years of experience, they are expected to have 2β more in salary as compared to those with no experience. Thus each additional year's worth of experience increases a player's expected salary by β.

The implication of writing the equation with $E(Y \mid X_i)$ is that it implies the understanding that *individual* values for Y, for given values of X_i, will not likely be exactly equal to $\alpha + \beta X_i$. To see this, we can return to Figure 1.2(b) and consider player i, who has 3 years of experience in MLB and earns a salary of Y_i. Notice that for this individual player, his actual salary Y_i is greater than the mean salary for his group, shown as $E(Y \mid X_i = 3)$. The difference between the actual and expected value for Y is shown as u_i. In terms of an equation, we can write a player's actual salary as

$$Y_i = E(Y \mid X_i) + u_i. \qquad (1.2a)$$

Or, using Equation 1.1, we can rewrite the last equation by replacing $E(Y \mid X_i)$, giving us

$$Y_i = \alpha + \beta X_i + u_i. \qquad (1.2b)$$

Every dot shown in Figure 1.2b, which represents a particular player's experience and his actual salary, can be expressed in a similar way. That is, every individual player's salary can be expressed as the sum of his group's expected salary, plus the specific player's value for u_i. What does u_i represent? The term u_i, which is called the **error term**, represents all the other factors that may affect player i's salary that are not taken into account by the simple model shown in Equation 1.1. There are, in fact, numerous other factors that enter into the determination of salaries. In baseball, for example, players are rewarded for their offensive (e.g., hitting) and defensive (e.g., fielding) abilities. The fact that these other important explanatory variables are not accounted for in our model means that player salaries would not likely fall exactly on the line shown in Figure 1.2b. To further illustrate why this is the case, consider two players who are identical in all measures, including years of experience, except that one player is a better hitter. This being the case, the better hitter would likely earn a greater salary because he is worth more to a team. What this means, then, is that although a player's experience may be an important factor in explaining his salary, experience alone cannot perfectly explain a player's salary. The error term included in Equation 1.2b is said to be **stochastic**, meaning that it is a random component of a player's salary, which varies from one player to another. Thus, if we again consider our specific player i, who has $X_i = 3$ years of playing experience, we see in Figure 1.2b that the vertical distance from the heavy dot on the line to the point representing this player's salary is the positive error u_i. This means that our player i is paid more than expected, perhaps because he is a better hitter, a factor not taken into account in our simple model. In a similar way, points below the line represent players whose salaries are less than expected (i.e., they have negative errors), perhaps because they are below-average hitters.

At this point, the reader may be wondering if it is possible to build a more elaborate model that takes into account these other factors that are missing from our model and that end up in the error term u_i. To a certain extent, this can and will be done in later chapters when we build on this simple model to include other explanatory measures such as hitting and fielding. In any case, it is not likely that *all* factors can be accounted for so that the error term is driven to zero.[4] This is true for a number of reasons. First of all, there may not be data available for many important variables (e.g., a player's speed in running the bases). Second, some factors that affect a player's salary may not be measurable (e.g., leadership ability or fan appeal). All of these factors that are not accounted for in our model end up in the error term, which will vary from player to player.

For now, we will continue to work with simple models like that shown in Equation 1.2b, which are referred to as **two-variable linear regression models** (also known as **bivariate linear regression models**) because they

---

[4] There is a case when the error term will, in fact, be zero. This is when an identity has been estimated. For example, suppose we collect data for distance measurements in meters and then collect data for the same distance measurements in inches. If we tried to estimate the relationship between meters and inches, we would find a perfect linear relationship and the errors would all be zero. This is the result because 1 meter is defined to be exactly 39.37 inches, and if measurements are made carefully enough, there should be no errors. There is no reason, however, to estimate an identity because these relationships are already known.

include only an intercept (α) and one slope term (β). These simple models will serve as a starting point from which we can discuss many of the issues regarding regression analysis. Bear in mind, though, that in most cases, a two-variable model will be too simplistic for our purposes and a more complex model will be needed.

Population Data Versus Sample Data

Before moving on, we need to clarify some aspects of our data sets, namely, their size. Typically, when we consider a theory, such as MLB salaries as a function of years of experience, there is a relevant population of data. In the baseball example, it may be all MLB players, past and present. For this population of data, when we formulate a mathematical model for the behavior of a dependent variable as a function of an independent variable, we are constructing what is called the **population regression function** (PRF) because it presents a hypothesis about the behavior of the population of data. Thus, for MLB, the model shown in Equation 1.1 is a population regression function for salary determination in MLB. In most cases, however, it is not possible to collect data for the entire population, perhaps because the data do not exist or because it would be practically impossible to collect the data.[5] As such, samples of data are collected from the population and analyzed with the hope that the information contained in the sample is a good representation of how the population behaves. In order to keep the distinction between sample analysis and population analysis clear, we will use the following **sample regression function** (SRF):

$$\hat{Y}_i = a + bX_i, \tag{1.3}$$

where $\hat{Y}_i$ is the sample version of the expression $E(Y \mid X_i)$, and a and b are the sample versions of the population's α and β. Figure 1.3 shows a graph of the sample regression function. As in the case for the population, given our sample, we can represent a specific player i's salary as the sum of what our model predicts his salary to be based on his experience, plus the error in prediction, e_i:

$$Y_i = \hat{Y}_i + e_i. \tag{1.4}$$

---

[5] Suppose, for example, we were studying the eating habits of the U.S. population. It would be nearly impossible to collect information from every individual given that the U.S. population is approximately 300 million.

Figure 1.3

Using Equation 1.3, we can rewrite this expression by substituting for $\hat{Y}_i$, giving us

$$Y_i = a + bX_i + e_i. \tag{1.5}$$

Thus, Equation 1.5 shows the linear relationship between Y_i and X_i, with the term e_i representing all other factors not accounted for in our model. This equation will be used in place of Equation 1.2b, which was for the population data, and the intercept term a is a sample estimate of the population's α and the slope term b is a sample estimate of the population's β. The term e_i is the error term (also called the **residual**) for our sample regression function and is analogous to the population's error term u_i.[6] As can be seen in Figure 1.3, the residual is simply the difference between player i's actual salary, Y_i, and the salary we would predict for a player with X_i years of experience, $\hat{Y}_i$ (i.e., the point on the line above X_i).

Hopefully, the sample's intercept and slope terms closely resemble the population's parameters α and β. If this is the case, then we can be confident

---

[6] Some authors reserve the term "residual" only for the sample regression function's error term (e_i) and use "error" or "disturbance" for the population regression function's error term (u_i). We will use both residual and error terms for e_i, remembering that these refer to sample results.

that by analyzing the sample's values for these parameters, we can understand the behavior of the population.

Presidential Elections

As a second example of a regression analysis model, we can consider the topic of presidential elections. Some academics, such as Yale economist Ray C. Fair, argue that the state of the economy is an important factor in describing the voting pattern in presidential elections (Fair, 1996; see also Kramer, 1971; Stigler, 1973). As Fair (1996) puts it, "Voters hold the party in the White House responsible for the state of the economy" (p. 90).[7] For example, if the current president is a Democrat, and the economy has grown substantially over his term, then the party in power is given partial credit for that economic success and voters would then reward the Democratic presidential candidate with votes. On the other hand, if the economy has suffered from recession in the years prior to the election, the reverse is true and the incumbent party candidate suffers. This theory can be evaluated using regression analysis. We can model voting for incumbent party candidates with the following sample regression function:

$$Y_t = a + bX_t + e_t. \tag{1.6}$$

In Equation 1.6, we now have the dependent variable, Y_t, representing the percentage of the two-party votes received by the candidate running for president who belongs to the same party as the incumbent (note that this could be the incumbent himself if he is running for a second term, such as Ronald Reagan, who ran for reelection in 1984, and Bill Clinton, who ran for reelection in 1996). The variable X_t now represents the economy's real percent growth rate over some specified period prior to the election at hand.[8] In this case, the error term, e_t, represents other factors not taken into account, such as the inflation rate prior to the election and perhaps other, immeasurable factors such as charisma of the candidate. Finally, note that in this case, we use the subscript t (as opposed to i used for the baseball example) to distinguish individual cases because now we are considering results of elections at different points in time. Graphically, this model would look similar to the one

---

[7] Indeed, Bill Clinton's 1992 presidential campaign used the phrase, "It's the economy, stupid!"

[8] The "real" growth rate is a term economists use to refer to the economy's growth rate adjusted for inflation.

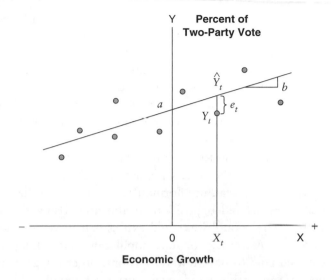

Figure 1.4

shown in Figure 1.3, except that the values for X_t, the real growth rate of the economy, can be negative. This is shown in Figure 1.4, which has a positive and negative range for X_t.

The value of a in this case would be the expected share of the two-party presidential vote received by the incumbent party candidate when the economy experienced no real growth (i.e., when $X_t = 0$). As for b, this would represent the increase (decrease) in the share of votes the incumbent party candidate would receive for a 1 percentage point increase (decrease) in the real growth rate. As in the case of baseball salaries, the actual data for Y_t would not likely fall exactly on the line, but would be "speckled" above and below the line as is shown in Figure 1.4. The vertical distance from these observations to the line shown would be the error term e_t, which, again, represents other factors affecting the share of the two-party votes the incumbent candidate received that are not taken into account in our simple model. As seen in Figure 1.4, for the given value X_t, the actual value of Y_t lies below the value predicted by the regression line, $\hat{Y}_t$. Thus, the associated error term e_t, which is equal to the actual value of Y_t minus its predicted value, would be negative.

Abortion Rates

Our third example of a regression analysis model deals with the socially sensitive issue of abortion. Abortion rates (the number of abortions performed per 1,000 women of childbearing age) differ, sometimes greatly, across the United States. Researchers have been interested in discovering what factors play a role in explaining why, in some states, the abortion rate may be relatively high, whereas in others it is relatively low. There are, of course, many factors that affect the abortion rate across states, but one of them would likely be the moral views of the state's residents. Other things being equal, the greater the moral aversion to abortion, the fewer would be expected to be performed.[9] The moral position that residents of a state hold with regard to abortion is difficult to measure. One way to measure it is to consider what percentage of the state's population belongs to the Catholic, Southern Baptist, Evangelical, or Mormon faiths. These are the four main religions that have a stated opposition to abortion. Using this measure, which we will call "religion," we would expect that if we compare states, those with a greater percentage of state population that belongs to one of these faiths would tend to have fewer abortions, other things being equal. This relationship can be expressed, again, using an equation like we have seen in our previous examples. In this case, Y_i would be the abortion rate in state i, and X_i would be the measure for "religion," equal to the percentage of a state's population that belongs to one of the four faiths mentioned above. In this case, the slope term, β, would be negative, indicating that states with a relatively large value for "religion" would tend to have a lower abortion rate, all else being equal. That is, we would have the following sample regression equation:

$$Y_i = a + bX_i + e_i. \tag{1.7}$$

In this case, the error term e_i would capture other factors omitted, such as income and legal differences across the 50 U.S. states. It should be noted that in this example, the subscript i is used to keep track of values for Y and X for states (not individuals, as was the case in the baseball example). Graphically, we would have something like Figure 1.5. As in the other examples, the vertical distance from a given point on the graph (e.g., Y_i, X_i) to the line would represent the error term e_i. In the example shown in Figure 1.5, the actual observation for the dependent variable, Y_i, lies below the predicted one, $\hat{Y}_i$, for the given value of the independent variable, X_i, and so the error term would be negative.

---

[9] Previous research on the determinants of abortion rates can be found in Medoff (1988) and Kahane (2000).

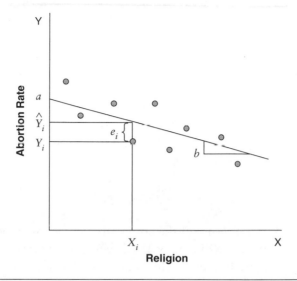

Figure 1.5

As for the intercept, a, it requires some additional discussion in this example. Technically speaking, the intercept represents the abortion rate that we would expect in the case where the variable religion is zero (i.e., $X_i = 0$). However, intuition would tell us that it is clearly not the case that the variable religion would take on the value of zero in any state, as this would require that *none* of a state's residents belonged to the Catholic, Southern Baptist, Evangelical, or Mormon faiths. As we can see in Appendix A, which presents the data for the variable religion, our intuition is correct in that the value of religion is not, in fact, zero in any state. What this means for our model shown in Equation 1.7 is that for this example, the intercept has no sensible interpretation. That is, the intercept term is technically necessary to "anchor" the line in the graph, but beyond that it is meaningless. (This fact that the intercept may have no meaningful interpretation is often the case in regression model analyses.)

As for the value for the slope term, b, in this case it represents the predicted change in the abortion rate as the measure for religion increases by 1 percentage point.

Crime Rates

Our next example deals with the issue of crime. Much of the modern theory on the determinants of crime can be traced back to the seminal 1968 work by economist and Nobel Laureate Gary Becker.[10] Becker viewed crime as a rational choice that individuals make after considering the costs and benefits of legal work versus criminal activities. As part of the computation of the benefits of legal work, individuals must consider the chances that legal work can indeed be obtained. A measure that can be used to gauge the ability that legal work may be available is the unemployment rate. Other things being the same, the higher the unemployment rate, the lower the chances are that legal work is available to the individual and hence, the greater the likelihood that the individual would pursue criminal activities. In terms of a sample regression equation, we would have

$$Y_i = a + bX_i + e_i, \tag{1.8}$$

where Y_i would be a measure of the crime rate (e.g., total crimes per 1,000 people) in location i and X_i would be the unemployment rate (in percent) in location i. In this case, the intercept term, a, would be the expected crime rate in the case where the unemployment rate, X_i, is zero. The slope term, b, would then represent the predicted change in the crime rate (e.g., change in the number of crimes per 1,000 people) for a 1 percentage point increase in the unemployment rate (see Figure 1.6).

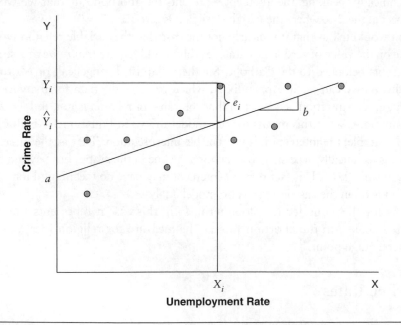

Figure 1.6

---

[10] See Freeman (1999) for a survey of research on the economics of crime.

In this case, the error term, e_i, represents other factors that may affect crime rates (e.g., police presence) that are not taken into account by the model.

Thus, we have four interesting examples that we can use to develop the basics of linear regression analysis. The graphs presented above for our four models show a line drawn through a scatter of points. At this point, two questions arise. First, what is the ultimate use of knowing such a line? The answer to this question is that, if we know this line, it can be used to predict values of the dependent variable, for given values of independent variables. For example, considering our model of MLB baseball salaries, if we know the values (i.e., the numbers) of the intercept, a, and the slope term, b, we could then use the line defined by them to predict a player's salary given his experience. This could be useful, for example, if a player is interested in knowing what his salary is expected to be as his experience increases. We will see in the following chapter how this kind of prediction can be accomplished. Of course, we must keep in mind that the predictions we make may not be entirely accurate because other factors that may be important in explaining a player's salary are not being considered. As we have already discussed, these excluded factors end up in the error term, e_i.

The second question that arises is, how can we find values for a and b so that the defined line "best fits" the scatter of points, which are our actual data? Recall that in our three examples of sample regression functions, we simply added a line to our graphs in such a way that the line seemed to fit the data well. This visual method, however, is imprecise, and there are better methods for accomplishing this task. This question of how we find the best fitting line to the data is, in fact, the subject of the next chapter.

Types of Data Sets

Finally, before moving on to the next chapter, we must say a few things about the various types of data sets. There are essentially three general varieties: **cross-sectional**, **time series**, and **pooled**. A cross-sectional data set fixes a point in time and looks across space. Our baseball example is a cross section because we collect data on salary and experience for a particular year and consider how salaries differ across players. In addition, our abortion example is a cross section because we consider a single point in time and look across the 50 states. A time series follows variables across time, while holding space constant. Thus, our presidential election example is a time series because we follow the breakdown of votes from one election to another. A pooled data set is a combination of both. For example, if we followed baseball salaries paid to all players *and* from year to year, we would have a pooled data set. In this case, if we follow the *same* set of players from year to year, then this represents what is called a **panel data set**.[11] Panel data sets are very rich data sets, but they often require special treatment. We consider some simple methods of how to work with panel sets in Chapter 6.[12]

PROBLEMS

1.1 Consider the following model:

$$Y_i = \alpha + \beta X_i + u_i,$$

where: Y_i is individual i's wage

X_i is individual i's years of education

a. What is the interpretation of α? Do you expect it to be positive or negative?

b. What is the interpretation of β? Do you expect it to be positive or negative?

c. What does the error term, u_i, capture in this case?

1.2 Consider the model for presidential elections shown in Equation 1.6, which shows the percentage of two-party votes received by the incumbent party candidate. What other factors might be important in determining Y_t besides the real growth rate?

1.3 There has been considerable research into the relevance of SAT scores as predictors of students' performance in college (e.g., see the research by Bridgeman, McCamley, & Ervin, 2000; Camara & Echternacht, 2000; and Rothstein, 2004). We can consider this issue with the following model:

$$Y_i = \alpha + \beta X_i + u_i,$$

where: Y_i is individual i's freshman college grade point average (GPA)

X_i is individual i's SAT score

a. What is the interpretation of β? Do you expect it to be positive or negative?

b. What does the error term, u_i, capture in this case?

---

[11] If we took a different sample of players each year for a number of years, this would be termed a "pooled cross-sectional" data set.

[12] Greene (2003) and Wooldridge (2002) provide advanced discussions on the handling of pooled data sets.

2

The Least-Squares Estimation Method

Fitting Lines to Data

In the various examples discussed in the previous chapter, lines were drawn in such a way as to best fit the data at hand. The question arises as to how we find the equation to such a line. This is the point of linear regression analysis: fitting lines to data. We can consider a number of approaches. For example, we could consider simply using a ruler and drawing a line that seems to fit the data best. This method, however, is not advisable because it is not a precise approach, and in some cases, the scatter of points does not suggest to the naked eye an obvious location for the line. A more systematic approach is needed.

One possibility would be to find a line that would minimize the sum of the error terms. This approach, however, is flawed. To see this, suppose we have a very small sample of just four data points, which are plotted in Figure 2.1.

The line shown seems to fit the data well using the criterion that the sum of the errors is minimized. In fact, if we calculate $e_1 + e_2 + e_3 + e_4$, it would come to approximately zero as the small positive errors (e_2 and e_4) would cancel with the small negative errors (e_1 and e_3), indicating a good fit. Unfortunately, under this criterion, the line shown in Figure 2.2 would serve just as well.

As in the previous case, the sum of the errors here is also approximately zero as the small positive error cancels with the small negative error (e_3 with e_2) and the large positive error cancels with the large negative error (e_4 with e_1). Thus, we have two very different lines that meet our criterion of minimizing the sum of the

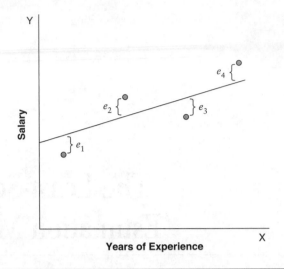

Figure 2.1

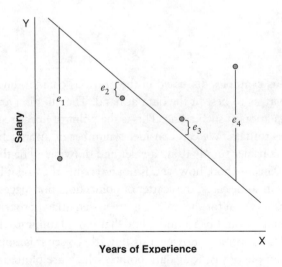

Figure 2.2

errors equally as well. In fact, there are any number of such lines that, when drawn, would give us a zero sum of errors. Obviously, this criterion will not do.

   The problem with the last method considered is the cancellation of positive errors with negative errors. A way of avoiding this problem would be to find a line such that the sum of the *squared* errors is minimized.[1] That is,

---

[1] We could consider minimizing the sum of the absolute value of the errors, but such a method is computationally difficult.

our task is to find a line determined by a and b such that the sum of the squared errors, $e_1^2 + e_2^2 + e_3^2 + e_4^2$, is as small as possible. This, in fact, is called the method of least-squares, sometimes called **ordinary least-squares (OLS)** so as to distinguish it from other specialized least-squares methods.[2] We can represent this task of minimizing the sum of squared errors mathematically by first noting that the error term e_i can be rewritten using Equation 1.5 in the following way:

$$e_i = Y_i - (a + bX_i). \tag{2.1a}$$

Thus, the error is decomposed into the difference between the observed value Y_i and the predicted value $(a + bX_i)$. Or, getting rid of the parentheses, we have

$$e_i = Y_i - a - bX_i. \tag{2.1b}$$

The OLS method finds a value for a and b that minimizes the sum of the squared errors; thus, we take the errors shown in Equation 2.1b, square them, and then take the sum over all observations in our sample (the sample size indicated by n). Doing this, we have

$$\sum_{i=1}^{n} e_i^2 = \sum_{i=1}^{n} (Y_i - a - bX_i)^2. \tag{2.2}$$

At this point, our task now becomes a calculus problem. We have an equation (Equation 2.2) that we want to minimize with respect to two parameters we can choose, a and b. To carry out this task, we use differential calculus and take the partial derivative of Equation 2.2 with respect to a and set it equal to zero, then do the same with respect to b. We then end up with two equations (the two partial derivatives) with two unknowns (a and b). The last step is to solve this system of equations simultaneously for a and b. Leaving out the details, what we end up with is the following formulas for b and a[3]:

$$b = \frac{\sum_{i=1}^{n} (X_i - \bar{X})(Y_i - \bar{Y})}{\sum_{i-1}^{n} (X_i - \bar{X})^2} \tag{2.3a}$$

---

[2] There are other, advanced methods, such as "two-stage least-squares" or "weighted least-squares," that are used in certain circumstances. These methods are beyond the scope of this book. See, for example, Gujarati (2003) or Wooldridge (2006) for a discussion of these techniques and others.

[3] For the full details of solving of the OLS estimators, see Gujarati (2003).

and

$$a = \bar{Y} - b\,\bar{X}, \qquad (2.3b)$$

where, in both Equations 2.3a and 2.3b, the bar above the variable stands for the mean of that variable (e.g., the sum of all X_i divided by the sample size, n). Thus, given values for X_i and Y_i, we can use these data to calculate a and b.

As an illustration, we can go back to our baseball example. Using the data on salary (Y_i) and years of MLB experience (X_i) provided in Table A1 in Appendix A, we can construct Table 2.1, which has the components needed for computing b and a.[4]

Viewing Table 2.1, we see that the sum at the bottom of the sixth column is the value needed for the numerator in Equation 2.3a. And the sum at the bottom of the fifth column is the value needed for the denominator. Plugging these values into our equation for b (and rounding to three decimal places), we have the following:

$$b = \frac{500.851}{763.500} = 0.656. \qquad (2.4a)$$

As for the intercept term, a, dividing the sums at the bottom of the first and second column by our sample size, $n = 32$, we find

$$\bar{X} = \frac{\sum_{i=1}^{n} X_i}{n} = \frac{284}{32} = 8.875$$

and

$$\bar{Y} = \frac{\sum_{i=1}^{n} Y_i}{n} = \frac{210.795}{32} = 6.587.$$

Using these values for the mean of X and Y, along with the value for b found in Equation 2.4a, we have for our intercept (again, rounding to three decimal places):

$$a = 6.587 - (0.656 \times 8.875) = 0.765. \qquad (2.4b)$$

---

[4] Our analysis will consider only nonpitchers because pitchers are evaluated with very different statistical measures.

Table 2.1

X_i	Y_i	$X_i-\bar{X}$	$Y_i-\bar{Y}$	$(X_i-\bar{X})^2$	$(X_i-\bar{X})(Y_i-\bar{Y})$
10	13.600	1.125	7.013	1.266	7.890
12	10.600	3.125	4.013	9.766	12.541
18	4.000	9.125	−2.587	83.266	−23.606
9	3.750	0.125	−2.837	0.016	−0.355
4	0.800	−4.875	−5.787	23.766	28.212
8	9.500	−0.875	2.913	0.766	−2.549
3	0.354	−5.875	−6.233	34.516	36.617
5	3.333	−3.875	−3.254	15.016	12.608
3	0.425	−5.875	−6.162	34.516	36.202
10	6.000	1.125	−0.587	1.266	−0.660
5	4.200	−3.875	−2.387	15.016	9.250
17	10.465	8.125	3.878	66.016	31.506
10	13.500	1.125	6.913	1.266	7.777
7	4.000	−1.875	−2.587	3.516	4.851
11	20.600	2.125	14.013	4.516	29.778
13	12.333	4.125	5.746	17.016	23.704
9	12.000	0.125	5.413	0.016	0.677
2	0.340	−6.875	−6.247	47.266	42.948
6	0.850	−2.875	−5.737	8.266	16.494
14	9.000	5.125	2.413	26.266	12.367
4	1.000	−4.875	−5.587	23.766	27.237
6	0.700	−2.875	−5.887	8.266	16.925
5	0.690	−3.875	−5.897	15.016	22.851
15	10.616	6.125	4.029	37.516	24.680
6	5.000	−2.875	−1.587	8.266	4.563
18	10.756	9.125	4.169	83.266	38.044
5	12.500	−3.875	5.913	15.016	−22.913
11	11.000	2.125	4.413	4.516	9.378
2	0.400	−6.875	−6.187	47.266	42.536
15	14.167	6.125	7.580	37.516	46.425
17	3.640	8.125	−2.947	66.016	−23.944
4	0.675	−4.875	−5.912	23.766	28.821
Sums: 284	210.795			763.500	500.851

Thus, putting it all together, we have for the OLS regression line

$$\hat{Y}_i = 0.765 + 0.656\ X_i, \tag{2.5a}$$

where the "hat" above Y_i denotes the predicted salary for player i. As an alternative way of reporting results, we can replace Y and X with their variable names:

$$\widehat{SALARY}_i = 0.765 + 0.656\ (YEARS_i). \tag{2.5b}$$

Interpreting these results, the intercept term, 0.765, is the predicted salary (in millions of dollars) for a player who has no MLB experience (i.e., a rookie). The value of b, 0.656, represents the added salary that a player earns, on average, for each additional year he plays in the MLB. Or, an additional year of experience adds on average about \$656,000 to salary, all else equal. Thus, a player who has 5 years of MLB experience is expected to earn

$$\widehat{SALARY}_i = 0.765 + 0.656\ (5) = 4.045. \tag{2.5c}$$

Comparing this predicted salary to MLB player David Eckstein, who has 5 years of experience (see Table A1), we see that his actual salary for the 2006 season was \$3.333 million, which is \$712,000 *less* than what his predicted salary would be according to Equation 2.5c. On the other hand, if we consider the salary for 5-year player Jay Gibbons, his actual salary was \$4.2 million, or \$155,000 *more* than predicted. The difference between these actual figures and the predicted ones is captured by the error term, e_i. Essentially, what we learn from this result is that years of experience may be important, but there are other factors in addition to experience that determine a player's salary.[5] Figure 2.3 shows the regression line (Equation 2.5a) plotted with the actual data for player salaries and years of experience. The fact that the plotted points do not fall precisely on the regression line illustrates this last point.

Applying the same least-squares method to our example for U.S. presidential elections, we can estimate the relationship between economic growth and presidential voting patterns. Using the data shown in Table A3 in Appendix A, we could plug the values for the dependent variable (the column of data labeled with *VOTES*) for Y_t and the values for the independent variable (the column of data labeled with *GROWTH*) for X_t into Equations 2.3a and 2.3b to determine the value for the slope, b, and the intercept, a, for the sample regression function shown in Equation 1.6. Although it was instructive

---

[5] Explaining part of the discrepancy between Eckstein's and Gibbons's salaries is the fact that Gibbons has a better career slugging average of 46.6 (through the 2005 season) compared to Eckstein's career slugging average of 36.2.

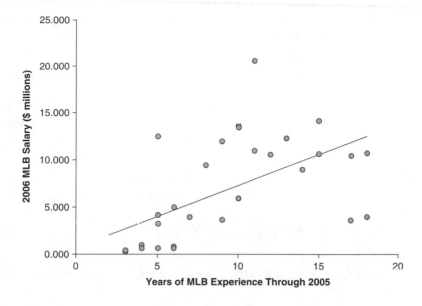

Figure 2.3

to do this calculation by hand in the previous example on baseball, these calculations can be performed more easily by using computer programs designed to carry out these tasks. There are *many* such programs that are capable of calculating sample regression lines.[6] Perhaps two of the most prevalent and commonly used programs are Microsoft Excel and SPSS. In order to give the reader experience in reading and interpreting regression analysis output from these programs, the examples presented from this point forward will use these two programs (on an alternating basis) to carry our calculations.[7]

Using Excel, we can input the data presented in Table A3 for the column labeled *VOTES* and the column labeled *GROWTH* into a spreadsheet. As shown at the bottom of Table A3, the variable *VOTES* is defined to be the percentage of the two-party vote received by the incumbent party candidate. This is our dependent variable Y_t in Equation 1.6. The data for *GROWTH* are the growth

---

[6] For example, some popular programs include SAS, TSP, EVIEWS, MINITAB, SHAZAM, and STATA.

[7] Microsoft Excel is a relatively easy program to use and performs the basic calculations we will need for this book. SPSS is specifically designed to do statistical calculations and is capable of carrying out more sophisticated analyses. Appendix B provides some basic instruction on how to perform regression analysis using Excel and SPSS. The reader is referred to the instruction manual and tutorial that accompany these programs for greater details on how to use these programs. Additionally, Einspruch (2005) gives detailed instruction on how to use SPSS.

rates of real gross domestic product (GDP) over the three quarters prior to the election.[8] This is our independent variable X_t shown in Equation 1.6.

Once the data have been input, we can then follow the steps for calculating the least-squares regression values for a and b. Doing so yields the results shown in Table 2.2.[9]

The first entry, "Observations," simply reports that we have 23 observations in our sample. Next, we see a column headed "Coefficients" and two rows labeled "Intercept" and "$GROWTH$." The entries are shown as 51.065 and 0.880 (rounding to three decimal places). These are the least-squares values for the intercept term, a, and the slope term, b (respectively), for Equation 1.6. Using these results, we can now write the predicted equation as

$$\hat{Y}_t = 51.065 + 0.880 \, X_t. \tag{2.6a}$$

Once again, we may reexpress our results using variable names in place of Y and X:

$$\widehat{VOTES}_t = 51.065 + 0.880 \, (GROWTH_t). \tag{2.6b}$$

This equation tells us that if the growth rate were zero over the three quarters prior to the election, then the incumbent party candidate is expected to receive approximately 51.065% of the two-party vote. In addition, for every 1 percentage point increase of real GDP over the three quarters prior to the election, the incumbent party candidate is expected to gain approximately 0.880 percentage points of the two-party vote. This, of course, works in the other direction as well. That is, for every 1 percentage point decline in the economy's real GDP, the incumbent party's candidate is expected to suffer a 0.880 percentage point loss of the two-party vote.

The last part of Table 2.2 shows predicted values and the associated residuals for 23 elections covered in our sample of data. The column headed "Predicted $VOTE$" shows the percentage of the two-party vote the incumbent party candidate was predicted to receive according to Equation 2.6b,

---

[8] The U.S. GDP is a measure used by economists to track the growth of the U.S. economy. It is defined as the total market value of all final goods and services produced inside the United States over a specified period of time.

[9] The results presented in Table 2.2 are an edited version of the actual output Excel produces. Much of the actual output the program produces was excluded in this example to make things easier for the reader. The full output will be presented in later examples as we progress.

Table 2.2

SUMMARY OUTPUT		
Observations	23	
	Coefficients	
Intercept	51.065	
GROWTH	0.880	
RESIDUAL OUTPUT		
Observation	Predicted VOTE	Residuals
1	53.000	−1.300
2	40.947	−4.847
3	47.634	10.566
4	55.112	3.688
5	38.220	2.580
6	61.358	1.142
7	54.232	0.768
8	54.936	−1.136
9	53.616	−1.216
10	51.769	−7.169
11	49.833	7.967
12	51.417	−1.517
13	55.552	5.748
14	55.552	−5.952
15	56.432	5.368
16	54.584	−5.684
17	47.898	−3.198
18	55.992	3.208
19	53.088	0.812
20	53.000	−6.500
21	53.440	1.260
22	52.472	−2.172
23	53.616	−2.416

plugging in the actual value of *GROWTH*. That is, for Observation 1 (the 1916 presidential election), the growth rate reported for that year is 2.2 (from Table A3). If we plug this value into Equation 2.6b, we would have the following predicted value for that election:

$$\widehat{VOTES}_1 = 51.065 + 0.880\,(2.2) = 53.000. \qquad (2.6c)$$

However, the actual value for that year was 51.7. The fact that our predicted value is not equal to the actual value again represents the fact that our very simple model is not capable of explaining the entire behavior of *VOTES*. The difference between actual values and the predicted values is what is shown in Table 2.2 as the "Residuals"—the "*e*" in our Equation 1.6. Thus, for the first observation, we have (rounding to one decimal place):

$$e_1 = VOTES_1 - \widehat{VOTES}_1 = 51.7 - 53.0 = -1.3. \qquad (2.7)$$

This result shows that our model overpredicted the actual percentage of the two-party vote received by the incumbent party candidate (Woodrow Wilson, in this case) by 1.3 percentage points. The residuals are calculated for each election in our sample and are reported in Table 2.2.

By plotting the regression line shown in Equation 2.6a, along with the actual values for Y_t and X_t, we have Figure 2.4.[10] As can be seen, the actual

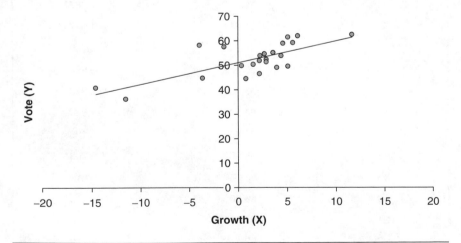

Figure 2.4

---

[10] This graph was created using the Excel program.

values do not fall precisely on the regression line, but are speckled above and below it. Again, this illustrates the imperfect relationship between Y_t and X_t, with the vertical distance from any dot to the regression line equaling the error in prediction.

Turning now to our example of state abortion rates, we can use the same tool of least-squares to estimate the sample regression function shown in Equation 1.7. Recall that for this model, the dependent variable, Y_i, is the abortion rate for state i, and the independent variable, X_i, is the measure for the variable called *RELIGION*. In this case, we will use the program SPSS to calculate the least-squares values for a and b in Equation 1.7. In doing so, we obtain the output shown in Table 2.3.[11]

Table 2.3

Coefficients[a]

Model		Unstandardized Coefficients		Standardized Coefficients	t	Sig.
		B	Std. Error	Beta		
1	(Constant)	23.825	3.979		5.988	.000
	RELIGION	−.099	.114	−.125	−.874	.386

a. Dependent Variable: ABORTION

We see in Table 2.3, under the "Unstandardized Coefficients" heading, that the intercept, or "constant" term, is 23.825. This is our value for a in Equation 1.7. The value for b is the coefficient for *RELIGION* and is shown to be −0.099. Using these values for a and b, we have the following sample regression function (rounded to three decimal places):

$$\hat{Y}_i = 23.825 - 0.099\, X_i, \tag{2.8a}$$

or, using variable labels,

$$\widehat{ABORTION}_i = 23.825 - 0.099\, (RELIGION_i). \tag{2.8b}$$

This equation for the sample regression function is plotted in Figure 2.5[12] along with the actual data.

---

[11] As in the previous example using Excel, the actual output produced by SPSS was edited so as to include only the results relevant for our discussion at hand. The full SPSS output will be presented in later chapters.

[12] Figure 2.5 was produced by the SPSS program.

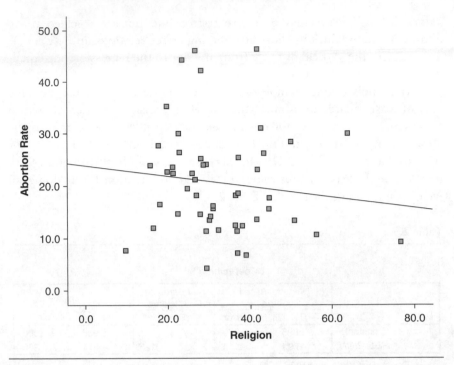

Figure 2.5

The squares representing actual observations are not closely speckled around the regression line, indicating that although X_i (religion) may explain some of the behavior of Y_i (the abortion rate), a great deal has been left unexplained. As we have discussed, this unexplained portion is captured by the error term e_i and is equal to the vertical distance from the dots shown to the regression line.

This example illustrates the point made in Chapter 1 that in many cases, our simple bivariate model will not be sufficient for explaining the behavior of a dependent variable, and a multivariate regression model will be needed. The subject of multivariate models will be taken up later in Chapter 4.

We now move to our crime example. Using data for 42 British police force areas for 2004, we can estimate the model presented in Equation 1.8 using our OLS method. The results, produced by SPSS, are shown in Table 2.4.

Using the output from Table 2.4, we can write the estimated sample regression function as

$$\hat{Y}_i = 51.772 + 10.218X_i, \qquad (2.9a)$$

Table 2.4

Coefficients[a]

Model		Unstandardized Coefficients		Standardized Coefficients		
		B	Std. Error	Beta	t	Sig.
1	(Constant)	51.772	5.698		9.085	.000
	UNEM	10.218	1.829	.662	5.588	.000

a. Dependent Variable: CRIME

or, alternatively,

$$\widehat{CRIME}_i = 51.772 + 10.218 \ (UNEM_i). \qquad (2.9b)$$

Recalling that CRIME is measured as the number of recorded crimes per 1,000 people, and UNEM is the male employment rate in percentages (both for the year 2004)[13], then interpretation of Equation 2.9b is straightforward. If UNEM were zero, then the estimated constant term tells us we would expect about 51.772 crimes per 1,000 people, all else being equal. The estimated coefficient to UNEM tells us that, all else being equal, a 1 percentage point increase in the male unemployment rate tends to increase crime by approximately 10.218 crimes per 1,000 people. In order to predict crime rates using Equation 2.9b, we can simply plug in a value for UNEM and compute the predicted value for CRIME. For example, we can consider the police force area "Avon & Somerset" (Avon for short) for 2004. The reported unemployment rate was 1.888%. Using this value in Equation 2.9b, we find

$$\widehat{CRIME}_{Avon} = 51.772 + 10.218 \ (1.888) = 71.064. \qquad (2.9b)$$

The actual reported crime rate for Avon in 2004, however, was 85.941 crimes per 1,000 people. Computing our error in prediction for 2004, we have

$$e_{Avon} = CRIME_{Avon} - \widehat{CRIME}_{Avon} = 85.941 - 71.064 = 14.877. \qquad (2.10)$$

In this case, we observe a rather large, positive residual. This result illustrates the fact that our model for crime shown in Equation 1.8 is much too simplistic and that many other factors (not included in the model) are important in determining crime rates. Figure 2.6a graphs the sample regression

---

[13] The male unemployment rate is used here because the vast majority of all crimes are committed by males in their late teens to early twenties.

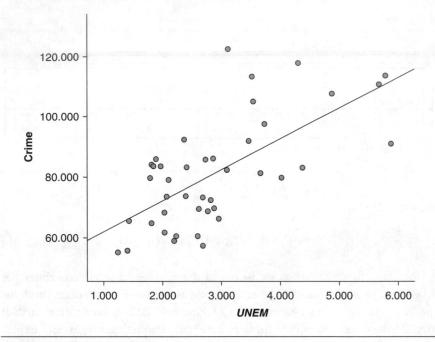

Figure 2.6a

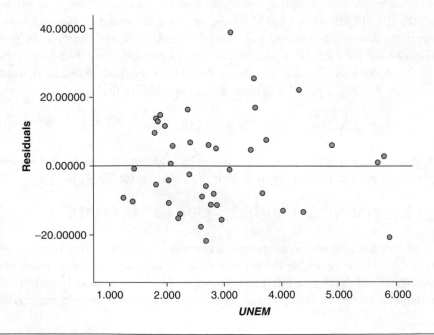

Figure 2.6b

function for Equation 2.9b and the actual values for 2004 crimes per 1,000 people and unemployment rates.

As one can see, the dots are widely spread around the sample regression function, further illustrating the limited ability of unemployment rates alone to explain the crime rates per 1,000 people across the 42 police force areas. Another visual method of showing the poor fit of the sample regression function is to plot the residuals against the unemployment rates, as shown in Figure 2.6b. A horizontal line corresponding with zero on the vertical axis is plotted along with the residuals. We can see that the residuals are fairly evenly spread above and below zero, but at the same time, the spread is quite wide. Again, this tells us that, although the unemployment rate may be able to partly explain crime rates, much is left unexplained.[14]

Regression Model Assumptions and the Properties of OLS

The OLS method of estimating regression lines is clearly a powerful research tool. The validity of the OLS results we obtain, however, depends on a series of assumptions, called the Classical Linear Regression Model (CLRM) assumptions, which we have yet to discuss. These assumptions are sketched briefly below.[15] The end result is that if these assumptions are satisfied, then the OLS estimated regression line gives us the best possible representation of the population's regression line.[16]

CLRM Assumptions

1. The average of the population errors (u_is) is zero. As seen in Figure 1.2b, some points will lie above the population regression function and will have positive errors, and some will lie below and have negative errors. On average, the errors should cancel each other, and thus the average of the errors should be zero.

2. The spread of the errors above and below the regression line (i.e., the **variance**) is uniform for all values of X. Graphically, this means that the

---

[14] A more formal discussion of how well an estimated sample regression function explains the behavior of the dependent variable (such as crime rates) will be presented in the following chapter.

[15] For a more detailed discussion of the regression model assumptions, see Berry (1993) or Wooldridge (2006).

[16] A formal proof that the OLS method is the best one is given by the famous **Gauss-Markov theorem**. For more details, see Greene (2003).

actual observations for Y_i, for given values of X_i, fall within a uniform band around the population regression function, as seen in Figure 2.7. As shown, the population regression function (PRF) has observations that are above and below it, but they are uniformly spread around the line, as the two darker, parallel lines above and below the PRF demonstrate. (The technical term is that the errors are said to be **homoscedastic**, meaning "equal variance." An example of when the assumption is violated is given later in Chapter 7.)

3. The error associated with one observation is not associated with errors from any other observations. Or, in technical terms, we assume no **autocorrelation** among the error terms. The basis for this assumption is straightforward. The errors are supposed to represent purely random effects for which our model is unable to control. If, however, one observation's error is somehow related to another observation's error, then this implies that there is some systematic relationship among the errors, and thus they are not purely random. The implication is that this systematic relationship contains information which we should use to improve the estimation of our model. If it is ignored, then we are not fitting the best line to our data. (An example of this kind of problem is considered in Chapter 7.)

4. The independent variable X_i is uncorrelated with the error term u_i. The reasoning behind this assumption can be understood if we recall our goal: to isolate the separate effects of changes in X_i on Y_i. Suppose, for example, that X_i and u_i are positively correlated, meaning that an increase in u_i would generally be associated with an increase in X_i. If this is the case, then it would be

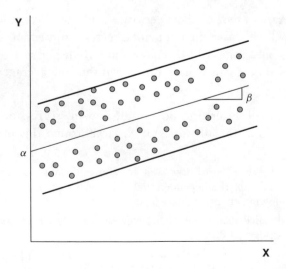

Figure 2.7

difficult to isolate the separate effects of an increase in X_i on Y_i because any increase in X_i could be due, in part, to an increase in u_i. An example of when this assumption is violated is when we have an "omitted variable bias," a topic we touch upon in Chapter 7.

5. The variables X_i and Y_i contain no measurement errors. Again, the necessity of this assumption is easy to understand. If X_i and Y_i are measured inaccurately, then the OLS values for a and b (which, as Equations 2.3a and 2.3b show, are derived from the values of X_i and $Y_{i,}$) are not likely to be accurate estimates of the population's α and β.

6. The model we put forth, such as the one in Equation 1.2b, is theoretically sound. This assumption can be violated in a number of ways, including omitting relevant independent variables. For example, if we consider our baseball salary model, we hypothesized that years of playing determine a player's salary. We know, however, that years alone do not determine baseball salaries. A player's offensive ability (e.g., hitting) or defensive ability (e.g., fielding) is also obviously important. If we do not take into account these important factors in our model, then our model will not be correctly specified (i.e., we commit a **model specification error**), and the values for a and b may not be reliable.

Another way we can misspecify our model is to use a functional form that is inappropriate. For example, we may fit a straight line to data when, in fact, a curve is appropriate. (We will have more to say about functional forms later in Chapter 5.)

7. Our last assumption has to do with how the population's error term, u_i, is distributed. We assume that the u_i follows a normal distribution (often referred to as the **normality assumption**). That is, the random errors follow the familiar bell-shaped curve that is well known from statistics. The importance of this assumption will be seen later in Chapter 3.[17]

If CLRM assumptions 1 through 6 are satisfied, then, as noted above, the OLS regression line provides the best possible estimate of the population regression line. Or, using the more common terminology, OLS is **BLUE**, which is an acronym for Best Linear Unbiased Estimator.[18] In order to

---

[17] The justification of this assumption comes from a theory from statistics called the Central Limit Theorem. Those interested in learning more about this theorem are referred to Greene (2003).

[18] Assumption 7, the "normality assumption," is not required for the BLUE property of the OLS estimation method. It is made for purposes of hypothesis testing, a topic we take up in the next chapter.

understand this property, we can begin by discussing what is meant by **linear** and **unbiased**. Linear simply means that we are estimating a value for the intercept (a) and the slope term (b) that are raised only to the power 1. Thus, our Equation 1.5 is an example of a linear regression model. However, consider the following equation:

$$Y_i = a + b^2X_i + e_i. \qquad (2.11)$$

In this case, b is raised to the power 2 and thus is not "linear" in the sense described here. On the other hand, we do allow for the independent variables to enter into our equation nonlinearly, as shown in the following equation:

$$Y_i = a + bX_i^2 + e_i. \qquad (2.12)$$

This is considered a linear estimation because a and b are raised to the power 1 and thus Equation 2.12 is a candidate for the BLUE property of OLS.[19]

Unbiasedness has to do with the fact that our sample estimate of b, the slope term, is a random variable. That is, given that we use a sample to calculate b, if we repeat the estimation with new samples, we will likely find different values for b. If we do so, we can then calculate *the average of all of these bs*. If it is true that the average of the bs is equal to the population's true β, then the estimator is said to be unbiased; similarly for a, the intercept term.[20]

Now that we know what is meant by linear and unbiased, we can explain what is meant by "best." If we consider all possible estimation methods that are linear and produce unbiased estimates of a and b, the OLS method is the best one in the sense that it gives us the most precise estimates of a and b. In order to understand the meaning of this statement, recall that the estimated parameters a and b "bounce" around from sample to sample (i.e., they are random variables). If they are unbiased, this means that as they bounce around, they have a mean value that is equal to the population's α and β. To be best, they will bounce around the least; any other linear unbiased estimation method will produce values of a and b that bounce around more than

---

[19] Our linearity requirement is only for the parameters to be estimated (i.e., a and b). The use of nonlinear independent variables, as shown in Equation 2.12, is discussed later in Chapter 5.

[20] Formally, if it is true that $E(a) = \alpha$ and $E(b) = \beta$, where "E" stands for expected value, then we say that a and b are unbiased estimators of α and β. It then follows that if $E(b) \neq \beta$, then b would be a biased estimator of β; similarly for the intercept term, a.

those calculated using the OLS method. In other words, of all linear unbiased estimation methods, the OLS method gives us the most precise estimates of α and β, or OLS is BLUE.[21]

Thus, we have powerful support for the use of OLS.

Summing Up

In this chapter, we have seen how we may use samples of data and employ the method of least-squares to estimate the linear relationship between a dependent variable and an independent variable. We have seen, however, that our estimated sample regression function does not completely explain the relationship between the dependent variable and the independent variable, and what is left unexplained shows up in the error term. The question we now turn to is that of model performance and reliability. That is, once we have estimated a relationship between a dependent variable and an independent variable, what can we say about *how well* we have estimated this relationship? This is the topic of the next chapter.

PROBLEMS

2.1 Consider the following data set:

Y_i	X_i
10.5	13
9.75	12
10.00	12
12.25	14
8.00	10

where: Y_i is individual i's hourly wage (in dollars per hour)
X_i is individual i's number of years of education

Use Equations 2.3a and 2.3b to calculate the OLS values for a and b and interpret your results.

2.2 Use Equation 2.5b and the data in Table A1 of Appendix A to predict the salary of Javy Lopez. What is the error in prediction (i.e., e_i)? What may account for this error?

---

[21] In technical terms, OLS estimates of the random variables a and b will have the smallest variance as compared to any other estimation method. For a more detailed discussion, see Gujarati (2003) or Wooldridge (2006).

2.3 Suppose we have the following model:

$$Y_i = \alpha + \beta X_i + u_i,$$

where, in this case, Y_i is the manufacturer's suggested retail price (*MSRP*) for a sports utility vehicle (SUV) and X_i is the horsepower of the SUV.

    a. What sign do you expect for α and β?

    b. Using SPSS or Excel (or an equivalent program), and the data provided in Table A5 in Appendix A, perform an OLS regression for the above model and interpret the estimated coefficients.

2.4 Recall the model discussed in Problem 1.3, which shows students' performance in college as a function of their SAT scores:

$$Y_i = \alpha + \beta X_i + u_i,$$

    where: Y_i is individual *i*'s freshman college grade point average (GPA)
                X_i is individual *i*'s SAT score

    a. Using Excel or SPSS (or an equivalent program) and the "GPA" data set, create a plot of the data with the variable GPA on the *Y*-axis and SAT on the *X*-axis. Does there appear to be any relationship between the two?

    b. Using SPSS or Excel (or an equivalent program), perform an OLS regression with GPA as the dependent variable and SAT as the independent variable. Interpret the estimated constant term and coefficient to SAT.

3

Model Performance and Evaluation

In the previous chapter, we learned how to use the method of least-squares to find a line that best fits a scatter of points. It can be shown that, given the right circumstances, there is no other method that is better at estimating such a line than least-squares. That is, if the CLRM assumptions are met, then OLS is BLUE. At this point, two other issues arise. First, suppose we have used least-squares to find a line that best fits the data. We can then ask *how well* the line fits the data. Finding the best fit is one thing, but how well our line fits the data is quite another. This is the issue of "goodness of fit," which we explore in the next section.

Another question we can ask is not how well the regression model as a whole performs, but how do the separate pieces of the model perform? That is, in the previous chapter, we learned how to calculate the least-squares values of a and b to determine the sample regression line. But because these values were derived from a sample, they may not be representative of the *population's* α and β. Thus, we can ask the question, how confident are we that our sample results are a good reflection of the population's behavior? We discuss this issue later in the chapter.

Goodness of Fit: The R^2

In Chapter 2, we estimated four sample regression lines, one for each of our examples. We then plotted these lines along with the actual data for the dependent variable, Y, and the independent variable, X. We have already accepted the fact that in each case, the dots representing the sample data will not fall exactly on the sample regression line, reflecting the fact that our model does not take into account all factors that affect our dependent variable. In general, however, we hope that the vertical distances from the dots to the regression line are small because if this is true, then our estimated line would be a good predictor of the behavior of Y.

Reviewing Figures 2.3, 2.4, 2.5, and 2.6a from the previous chapter, we can see some qualitative differences. In Figure 2.3, which is for our baseball salary example, we see that the plotted data points are somewhat broadly scattered around the sample regression line. This indicates that the model explains some of the behavior of Y, but much is left unexplained. Comparing this to Figure 2.4, which is for the presidential voting model, we see that the plotted points in this case are more closely cropped around the regression line. Thus, for this example, the regression line seems to tell us a lot about the behavior of the dependent variable, Y. Finally, in Figures 2.5 and 2.6a, we see that the plotted data for state abortion rates and crime in California are spread very broadly around their respective regression lines. In the case of abortion, we can conclude that although religion may be an important factor in determining abortion rates, there are many other important factors we need to consider. The same can be said for the case of British crime rates: Unemployment rates may be one of the determining factors, but there are obviously other causal factors not present in the model.

Even though the least-squares regression method produces the best possible line to fit our data,[1] this means only that we have done the best we can, and the overall performance of the model is not guaranteed to be good. In order to judge how well the model fits the data, we can employ a measure called the **R^2** (read as the **R squared**).[2] The technical derivation of this measure can be a little hard to follow, but the intuition of it is not too difficult to understand.

Our basic approach, as set out in Chapter 1, is to understand the behavior of Y, the dependent variable, by observing the behavior of X, the independent variable. As the value of X differs from one observation to another, we expect that this difference in X will explain, at least in part, the differences in Y from one observation to another. This approach is summarized by Equation 1.5.

---

[1] Again, this will be true only if the CLRM assumptions are met. As we see in later chapters, our simple models may not satisfy all of the necessary conditions that are needed before we can say that we have found the best possible line to fit our data. In order to continue with our discussion, however, we will assume that all conditions have been satisfied and our least-squares estimates are the best possible.

[2] The R^2 is also referred to as the "coefficient of determination."

We hope that by observing the behavior of X, we learn a great deal about the behavior of Y. The behavior of Y that is not explained by X will be captured by the error term in Equation 1.5. *The R^2 simply is a measure that tells us what proportion of the behavior of Y is explained by X.*

We can easily consider the bounds for the R^2. If, by observing the behavior of X, we know exactly how Y behaves, then the R^2 would be equal to 1 (100%). This outcome is very unlikely.[3] On the other hand, observing X may tell us nothing about Y, in which case the R^2 would be equal to 0 (0%). Thus, the R^2 is bounded between 0 and 1. Values close to 1 mean that by observing the behavior of X, we can explain nearly all of the behavior of Y. This would indicate that our estimated sample regression function is performing well overall. Values close to 0 would have the opposite implication.

The above discussion gives us an intuitive understanding of the R^2. In order to understand the technical derivation of this measure, we need to define what is meant by the "behavior" of Y. The dependent variable Y will have a mean (average), and of course, some values of Y will fall above this mean and some below. As a graphic example, we can consider Figure 3.1.

As we can see in Figure 3.1, a particular point is plotted for observation Y_i for a given value of X_i. Of course, there would normally be many other observations plotted on the graph, but they are not shown in this case so that we may focus on this single observation. The mean value for the dependent variable, $\bar{Y}$, is a horizontal line. The sample regression function (SRF) is also plotted. Notice that the plotted point Y_i lies above $\bar{Y}$ (i.e., it is above the horizontal line). Thus, the value of Y for this particular observation is above the sample's average value for Y. The amount by which Y_i exceeds $\bar{Y}$ is shown as the distance from the horizontal line to the point Y_i and is denoted as $(Y_i - \bar{Y})$. This deviation of Y_i from its mean can be broken up into two pieces: the amount of the deviation that is predicted by our model, and the amount that our model does not predict. That part of the deviation that our model predicts is shown as the vertical distance from the mean of Y ($\bar{Y}$) to the value the model would predict for Y ($\hat{Y}_i$) for the given X_i. This distance is denoted $(\hat{Y}_i - \bar{Y})$. The second piece is the part of the total deviation that was not predicted by our model, shown as the vertical distance from the point on the sample regression function, $\hat{Y}_i$, to the observation Y_i, and this distance is denoted as $(Y_i - \hat{Y}_i)$, which is simply our error term, e_i. Thus, suppose this observation is from our baseball example. Then the salary for player i, Y_i, is above the average salary for all players in our sample. Part of the amount by which player i's salary exceeds the average is explained by our model. That is, it can be explained by the number of years player i has

---

[3] If the R^2 turns out to be equal to 1, the most likely reason is that the model that was estimated was, in fact, an identity. (See footnote 4 in Chapter 1.)

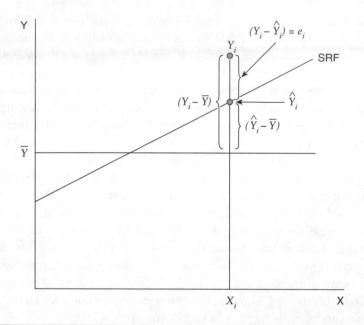

Figure 3.1

played in MLB. The rest is not explained by our model and is captured by the residual, e_i. It should be obvious that the greater the proportion of the deviation of the observation from its mean value that is explained by our model, the better our model is performing because this would mean that the proportion accounted for by the error term is smaller. On the other hand, if our model does a poor job of explaining the deviation of Y_i from its mean, then our error term will be larger. This kind of breakdown of the total deviation of Y_i from its mean into the explained portion and the unexplained portion can be done for all observations in our sample.

Now, as noted above, the R^2 is a measure that tells us what proportion of the behavior of Y is explained by X. We can now use the method described above to give a more precise meaning to the "behavior of Y." We can define this behavior of Y as the *variation* in Y, and it is calculated according to the following equation:

$$TSS = \sum_{i=1}^{n}(Y_i - \overline{Y})^2. \tag{3.1}$$

That is, the variation in Y is the sum of the squared deviations of Y around its mean. We will call this sum the "Total Sum of Squares," or TSS for short. Essentially, it is a measure that tells us by how much the values of Y

"bounce" around its mean. The deviations are squared so as to prevent cancellation of positive values with negative ones (recall that this was also done when we derived the OLS method in Chapter 2).

Part of this behavior of Y (i.e., the TSS) is explained or "predicted" by our model, and the rest is left unexplained. The part of this variation that is explained is

$$\text{ESS} = \sum_{i=1}^{n} (\hat{Y}_i - \bar{Y})^2. \tag{3.2}$$

We call this value the "Explained Sum of Squares," or ESS for short. It represents the explained behavior of Y about its mean.

Finally, as we have noted, the error term represents what is not explained by our model:

$$\text{RSS} = \sum_{i=1}^{n} e_i^2. \tag{3.3}$$

We call this sum the "Residual Sum of Squares," or RSS. Using these measures, we can represent the behavior of Y in the following way:

$$\text{TSS} = \text{ESS} + \text{RSS}. \tag{3.4}$$

That is, the behavior of Y (TSS) can be broken up into two pieces: that which is explained by the model (ESS) and that which is unexplained (RSS). The R^2 is thus defined as the proportion of TSS explained by the model, or

$$R^2 = \frac{\text{ESS}}{\text{TSS}}. \tag{3.5a}$$

As an illustration of how to use the R^2, we can return to our second example, which looks at presidential voting. Looking at Table 2.2, we see the reported predicted values (i.e., the $\hat{Y}_i$ values). In Table A3 in Appendix A, we have the actual values for the percentage of two-party votes (i.e., the Y_i values) as well as the mean (i.e., the value for $\bar{Y}$). Thus, we have all the ingredients needed for calculating the R^2. Plugging these values into Equations 3.1 and 3.2, we find that TSS is 1023.61 and ESS is 539.52. Using Equation 3.5a, we have

$$R^2 = \frac{539.52}{1023.61} = 0.527. \tag{3.5b}$$

The result in Equation 3.5b means that approximately 53% of the variation in Y is explained by our model. This, in turn, tells us that about 47% of the behavior of Y is not explained by our model. These results suggest that our model is moderately successful, overall, in explaining the variation in the percentage of two-party votes received by incumbent party candidates.[4]

Virtually all computer packages that are capable of performing OLS regression will calculate the R^2. For example, Table 3.1 shows the OLS output generated by Excel for our baseball model.

As we can see, Table 3.1 provides a great deal of information.[5] We can see under the heading "Coefficients" the values for our intercept term, a (0.765), and the slope term, b (0.656), shown in Equation 2.5a. At the top of the table, we see the heading "Regression Statistics," below which we find "R Square," which is reported as 0.345. This is our measure of the "goodness of fit" discussed above. The interpretation of this number is that about 34.5% of the behavior (i.e., variation) of baseball salaries is explained by our model. This means that about two thirds of the variation in baseball salaries is left unexplained. This somewhat poor result should not be too surprising because, as was pointed out in Chapter 1, the two-variable model is too simplistic in most cases, and a more complex model is warranted.

Also shown in Table 3.1 is a section labeled "**ANOVA,**" which stands for "*AN*alysis *O*f *VA*riance." Focusing on this section for a moment, we see a column headed "SS." This is short for "sum of squares" and is a breakdown of the variation of Y (baseball salaries) into its separate pieces as described in Equation 3.4.[6] The first entry for "Regression," 328.555, is our ESS in Equation 3.4. The second entry, labeled "Residual" (623.445), is our RSS in

---

[4] It should be pointed out that there is no benchmark R^2 value that needs to be achieved before we declare a model to be successful. There are some areas of research where an R^2 of 0.527 would be considered quite good (e.g., models of wage determination in industries other than MLB), whereas in other areas of research, it would be considered a weak result (e.g., models that forecast national income). These differences arise for a variety of reasons. It may be due to differences in the availability and quality of data, or it may simply be the case that some relationships naturally have a larger random component (i.e., u_i) than others.

[5] The output shown, as in earlier examples, has been edited to include only the relevant information needed for the present discussion. In addition, values were rounded to three decimal places.

[6] The column headed "MS" is simply the calculated mean of the sum of squares values. The MS values are not of particular use for us in this book.

Table 3.1

SUMMARY OUTPUT				
Regression Statistics				
Multiple *R*	0.587			
R Square	0.345			
Adjusted *R* Square	0.323			
Standard Error	4.559			
Observations	32			
ANOVA				
	df	SS	MS	
Regression	1	328.555	328.555	
Residual	30	623.445	20.782	
Total	31	952.000		
	Coefficients	Standard Error	*t* Stat	*P* value
Intercept	0.765	1.671	0.458	0.650
YEARS	0.656	0.165	3.976	0.000

Equation 3.4. And finally, "Total," given as 952.000, is our TSS (= ESS + RSS) discussed earlier. Thus, using our definition of the R^2 in Equation 3.5a, we have

$$R^2 = \frac{328.555}{952.000} = 0.345, \qquad (3.5c)$$

which is indeed our reported "R square" in Table 3.1.[7]

Several other measures are shown in Table 3.1 under the heading of "Regression Statistics," and we can discuss them briefly. The **standard error**, shown as approximately 4.559, is the positive square root of the variance of the errors. It is essentially a measure of the typical size of the error (our e_i) in prediction. "Observations" simply tells us the sample size (32 in this case) used in the regression.

---

[7] "Multiple R," reported as 0.587, is simply the square root of the R^2 and is the absolute value of the correlation between Y and X. This statistic is not often used in our assessment of the model's overall performance.

Sample Results and Population Parameters

In addition to judging the overall performance of our model, we can consider the separate performance of estimated parameters a and b. It was pointed out in Chapter 2 that we typically are working with samples of data, not the population. Thus, we collect a sample and use it to calculate OLS values for a and b; these values then define a sample regression line. The hope is that our sample values of a and b are a good representation of the true, but unknown, values of the population parameters α and β shown in Equation 1.2b.

Suppose we replaced our original sample and collected a new one. This new sample could then be used to calculate OLS values for a and b. Obviously, because this second sample would not likely be identical to the previous one, these values for a and b would likely be different from those of the first sample. Different samples have different information contained in them; thus, as samples change, so will the OLS-calculated values for a and b. In other words, these sample values for a and b are random variables that "bounce around" from sample to sample and we can thus study their behavior. To illustrate the fact that a and b typically change from sample to sample, we can return to our baseball example. Suppose we draw two subsamples of size 16 from our 32 observations. We can then calculate OLS values for a and b for each subsample. For observations 1 through 16 (rounding to three decimal places), we have

$$a = 1.177, \qquad b = 0.680,$$

and for observations 17 through 32, we have

$$a = 0.352, \qquad b = 0.631.$$

As we can see, we have substantially different values for these estimated parameters from one sample to the next.[8]

Understanding that the OLS-calculated values for a and b are, in fact, random variables is important because we use them as estimates of the population's α and β. If the calculated values of a and b change a lot from sample to sample, then we would not have much confidence in any single sample's results being representative of α and β. On the other hand, if the OLS estimates of a and b differ only slightly from one sample to another, then we can be fairly confident that a single sample's results are a good representation of the population's parameters. The measures used to judge the

---

[8] The reader is invited to verify these results.

reliability of a and b as estimates of their population counterparts are the standard error of the coefficient estimates.[9] Essentially, they are measures of how a and b bounce around from sample to sample. The *smaller* the standard error, the *more reliable* are the sample values of a and b as estimates for α and β. In our baseball example, we can see in Table 3.1 that the column headed "Standard Error" for the "Intercept" (i.e., a) is shown as 1.671 and for "YEARS" (i.e., b) we have 0.165, after rounding to three decimal places. We need to keep in mind two things with these standard errors. First, they are in the same units as the dependent variable (millions of dollars in our case). Second, it is their size *relative* to the value of the estimated coefficient that is important for us. That is, consider the value for b, which is shown in Table 3.1 to be 0.656. Comparing this number to its standard error of 0.165, we see that the coefficient is nearly four times as large as the standard error. In other words, the sample value for b appears to be a fairly reliable estimate of the population's β.[10]

Given the values of the standard errors of our a and b, we can use them to test various ideas or "hypotheses." One of the most common tests is the "zero hypothesis" test. This test, in some sense, looks into the "soundness" of our model. Recall in Chapter 1 where we introduced the four examples. In each case, we specified a dependent (Y) variable and an independent (X) variable that we believed (or "hypothesized") should explain at least part of the behavior of the dependent variable. Take, for example, our model of voting patterns in presidential elections. In building this model, we hypothesized for the population data that the percentage of two-party votes received by the incumbent party candidate is determined, in part, by the economy's health as measured by the growth rate. This relationship between votes and growth is not an established fact; rather, it is a theory or hypothesis that we put forth. It could be wrong; there may be no relationship between votes and growth. Part of our task in regression analysis is to test this hypothesis. We do this by collecting a sample, estimating the sample regression function, and then analyzing our results to see whether the hypothesis is supported. More specifically, consider our model shown in Equation 1.6, except now for the population of data: $Y_t = \alpha + \beta X_t + u_t$.

If economic growth (i.e., variable X_t) is an important factor in explaining voting patterns (i.e., Y_t), then the population's value for β should be positive.

---

[9] See Gujarati (2003) for details on how the standard errors for the OLS parameter estimates are calculated.

[10] Generally speaking, if the absolute value of the estimated parameter (e.g., a or b) is twice (or more) the size of the associated standard error, then the estimated parameter is considered to be a fairly reliable estimate of the population parameter (e.g., α or β).

On the other hand, suppose that the economic growth rate has nothing to do with the way people vote; in that case, β would be zero. If β is truly zero, then βX_t would be zero, meaning that X_t has no impact on Y_t.

Whether or not β is zero is a hypothesis made for our population of data. Stating the hypothesis a bit more formally, we can write

$$H_0: \beta = 0$$

$$H_1: \beta \neq 0,$$

where H_0 is called the **null hypothesis** and H_1 is the **alternative hypothesis**. If we find that H_0 is true, then our hypothesis that economic growth is an important factor in explaining voting patterns would be false. On the other hand, if we find that H_1 is true, then our hypothesis is correct. Unfortunately, we typically cannot prove that either H_0 or H_1 is true. This is because we typically do not have the population data and are working only with a sample. Because our sample result for b is not a perfect predictor for β, our sample results can only support or fail to support our hypotheses over β.[11]

In order to see how we can use our sample regression results to test the above hypothesis, we can use the information in Table 3.2, which contains the OLS output (produced by Excel) for our voting model.[12]

We see in Table 3.2 that the estimated values for a and b are, as we saw earlier, 51.065 and 0.880, respectively. We can also see that the standard errors for these values of a and b are approximately 1.035 and 0.182, respectively. If we next consider the column headed "t stat" (short for **t statistic**), we see the rounded value of 49.339 for the intercept, a, and 4.838 for the coefficient to $GROWTH$, or b. The basis of the t statistic actually stems from the normality assumption that was introduced in Chapter 2 in CLRM Assumption 7. Although the discussion of the use of the t statistic is somewhat advanced, it boils down to this: If the population errors, u_i, are normally distributed, then it can be shown that the sample estimates for a and b follow a t distribution.[13] Given this result, then we can use the t distribution to test hypotheses over the population parameters α and β with our sample estimates. In other words, the

---

[11] It should be understood that β is a fixed parameter, not a random variable. The value for b from our sample regression, on the other hand, is not a fixed parameter but is a random variable that we use to estimate β.

[12] Table 3.2 is similar to Table 2.2, except that the prediction errors and predicted values are omitted and other relevant statistics are now included.

[13] See Gujarati (2003) for the proof of this result.

Table 3.2

SUMMARY OUTPUT				
Regression Statistics				
Multiple R	0.726			
R Square	0.527			
Adjusted R Square	0.505			
Standard Error	4.801			
Observations	23			
ANOVA				
	df	SS	MS	
Regression	1	539.524	539.524	
Residual	21	484.088	23.052	
Total	22	1023.612		
	Coefficients	Standard Error	t stat	P value
Intercept	51.065	1.035	49.339	0.000
GROWTH	0.880	0.182	4.838	0.000

normality assumption introduced in Chapter 2 now justifies our use of the t stat here.

As for the value for each t stat shown, it is calculated by dividing a coefficient by its associated standard error. That is, for the intercept, if we divide 51.065 by 1.035, we get 49.339, which is the t stat value shown (allowing for rounding differences). Similarly, for the coefficient to GROWTH (i.e., our b), we have 0.880, which, if divided by its standard error of 0.182, gives us 4.838, the reported t stat for GROWTH. As noted earlier, the size of the standard error relative to the estimated coefficient is what is important for us. This is exactly what the reported t stat shows: the coefficient divided by its own standard error. In the case of the intercept, our t stat of 49.339 tells us that our calculated value of a is about 49 times larger than its standard error. In other words, the OLS value for a is a reliable estimate of the population's α because it bounces around very little from sample to sample. As for b, this coefficient is approximately 4.8 times larger than its own standard error, indicating that this sample value for b is a very reliable estimate for the population's parameter β. Exactly how reliable are these estimates? The answer to this question is our next task.

The column next to the *t* stat column in Table 3.2 is headed "**P value.**" The numbers shown here for *a* and *b* are calculated using the *t* stat.[14] These numbers represent *probabilities*, based on the associated *t* stat, that we can use to test the zero hypotheses discussed earlier. The interpretation of these numbers is a little tricky. They represent what the probability would be of finding the values of *a* and *b* shown if, in fact, *for the population,* the null hypothesis was true. In other words, it sets up a straw man that we hope we can knock down, and this straw man says that, for the population, *X* has no relationship to *Y*.

In order to make this clear, let's focus on the value for *b* shown in Table 3.2. This coefficient to *GROWTH* is estimated to be 0.880, based on our sample OLS results. This number, as we have discussed, is only an estimate of the true value of the population's β. Furthermore, we have learned that this result for *b* will likely differ from sample to sample (i.e., it is a random variable). This being the case, the value of 0.880 could be quite different from β. We can therefore consider the following question: Could it be the case that the true value for β is, in fact, zero, and that our value of 0.880 was merely a result of our sampling? This is the question that the *P* value addresses: What is the likelihood of getting a sample value of 0.880 when, in fact, it is true that β is zero? In our case, the *P* value for *b* is shown as 0.000 after rounding to three decimal places. If we allow for a greater number of decimal places, say six, we would find this *P* value to be 0.000088.[15] That is, the probability of getting the value of 0.880 for *b* when it is true that β is zero is about 0.000088 (or about a 0.0088% chance).[16] This is quite small,

---

[14] The probabilities shown under the *P* value column are calculated by plugging the given *t* stat into the *t* probability distribution function. This, again, is a complicated matter that goes beyond the scope of this book. Those interested in learning more about the specifics of probability distribution functions are referred to Gujarati (2003) or Greene (2003).

[15] In fact, the Excel output produces the following *P* value for the coefficient to *GROWTH*: 8.79747E-05. This number is expressed in scientific notation and could be rewritten as 8.79747×10^{-5} or, in nonscientific notation, as 0.0000879747.

[16] This interpretation is not strictly correct. The hypothesis test we are conducting is whether or not β is statistically different from zero. To reject this null hypothesis, we need to get a sample result for β that is sufficiently different from zero, that is, sufficiently larger *or* sufficiently smaller than zero. In our case, our sample result was 0.880, but if our sample gave us a value of −0.880, this too would be sufficiently different from zero (in this case, smaller than zero) to reject our null hypothesis. Thus a more accurate interpretation of the *P* value in this example would be: The probability of obtaining a sample value of 0.880 or greater *in absolute value terms,* when the true population's value is zero, is approximately 0.000088.

indicating that the hypothesis that β is zero is probably not true. In other words, we would likely reject H_0: $\beta = 0$ in favor of H_1: $\beta \neq 0$.

We can also perform a similar test for the intercept term, α. That is, we can consider the hypothesis that the population's intercept is really equal to zero. Putting it formally, we would have

$$H_0: \alpha = 0$$

$$H_1: \alpha \neq 0.$$

In order to test this hypothesis, we need only consider the P value for a, which is given as approximately 0.000. Or, again, allowing for a greater number of decimal places, the Excel program reports 3.3542E-23. This is in scientific notation, which means we move the decimal 23 places to the left. Obviously, this is an extremely small number. In terms of our hypothesis test, this means that the probability of obtaining a value for a of 51.065 from our sample when the value for α is truly zero is 3.3542E-23 (or a 3.3542E-21% chance). In other words, it means we can be quite confident that the true population's intercept α is not zero.

In the above example, we found very small P values, which indicated that we can reject H_0 for both the intercept and slope terms with great confidence. Suppose, however, that we were not able to be so confident. That is, suppose the P value for b turned out to be 0.20. This would mean that the chance of getting the value of b we found (or greater, in absolute terms), when in fact the population's β is zero, is about 20%. Would we be sufficiently confident that β is not zero with this result? In other words, how large of a P value are we willing to accept before concluding that we cannot reject H_0? If the P value is 0.20 and we declare that we reject H_0, then this means we have a 20% chance that our declaration is wrong.[17] How prudent we are in rejecting the null hypothesis (i.e., accepting the estimated relationship) may vary with circumstances. For example, in a model exploring the usage of a particular drug and the possibility of its use causing birth defects, we would want to be quite sure that a real relationship exists. It is standard practice to reject the zero hypothesis when the associated P values are 0.05 or smaller (in some cases, P values of 0.10 or smaller are used).

In order to solidify the concept of hypothesis testing, we can apply these tools to our third example. Recall that this model, which is shown in Equation 1.7, hypothesizes that abortion rates across the 50 states differ, in

---

[17] If we reject a hypothesis when it is actually true, we are committing what is called a "Type I error." (Accepting a hypothesis when it is actually false is called a "Type II error.") The P value thus represents the probability of committing a Type I error.

part, because the moral views on abortion differ across the states. We use the variable *RELIGION*, which shows the percentage of the population that is Catholic, Southern Baptist, Evangelical, or Mormon, to capture the moral differences. As *RELIGION* (X_i) increases from one state to another, we expect that the abortion rate (Y_i) would be smaller, other things being equal. As in the previous example, this is a hypothesis that we put forth. It could be wrong, meaning that *RELIGION* tells us nothing about abortion rates. That is, it may be the case that β is zero for the population. We can test this hypothesis by evaluating the *P* value from the OLS regression. Table 3.3 shows the output from our earlier regression, but with more details in this case.

The three panels of output shown in Table 3.3 were produced by the program SPSS. The output provided is similar to that produced by the Excel program. We can see in the first panel, titled "Model Summary," that the *R* squared is reported as 0.016. This result tells us that approximately 1.6% of the behavior of abortion rates (Y_t) is explained by our model. This is

Table 3.3

Model Summary

Model	R	R Square	Adjusted R Square	Std. Error of the Estimate
1	.125[a]	.016	−.005	10.0829

a. Predictors: (Constant), *RELIGION*

ANOVA[b]

Model		Sum of Squares	df	Mean Square
1	Regression	77.691	1	77.691
	Residual	4879.935	48	101.665
	Total	4957.626	49	

b. Dependent Variable: ABORTION RATE

Coefficients[a]

Model		Unstandardized Coefficients		Standardized Coefficients		
		B	Std. Error	Beta	t	Sig.
1	(Constant)	23.825	3.979		5.988	.000
	RELIGION	−.099	.114	−.125	−.874	.386

a. Dependent Variable: ABORTION RATE

clearly a very poor result, because it means that approximately 98.4% of the behavior (i.e., variation) of our dependent variable is not explained. This result is mirrored in the second panel, titled "ANOVA," which shows that the residual sum of squares, RSS (reported as 4879.935), makes up nearly all of the total sum of squares, TSS (reported as 4957.626). In sum, the model, as it stands, fits the data very poorly.

Turning to the separate components of the model, we find similarly weak results. In the panel titled "Coefficients," we find the estimate of a to be 23.825 with a standard error of 3.979, and the estimate of b to be −0.099 with a standard error of 0.114. In the case of the constant term a, dividing the coefficient by its standard error (i.e., 23.825/3.979) gives us a reported "t" (which is the same as Excel's "t stat") of 5.988. This t then translates into a "Sig." (short for **significance level**, which is the equivalent of Excel's P value) of 0.000. This result tells us that we can reject the hypothesis that the constant term for the population, α, is truly zero with a very high degree of confidence.[18]

As for the coefficient to *RELIGION* (i.e., b), the results are quite different. The coefficient has the negative sign that was hypothesized, supporting the idea that as *RELIGION* increases from state to state, abortion rates tend to be smaller, other things being equal. However, the value for b appears not to be very different from zero. Again, we can ask the question: Is it true that the population value for β is really zero and that our result for b of −0.099 is from a sample that does not perfectly reflect the population? In other words, is −0.099 *statistically* different from zero? The fact that the magnitude of our b is small is not enough to make any conclusions about whether it is not statistically different from zero. We must compare the value for b to its standard error. The reported standard error of b is *larger* than (the absolute value of) b. In other words, for this model, the random variable b tends to bounce around a great deal, and as such the computed value is not a very reliable predictor of β. We can see this clearly by observing the Sig. value for b, shown as 0.386. What this number means is that there is a 38.6% chance of finding a sample value of 0.099 or larger (in absolute terms) for b when, in fact, the population's β is truly zero.[19]

---

[18] The Sig. value of 0.000 represents a rounded figure; it is not perfectly equal to zero, just very close. The fact that the intercept term is significantly different from zero, however, is not of great importance to us because the interpretation of the intercept in this case is not very meaningful.

[19] A word on terminology: In determining whether we reject or do not reject the null hypothesis, the P value (or Sig.) tells us at what probability the coefficient is "significantly" different from zero. For example, a P value of 0.10 means that we can reject the hypothesis that the associated coefficient is zero at the 10% "significance level." Equivalently, we can say that the null hypothesis is rejected at the 90% "confidence level." The terms *significance level* and *confidence level* are used interchangeably, and the confidence level is simply 100 minus the significance level.

In other words, we cannot confidently rule out the possibility that *RELI-GION*, on its own, has nothing to say about state abortion rates.

On some occasions, we must work directly with the t statistic in order to test hypotheses. This may occur, for example, if the software program with which we are working does not produce a P value (or significance level) for estimated coefficients.[20] Alternatively, we may wish to test a hypothesis other than the "zero hypothesis" test we have been performing. In both cases, we need to do some work by hand to perform a hypothesis test for our estimated coefficients. In order to see how we can work directly with the t statistic, we can return to our crime example. Table 3.4 reports the same results as Table 2.4 except we now include more detailed output.

Using the data in Table 3.4, we can write down the estimated equation, which is the same as we saw in Equation 2.9b but now including the standard error ("*se*" for short) for the intercept and coefficient to $UNEM_i$ shown in parentheses below the estimated coefficients[21]:

$$\widehat{CRIME_i} = 51.772 + 10.218\,(UNEM_i)$$

$$se = (5.698) \quad (1.829)$$

Suppose we wanted to perform a zero hypothesis test for the estimated coefficient to *UNEM*, b, but we did not have a P value to use. In order to do so, we can use the standard errors provided to compute the t statistic, and then we can compare it to a table of t values that is provided in Appendix C of this book. Before describing how to use the table of t values, however, we can explore the intuition behind this procedure.

Recall that the value of b is a sample's estimate of the population's coefficient to *UNEM*, β. The standard error of b is a measure of how precise our estimate is: the larger the standard error, the less precise our estimate. We noted that the "t stat" reported by Excel (or the "t" reported by SPSS) is calculated by dividing the estimated coefficient by its standard error. That is, for the coefficient to *UNEM*, we have

$$t\,\text{statistic} = \frac{b}{se(b)}. \tag{3.6a}$$

---

[20] Some older software programs simply provided the standard error for each coefficient estimated, and the researcher then had to perform calculations and hypothesis tests by hand. Most software programs now routinely generate t statistics and P values (or significance levels).

[21] Putting the standard errors in parentheses below their respective estimated coefficients is a common way to report regression results.

Table 3.4

Model Summary

Model	R	R Square	Adjusted R Square	Std. Error of the Estimate
1	.662[a]	.438	.424	13.610087

a. Predictors: (Constant), *UNEM*

ANOVA[b]

Model		Sum of Squares	df	Mean Square	F	Sig.
1	Regression	5783.392	1	5783.392	31.222	.000[a]
	Residual	7409.379	40	185.234		
	Total	13192.77	41			

a. Predictors: (Constant), *UNEM*

b. Dependent Variable: CRIME

Coefficients[a]

Model		Unstandardized Coefficients		Standardized Coefficients		
		B	Std. Error	Beta	t	Sig.
1	(Constant)	51.772	5.698		9.085	.000
	UNEM	10.218	1.829	.662	5.588	.000

a. Dependent Variable: CRIME

Focusing on Equation 3.6a for the moment, we see that for any given value for b, the larger the se(b), the smaller the t statistic. Therefore, the smaller the t statistic, the less reliable our value of b is as an estimate of the population's coefficient, β. In other words, a "small" absolute value of the t statistic means that our value of b bounces around a lot from sample to sample. This, in turn, means that the population's value for β may truly be zero and that our sample estimate of the coefficient was simply off the mark. Putting this formally, we can state the following two hypotheses:

$$H_0: \beta = 0$$

$$H_1: \beta \neq 0.$$

In this case, the "smaller" the absolute value of the t statistic, the more likely it is that we would not reject H_0 (i.e., that the population's regression line has a zero coefficient to *UNEM*). On the other hand, the "larger" the absolute value of the t statistic, the more likely it is that we would reject H_0 in favor of H_1 (i.e., that the population's regression line has a nonzero coefficient for *UNEM*). The question that arises is, how "large" does the t statistic have to be to reject H_0? The answer to this question depends on how confident we want to be in our test's result. It is standard practice that researchers settle on 90% or 95% confidence levels, or equivalently, 10% or 5% significance levels (see footnote 19). Thus, if we choose a significance level of 10% as our cutoff, we can then determine if our t statistic is large enough to reject H_0 for this level. To carry out this test, we can refer to Table C1 in Appendix C. In the first column of this table, we see the heading "df." This is short for **degrees of freedom**, which are calculated by taking our sample size and subtracting from it the number of parameters we have estimated.[22] Thus, for our 2004 crime example, we have a sample size of 42 police force areas and we are estimating two parameters (a and b), leaving us with 40 degrees of freedom.[23] Referring to Table C1, we see that the first column is headed "df" for degrees of freedom. For this test, we go down to the row for 40 degrees of freedom.[24] Across the top of Table C1, we see the heading "Confidence Level." Below this. we see "Probability," which, if multiplied by 100, is our significance level. Staying with our chosen 10% significance level, this means we go over to the column headed by 0.1 (i.e., 10%). We see, then, that for 40 degrees of freedom and a significance level of 0.10, we have the number 1.684 in Table C1. This number is a t value, and it represents the minimum value

---

[22] The meaning of the degrees of freedom is somewhat difficult to explain. The easiest way to think about the degrees of freedom is that they measure how much useable information we have left over from our sample after already performing certain tasks. That is, when we have a sample of data, this data set contains a finite amount of information. If we use part of this information to perform certain calculations, such as estimating a and b in a sample regression function, then we have less information left over to carry out other tasks, such as hypothesis tests. Thus, the degrees of freedom keep track of how much information we have left for such tasks.

[23] Note that both Excel and SPSS routinely report the degrees of freedom. Both programs provide several values for the degrees of freedom, shown as "df," in the ANOVA portion of their output. The relevant value for the purpose of performing t tests are the ones reported for the "Residual." Thus, we see in Table 3.4 a value of 40. In the case of our abortion model, with a sample size of 50, we have degrees of freedom equal to 48 (see Table 3.3).

[24] Other, more extensive t tables have a greater number of values for degrees of freedom.

that the absolute value of our t statistic must achieve before we can reject H_0.[25] That is, if

$$|t \text{ statistic}| \geq t \text{ value},$$

then we can reject H_0, meaning that the coefficient to UNEM is statistically different from zero at the 10% significance level.

Returning to our crime example, we have

$$t \text{ statistic} = \frac{10.218}{1.829} = 5.587,$$

which is the same value reported for the t statistic in Table 3.4 (allowing for some minor difference due to rounding) for the coefficient to UNEM. Because this t statistic is greater than 1.684, the t value, we can reject H_0 at the 10% significance (90% confidence) level. In fact, we can see that we can achieve even a smaller significance (or higher degree of confidence) with our given t statistic. Our t statistic is larger than the t value of 0.05 (shown as 2.021 in Table C1) and is also larger than the t value for 0.01 (shown as 2.704). Thus, we can reject H_0 at a significance level that is smaller than 1%. What is the exact significance level we can achieve? This is, in fact, what the Sig. value tells us. Referring back to Table 3.4, the Sig. value is shown as 0.000, which is rounded to three decimal places. Carrying the Sig. value out to 6 decimal places, we have 0.000002 as our significance level. This Sig. value tells us that we can reject H_0 at less than the 0.0002% level of significance. This example illustrates the linkage between the t statistic reported by the program and the associated Sig. value. Furthermore, it provides us with strong evidence that unemployment is truly an important determining factor of British police force area crime rates in 2004.

We can also use t statistics to perform hypothesis tests other than the zero hypothesis. For example, we saw in our voting regression (see Table 3.2)

---

[25] If the value for a or b happens to be negative, then the t statistic will be negative (e.g., the value for b in our abortion regression shown in Table 3.3). The t tables, however, show only positive values. This is because the t distribution is symmetric and centered around zero, so if we compute a t statistic and find it is negative, we can take the absolute value of this number and compare it to the positive t values shown in Table C1. For a more detailed discussion of the t distribution, see Gujarati (2003).

that the OLS estimation of the slope term, b, yielded a value of approximately 0.880 with a standard error of about 0.182 (rounding to three decimal places). The "t stat" and the associated "P value" show that the population's β is different from zero at a very small significance level (or high confidence level). We can, however, ask the following question: Is the population's β different from 1? The value of 0.880 is not too far off from 1, and given the fact that our value for b is from a sample, it seems possible that if we had the population data and calculated the population regression function, we could perhaps end up with β equal to 1. Recall, however, that we cannot simply consider the size of b; we must also consider its size relative to its standard error. Thus, a more formal test is needed. We can state our hypothesis more formally as

$$H_0: \beta = 1$$
$$H_1: \beta \neq 1.$$

We can perform this test using the t statistic in a similar way as we did above. In this case, however, we need to recalculate the t statistic to make it conform to our new hypothesized value of β. We calculate this new t statistic using the following equation:

$$t\text{ statistic} = \frac{b - h}{se(b)}, \tag{3.6b}$$

where b is the OLS sample result for the slope term and h is our hypothesized value for β.[26] Using the values from our voting regression, we have

$$t\text{ statistic} = \frac{0.880 - 1}{0.182} = -0.659, \tag{3.6c}$$

and taking the absolute value for this t statistic, we have 0.659. Turning to Table C1 and locating the row for 21 degrees of freedom (23 observations

---

[26] This equation is very similar to that shown in Equation 3.6a, except that we are subtracting h in the numerator. However, this is only an apparent difference. Recall in Equation 3.6a that we were calculating a t statistic for use in testing a hypothesized value of zero for our population parameter β. In that case, then, h was zero, and so b minus h would simply be equal to b.

minus two estimated parameters), we see that for a significance of level of 10% (or confidence level of 90%), the t value is 1.721. Comparing the absolute value of our t statistic to this t value, we see that it is less than the t value, and so we cannot reject H_0, that β is truly 1 for the population at the 10% level of significance. In fact, we see that the absolute value of our calculated t statistic is smaller than all the values reported for 21 degrees of freedom. The bottom line is that we cannot confidently reject the hypothesis that β is equal to 1.

Summing Up

In building regression models, the researcher is responsible for specifying what factors are important in explaining the behavior of a dependent variable. Whether or not the researcher has built a sound model depends on a number of things. Ultimately, though, the model must have some logic to it. In our four examples, we put forth hypotheses about how Y can be explained by the related X variable. Using samples of data, we then calculated the OLS regression for each model and asked the following questions: How well does the model fit the data as a whole? And how do the separate components of the model (i.e., a and b) perform? We have seen that the first question can be answered by using the R^2 value. If the R^2 is "large" (i.e., close to 1), then our model works well, and if it is "small" (i.e., close to 0), then our model performs poorly. What value of the R^2 is large enough so that we can claim a good fit is subjective.[27]

With regard to the second question, we have seen that an estimated coefficient's standard error can be used to determine if the coefficient is reliably different from zero. Using the P value (or Sig. in the case of SPSS), we have determined that the smaller its value, the more confident we are that the variable included in the model is truly important in explaining the behavior of the dependent variable. We have also seen that we can test other hypothesized values for our parameters by calculating t statistics and comparing them to t values provided in Table C1 in Appendix C.

---

[27] It should be noted that it is possible for a model to produce a relatively large R^2 even though each separate estimated coefficient fails to achieve a sufficient level of significance. It is also possible to achieve a low R^2 when each estimated coefficient is highly significant.

PROBLEMS

3.1 Use Excel (or another program) and the data shown in Table A6 in Appendix A to calculate the OLS estimation of the following model:

$$Y_i = \alpha + \beta X_i + u_i$$

where: Y_i is hourly wage

X_i is years of education.

Interpret the estimated values for α and β. What is the R^2 for this regression? What is its interpretation?

3.2 Use the regression output from Problem 3.1 to perform the following hypothesis tests:

a. H_0: $\alpha = 0$, H_1: $\alpha \neq 0$, at the 5% significance (or 95% confidence) level.
b. H_0: $\beta = 0$, H_1: $\beta \neq 0$, at the 1% significance (or 99% confidence) level.

3.3 Use the output shown in Table 3.4 and the t table presented in Appendix C to test the following hypothesis:

H_0: $\beta = 9$, H_1: $\beta \neq 9$, at the 5% significance (or 95% confidence) level. [Hint: You should use Equation 3.6b to conduct this test.]

3.4 Using SPSS or Excel (or an equivalent program), perform an OLS regression with GPA as the dependent variable and SAT as the independent variable and conduct the following hypothesis test:

H_0: $\alpha = 0.8$, H_1: $\alpha \neq 0.8$, at the 5% significance (or 95% confidence) level. [Hint: You should use Equation 3.6b to conduct this test.]

4

Multiple Regression Analysis

The two-variable model with which we have been working is the simplest model we can construct. Most things in life, however, are more complicated. Take our baseball example, which hypothesizes that player salaries are a function of how many years a player has played in the major leagues. It should be obvious that this model is too simple. Years of experience may be important in explaining salaries, but clearly other factors are important. In fact, reviewing the data in Appendix A (Table A1), we see that there are four players with 5 years of experience whose salaries range from $0.690 million (Nick Punto) to $12.5 million (Ichiro Suzuki). Years of experience doesn't explain this difference in salary. The data also show that Eric Chavez, who has played 8 years in the major leagues, earned $9.5 million in 2006, whereas Omar Vizquel has played for 17 years but earned only $3.64 million, or a little more than a third as much as Chavez. Time on the job may be important, but so are other factors. In order to improve our model and take into account other important factors, we now begin to discuss the **multiple regression** model. We shall see that in all four of our examples, a richer model is in order.

Baseball Salaries Revisited

A multiple regression model is simply a model that has two or more independent variables. For example, we can build upon our baseball model to include another measure that theoretically should affect baseball salaries: offensive performance. If we consider players with the same number of years of experience in the MLB, then players who perform better offensively may be rewarded with a higher salary, other things being equal. Thus, we can take our original model, shown in Equation 1.2b, and add to it, giving us the following model:

$$Y_i = \alpha + \beta_1 X_{1i} + \beta_2 X_{2i} + u_i, \qquad (4.1)$$

where Y_i represents player i's salary and X_{1i} is the number of years player i has been in MLB. The variable X_{2i} is the player's career slugging average (multiplied by 100). Defined as the average number of bases reached per 100 at bats, this variable is a measure of a player's offensive ability. Finally, u_i is the error term. Notice that we have now added a subscript to the βs and a second subscript to the Xs. This is done so that we know, for example, that β_1 is the coefficient to the variable X_{1i}. The interpretation of β_1 is essentially the same as it was for our previous model. That is, β_1 shows how player salaries increase, on average, as years of MLB experience increase, other things (such as slugging average) being equal. The value for β_2 shows how player salaries increase, on average, as slugging average increases, other things (such as years of MLB experience) being equal. We would expect a positive value for β_2 because the larger a player's slugging average, the more he contributes to a team's offensive production, and as such he should command a higher salary. In sum, each β shows the separate effects of a one-unit increase in its respective X variable on the dependent variable Y while all other things are held constant. We can take the population regression function shown in Equation 4.1 and write the associated sample regression function as

$$Y_i = a + b_1 X_{1i} + b_2 X_{2i} + e_i, \qquad (4.2)$$

where a, b_1, and b_2 are sample estimates for α, β_1, and β_2, respectively.

Given data on Y_i, X_{1i}, and X_{2i}, our goal then is quite similar to the two-variable case: We want to find values for a, b_1, and b_2 such that the sum of the squared errors is as small as possible. Formally, we have the following equation for the sum of the squared errors:

$$\sum_{i=1}^{n} e_i^2 = \sum_{i=1}^{n} (Y_i - a - b_1 X_{1i} - b_2 X_{2i})^2. \qquad (4.3)$$

We can see that Equation 4.3 is very similar to Equation 2.2, except we now have a second X variable on the right-hand side. At this point, as we saw in Chapter 2, we now essentially face a calculus problem where we would find values of a, b_1, and b_2 that minimize the sum of squared errors. The details of the solution to this calculus problem are somewhat complicated and need not concern us here.[1] Suffice it to say that the solution would yield formulas for calculating a, b_1, and b_2, which we could use to define an OLS regression line. Fortunately, software programs such as Excel and SPSS can carry out such calculations for us.

The regression model shown in Equation 4.1 takes our original two-variable model one dimension further and allows us to consider differences in offensive ability. Even this model, however, may not adequately explain differences in salary for players who have the same years of MLB experience and the same offensive ability. Another important factor in determining salary may be defensive ability (i.e., the ability to prevent the opposing team from scoring). If we consider two players with the same years of experience and same offensive ability (i.e., slugging average), if one player is a better defensive player than the other, he would likely command a higher salary. Thus, we can add to the model shown in Equation 4.1 a variable that captures differences in defensive ability. For example, we may include fielding percentage, which measures a player's ability to make a defensive play without committing an error.[2] Doing so gives us the following sample regression function:

$$Y_i = \alpha + \beta_1 X_{1i} + \beta_2 X_{2i} + \beta_3 X_{3i} + u_i, \tag{4.4}$$

where X_{3i} is player i's fielding percentage and β_3 shows the separate effect of an increase in a player's fielding percentage on his salary, other things being equal. We would expect a positive value for β_3 because better defensive players (i.e., players with larger fielding percentages) should earn higher salaries, other things being equal. The associated sample regression function would be

$$Y_i = a + b_1 X_{1i} + b_2 X_{2i} + b_3 X_{3i} + e_i. \tag{4.5}$$

Our goal now is to find values of a, b_1, b_2, and b_3 that would minimize the sum of squared errors and give us the best fitting equation for our data. Specifically, we can augment Equation 4.3 to include our third X variable, giving us the following equation for the sum of squared errors:

$$\sum_{i=1}^{n} e_i^2 = \sum_{i=1}^{n} (Y_i - a - b_1 X_{1i} - b_2 X_{2i} - b_3 X_{3i})^2. \tag{4.6}$$

---

[1] The interested reader can find the details for calculating a, b_1, and b_2 in Gujarati (2003).

[2] See the footnote to Table A1 for a definition of fielding percentage.

Again, applying differential calculus methods to Equation 4.6, we can find the OLS values for a, b_1, b_2, and b_3. Both Excel and SPSS are capable of performing these complicated calculations quite easily. For example, using Excel to estimate the sample regression model shown in Equation 4.5 yields Table 4.1.

Table 4.1 provides us with a great deal of information. We can see under the column headed "Coefficients" a value given for the Intercept, *YEARS*, *SLUGGING*, and *FIELDING*. These values are the OLS estimates for a, b_1, b_2, and b_3, respectively. Thus, the estimated sample regression function (after rounding to three decimal places) is

$$\hat{Y}_i = -30.913 + 0.298\ X_{1i} + 0.430\ X_{2i} + 0.157\ X_{3i}. \qquad (4.7a)$$

Replacing Ys and Xs with variable names, we have

Table 4.1

SUMMARY OUTPUT					
Regression Statistics					
Multiple R	0.740				
R Square	0.548				
Adjusted R Square	0.500				
Standard Error	3.919				
Observations	32				
ANOVA					
	df	SS	MS	F	Significance F
Regression	3	521.937	173.979	11.327	0.000
Residual	28	430.063	15.359		
Total	31	952.000			
	Coefficients	Standard Error	t stat	P value	
Intercept	−30.913	61.552	−0.502	0.619	
YEARS	0.298	0.174	1.710	0.098	
SLUGGING	0.430	0.123	3.499	0.002	
FIELDING	0.157	0.612	0.256	0.800	

$$\widehat{SALARY}_i = -30.913 + 0.298\,(YEARS_i) + 0.430\,(SLUGGING_i)$$
$$+ 0.157\,(FIELDING_i). \tag{4.7b}$$

Interpreting Equation 4.7b, we see that the intercept term is a very large negative number. Technically, it means that a player with zero years of experience, zero slugging average, and a zero fielding percentage would earn on average −$30.913 million! Obviously, this value for a is meaningless because a player realistically cannot earn a negative salary. This result for a exemplifies the point made in Chapter 1 that the intercept does not always have a sensible interpretation.

Moving on to the coefficient for YEARS (i.e., b_1) we see that on average, a player's salary increases by approximately $0.298 million ($298,000) for each additional year of MLB experience, other things being equal. The coefficient for SLUGGING (i.e., b_2) tells us that on average, if a player's slugging average increases by one unit (i.e., one more base per 100 at bats), his salary rises by approximately $0.430 million ($430,000), all else considered. And finally, the coefficient for FIELDING (i.e., b_3) tells us that on average, if a player's fielding percentage increases by 1 percentage point, his salary is expected to increase by about $0.157 million ($157,000), but as we shall see, we need to be careful about this interpretation of the FIELDING coefficient.

Our results in Table 4.1 were, of course, derived from a sample of data. Thus, we face the same issues raised earlier in Chapter 3 regarding the reliability of the values of a, b_1, b_2, and b_3 as estimates of the population parameters α, β_1, β_2, and β_3. That is, are the values for the estimated parameters statistically different from zero? We can answer this question by referring to the P values provided for each estimated coefficient. As we can see, the P values for YEARS and SLUGGING are less than 0.10, meaning we can reject the hypothesis that the population parameters β_1 and β_2 are equal to zero at the 10% level of significance. However, the P value for FIELDING is 0.800, which, given its size, does *not* allow us to reject the hypothesis that β_3 is equal to zero at a reasonable significance level. In other words, there is evidence that YEARS and SLUGGING are significant determinants of a player's salary, but we cannot say this for FIELDING.[3]

Table 4.1 also provides us with the R^2, reported as approximately 0.548, which we can use to evaluate the overall goodness of fit. In this case, the R^2

---

[3] Note that, as we saw in Chapter 3, we can work directly with the t statistics to perform zero hypothesis tests as well as testing nonzero hypotheses.

tells us that about 54.8% of the variation of salaries can be explained by the variables *YEARS, SLUGGING*, and *FIELDING*. Referring back to Table 3.1, we can recall that our simple two-variable model yielded an R^2 of approximately 0.345, or 34.5%. Thus, the R^2 has achieved a marked improvement by adding *SLUGGING* and *FIELDING* to our model. A word of caution, however: *We cannot directly compare the R^2 from our two-variable model to that of our multiple regression model.* In comparing R^2s, there are essentially two rules. First, it is appropriate to directly compare R^2s from two different models only if the dependent variable (Y) is the same in both models *and* the number of independent variables (Xs) is the same in both models.[4] Second, if the dependent variables are the same but the number of X variables is not the same, then each R^2 must be adjusted before we can compare them. This adjustment is needed because of a particular characteristic of the R^2 measure. It can be shown that the R^2 is a nondecreasing function of the number of X variables that appear in our model, regardless of their importance.[5] That is, the R^2 can be artificially inflated by simply adding more X variables to our model, even if adding those X variables is not theoretically justified. The **adjusted R^2** simply takes the regular R^2 and adjusts it downward depending on how many X variables we have. Virtually all software programs that perform regression analysis, including Excel and SPSS, report both the R^2 and the adjusted R^2. Looking at Table 4.1, we see that below the R^2 entry, the adjusted R^2 (i.e., "Adjusted R Square"[6]) is reported as 0.500. Referring back to Table 3.1, we can see for our two-variable model that the adjusted R^2 for that regression is given as approximately 0.323. Thus, based on adjusted R^2s, the multiple regression model performs better than our simple two-variable model.

In dealing with a multiple regression model, a test is commonly carried out to consider the significance of the model *as a whole*. This kind of test

---

[4] For example, we could compare the R^2 from the two-variable model estimation shown in Table 3.1 to the R^2 found from a sample regression where salaries are modeled as a function of slugging average *instead* of years in MLB. In this case, the dependent variable would be the same (player salaries), and both models would have just one X variable. In fact, running this regression (salaries as function of slugging average alone) yields an R^2 of approximately 0.499. This R^2 is more than the one found in Table 3.1, where it was reported as approximately 0.345. Thus, in comparing these two models, we prefer the one that uses slugging average. As we shall see, however, both of these two-variable models are inferior to the multiple regression model shown in Equation 4.4.

[5] For more details regarding this fact, see Gujarati (2003), p. 217.

[6] The adjusted R^2 is sometimes denoted by putting a bar above the regular R^2, that is, $\bar{R}^2$.

becomes important when we may have somewhat high P values (i.e., small t stats) for our estimated bs, indicating that some of our X variables, separately, may not be statistically important. In this event, we may question whether our model actually has anything to say about the dependent variable, Y. It may be the case, however, that despite weak results for the separate X variables, taken together as a group the X variables are *jointly* important. Or, in other words, it may be that each piece of our model is weak, but taken as a group they may be strong. Writing this as a formal hypothesis, we have

$$H_0: \beta_1 = \beta_2 = \beta_3 = 0;$$

that is, the hypothesis that all the population parameters to the X variables are truly and jointly equal to zero, meaning that our model as a whole has no ability to explain the behavior of Y.[7] As for the alternative hypothesis, it would simply be that one or more of the βs is not simultaneously equal to zero.[8] This test of the overall significance of a regression model is called the F **test of significance**, the details of which are somewhat complicated. Fortunately, however, most software programs routinely provide the necessary information, making this test quite easy. Referring to Table 4.1, we see under the ANOVA heading a column headed "F" (short for F **statistic**) with the value 11.327. Next to this column, we see another headed **Significance** F with the value 0.000, which has been rounded to three decimal places.[9] The Significance F is analogous to the P value, which was used to assess the significance of each X variable separately, except that the Significance F is used to assess the significance of the X variables taken as a group. The Significance F tells us the probability that H_0 is true, given our sample results for the regression. In this case, we see that this is an extremely small probability. In other words, we can be quite confident that the model as a whole has something to say about the behavior of Y.

---

[7] This kind of test is unnecessary for the two-variable model we saw in earlier chapters. This is because in the two-variable case, there is only one β, and so the simple P value test is sufficient.

[8] Although the R^2 tells us in some sense how well our model is performing as a whole, it is not a statistical test per se. It can be shown, however, that the testing hypothesis, $H_0: \beta_1 = \beta_2 = \beta_3 = 0$, is equivalent to testing the hypothesis $H_0: R^2 = 0$ (e.g., see Gujarati, 2003, p. 258).

[9] If we increase the decimal places, we have the value 4.86 E-05, reported using scientific notation. The F statistic follows an F distribution, which, in turn, can be used to generate the Significance F. For more details on F distributions and the F statistic, see Gujarati (2003).

Presidential Elections Revisited

Returning to our presidential election example, recall that our two-variable regression model hypothesized that the percentage of two-party votes received by the incumbent party candidate (Y) was a function of the real growth of the economy during the period before the election (X). Although real growth was found to be an important predictor for the votes received, there are other economic measures that we can consider. For example, inflation, defined as the rise in the average price level, is an economic evil because it erodes the value of our income, savings, and other assets that are denominated in dollars. Therefore, even if real incomes have grown, a high rate of inflation may bring economic harm to voters who have dollar-denominated assets, and so these individuals may be less likely to reward candidates from the incumbent party with votes. Thus, we can consider the following multiple regression model that includes both real growth and inflation:

$$Y_t = \alpha + \beta_1 X_{1t} + \beta_2 X_{2t} + u_t. \tag{4.8}$$

The associated sample regression model is

$$Y_t = a + b_1 X_{1t} + b_2 X_{2t} + e_t, \tag{4.9}$$

where X_{1t} is the real percent growth rate of GDP over the three quarters prior to the election and X_{2t} is the inflation rate over the 15 quarters prior to the election. We expect b_2, the coefficient to X_{2t}, to be negative, implying that, other things being equal, an increase in inflation prior to the election would reduce the percentage of two-party votes received by the incumbent party candidate.

The procedure for estimating this model is the same as we saw in the baseball example. We employ the OLS method to find the values for a, b_1, and b_2 so that the sum of squared errors is minimized. Using SPSS to perform this regression, we obtain the results shown in Table 4.2.

Reviewing Table 4.2, we can see in the "Model Summary" panel that the model explains about 57% of the variation in Y, according to the R^2. We can also see that this model outperforms the two-variable one we had before as the adjusted R^2 increased from 0.505 to 0.527 (see Table 3.2). Under the panel headed "ANOVA," we see the F statistic, equal to 13.250, and the associated "Sig." (short for Significance F), which can be used to perform a

Table 4.2

Model Summary

Model	R	R Square	Adjusted R Square	Std. Error of the Estimate
1	.755[a]	.570	.527	4.6918

a. Predictors: (Constant), *INFLATION, GROWTH*

ANOVA[b]

Model		Sum of Squares	df	Mean Square	F	Sig.
1	Regression	583.344	2	291.672	13.250	.000[a]
	Residual	440.268	20	22.013		
	Total	1023.612	22			

a. Predictors: (Constant), *INFLATION, GROWTH*
b. Dependent Variable: *VOTE*

Coefficients[a]

Model		Unstandardized Coefficients		Standardized Coefficients	t	Sig.
		B	Std. Error	Beta		
1	(Constant)	53.365	1.919		27.811	.000
	GROWTH	.705	.217	.581	3.250	.004
	INFLATION	.478	.339	−.252	−1.411	.174

a. Dependent Variable: *VOTE*

test of overall significance. According to the Sig. value, we can reject the hypothesis H_0: $\beta_1 = \beta_2 = 0$ at a very small level of significance (or, equivalently, at a very high level of confidence).[10] That is, we have a statistically significant regression.

The OLS values for a, b_1, and b_2 are given in the third panel, headed "Coefficients." Using these values, we can write the equation for the predicted percentage of two-party votes received by the incumbent party candidate as

$$\hat{Y}_t = 53.365 + 0.705\ X_{1t} - 0.478\ X_{2t}. \qquad (4.10a)$$

---

[10] The "Sig" value shown as .000 is rounded to three digits and means that we can reject H_0: $\beta_1 = \beta_2 = 0$ at the less than 0.01% level of significance.

Or, using variable names, we have

$$\widehat{VOTES_t} = 53.356 + 0.705 \ (GROWTH_t)$$
$$- \ 0.478 \ (INFLATION_t). \tag{4.10b}$$

The coefficient to $GROWTH$ is positive and has a Sig. value of 0.004, meaning that it is significantly different from zero at better than the 1% level of significance (or 99% level of confidence). Its value of 0.705 tells us that a 1 percentage point increase in the growth (as measured here) increases the percentage of two-party votes received by the incumbent party candidate by about 0.705 percentage points, all else being equal. The coefficient to $INFLATION$ is negative and has a Sig. value of 0.174, meaning that the estimated coefficient is statistically different from zero at only the 17.4% level of significance (or 82.6% level of confidence). The coefficient's value of -0.478 means that if inflation (as measured here) increases by 1 percentage point, the percentage of two-party votes received by the incumbent party candidate falls by approximately 0.478 percentage points, all other things considered. This last comment, however, is made with caution due to the weak results for the Sig. value for this coefficient. Recall that a Sig. value of .174 means that there is a 17.4% chance of obtaining a b_2, in absolute terms, of 0.478 or greater when, in fact, the true population's $\beta_2 = 0$. This significance level is larger than the 10% cutoff that is commonly used. Ultimately, however, it is up to the individual researcher or reader to judge whether this result is too weak.[11]

Abortion Rates Revisited

The two-variable model of abortion rates that we estimated in Chapter 3 performed poorly judging by the R^2, which was only 0.016 (see Table 3.3). Recall that the coefficient $RELIGION$ was negative, as expected, but was significantly different from zero at only the 38.6% level of significance (or 61.4% confidence level). By any standard, this result is weak, suggesting that there is a strong chance that the religious makeup of a state (as measured by $RELIGION$) tells us nothing about a state's abortion rate. Clearly, this two-variable model is inadequate.

We can imagine many factors that may affect the abortion rate in a state beyond its religious breakdown. For example, the field of economics tells us

---

[11] Some researchers, in fact, insist on 5% as the cutoff before declaring a coefficient statistically different from zero.

that several factors affect the demand for a particular good or service.[12] In particular, the price of the service should be an important factor. That is, other things being equal, as the price of an abortion increases, the demand for the service should decrease.[13] In addition, income that individuals have to spend on abortions may also affect the demand for abortion services. Specifically, controlling for other factors (i.e., price and religion), as incomes rise, the service becomes more affordable and thus the demand for it increases. Yet, with regard to the effects of income, another, competing theory arises. As incomes rise, all else being constant, the ability of a parent to be able to afford to care for a child also increases, and thus the demand for abortion services may actually *fall*. Which theory for income is correct? We cannot say at the outset, and we allow the regression results to give us guidance.

Another factor that may affect the demand for abortion services is antiabortion activity. As we know, abortion is a divisive, socially sensitive issue. It has prompted some individuals to join together in opposing the provision of such services. In fact, many clinics that provide abortion services have been picketed by groups of individuals who oppose abortion. This being the case, in states where this kind of activity occurs frequently, one would expect that the abortion rate may be lower as both providers and consumers of the service face opposition, all else being equal. In order to control for this factor in our multiple regression model, a variable called *PICKET* is included and is equal to the percentage of clinics in a state that have reported experiencing picketing (including contact with patients and/or providers). Other things being equal, we expect that states with a higher value for *PICKET* will have a lower abortion rate.

Given the above discussion, we can write our sample regression function for abortion as follows:

$$Y_i = a + b_1 X_{1i} + b_2 X_{2i} + b_3 X_{3i} + b_4 X_{4i} + e_i, \qquad (4.11)$$

where Y_i is the abortion rate in state i, X_{1i} is the value of *RELIGION* in state i, X_{2i} is the average *PRICE* of an abortion in state i, X_{3i} is the value of

---

[12] I do not wish to trivialize the socially important issue of abortion by considering it a service that is bought by a consumer. Thinking in this way simply allows us to consider economic factors that may have an impact on abortion rates. For an extensive survey of the economics of abortion, see Kahane (2005).

[13] Economists call this inverse relationship between price and the quantity demanded the "law of demand."

average *INCOME* in state i, and X_{4i} is the value for *PICKET* in state i.[14] Given the above discussion, we expect negative signs for b_1, b_2, and b_4. As for b_3, we have competing theories, and so it could be positive or negative.

Table 4.3 shows the OLS estimation for this multiple regression model. The reported R^2 of 0.539 tells us that our model explains about 53.9% of the variation in abortion rates across states. The adjusted R^2 is shown as 0.498, whereas for the two-variable model, it was -0.005; thus, we clearly

Table 4.3

Model Summary

Model	R	R Square	Adjusted R Square	Std. Error of the Estimate
1	.734[a]	.539	.498	7.1254

a. Predictors: (Constant), *PICKET, PRICE, RELIGION, INCOME*

ANOVA[b]

Model		Sum of Squares	df	Mean Square	F	Sig.
1	Regression	2672.943	4	668.236	13.162	.000[a]
	Residual	2284.683	45	50.771		
	Total	4957.626	49			

a. Predictors: (Constant), *PICKET, PRICE, RELIGION, INCOME*
b. Dependent Variable: ABORTION

Coefficients[a]

Model		Unstandardized Coefficients		Standardized Coefficients	t	Sig.
		B	Std. Error	Beta		
1	(Constant)	-5.869	9.182		$-.639$	.526
	RELIGION	.0004	.083	.001	.005	.996
	PRICE	$-.045$	.022	$-.219$	-2.047	.046
	INCOME	.002	.000	.668	6.203	.000
	PICKET	$-.109$	.040	$-.286$	-2.727	.009

a. Dependent Variable: ABORTION

---

[14] See the footnote to Table A4 for a description of these variables, including source.

have a better fit in this case.[15] The F statistic (13.162) and the associated Sig. value (0.000) shown in the ANOVA panel indicate that the regression as a whole is statistically significant at better than the 0.1% significance (or 99.9% confidence) level. Using the OLS coefficients shown for our model, we can write the following predicted equation (after rounding):

$$\hat{Y}_i = -5.869 + 0.0004\ X_{1i} - 0.045\ X_{2i} + 0.002\ X_{3i} - 0.109\ X_{4i}. \quad (4.12a)$$

Rewriting using variable labels, we have

$$\widehat{ABORTION}_i = -5.869 + 0.0004\ (RELIGION_i) - 0.045\ (PRICE_i)$$
$$+ 0.002\ (INCOME_i) - 0.109\ (PICKET_i). \quad (4.12b)$$

Of the four coefficients to the X variables, the one for $RELIGION$ clearly has the wrong sign. It is positive, whereas we hypothesized that it should be negative. This point, however, becomes moot in light of the fact that the small t statistic (0.005) and the large associated Sig. value (0.996) provide strong evidence that $RELIGION$ is not statistically important in this regression. This outcome illustrates an important point. Namely, in cases where an estimated coefficient is not statistically different from zero at an acceptable level of significance, interpretation of the estimated coefficient's sign and size is often ill-advised because it may imply to the uninformed reader that the variable is statistically important, when in fact it is not.

The coefficient to $PRICE$, on the other hand, has the expected negative sign, and it is statistically different from zero at the 4.6% level of significance. This result supports the hypothesis that, all other things considered, as the price of an abortion increases from one state to another, the abortion rate falls. Specifically, a $1 increase in $PRICE$ tends to reduce the abortion rate by 0.045, all else being equal.

As for $INCOME$, recall that we had competing theories as to whether it would have a positive or negative effect on the abortion rate. The estimated coefficient is found to be positive and significantly different from zero at better than the 0.1% level. This result lends support for the theory that,

---

[15] A negative adjusted R^2 can occur in cases where we have a particularly poor fit, as was the case in the two-variable model for abortion rates.

other things being equal, higher incomes make abortions more affordable and thus cause an increase in the abortion rate.[16] That is, according to our results, as incomes rise by \$1 (from one state to another), the abortion rate tends to increase by 0.002.

Finally, the coefficient for *PICKET* has the expected negative sign. The *t* statistic of −2.727 and Sig. value of 0.009 show that this estimated coefficient is statistically different from zero at better than the 1% significance (or 99% confidence) level. These results support the hypothesis that antiabortion activities (as measured here) have worked to reduce the demand for abortion services, all other things considered. The estimated coefficient predicts that a 1 percentage point increase in reported picketing (from one state to another) leads to a 0.109 drop in the abortion rate, all else being equal.

British Crime Rates Revisited

Our regression for 2004 British police force area crime rates presented in Chapter 3 had only one *X* variable, the unemployment rate, *UNEM*. The estimated coefficient to *UNEM* was positive (as hypothesized) and significant at better than the 1% level. Although the unemployment rate appears to be an important determining factor of crime rates, judging by the reported R^2 of 0.438, there are other factors that need to be considered when modeling crime rates.[17] Several possibilities come to mind. For example, wealth may affect crime. Other things being equal, greater wealth may indicate that individuals are economically better off and hence have a lesser need to supplement their income via criminal activities. On the other hand, greater wealth may represent greater potential gains to criminal activities (i.e., there's more "loot" to be had for those committing crimes).[18] Thus, we have two competing theories about the effects of wealth, and we shall let the

---

[16] There is, in fact, another interpretation for the positive effect of income on the abortion rate. Economists use the term *opportunity cost* when discussing what one gives up in order to pursue something else. In this case, in order to carry a pregnancy to term and raise a child, it is likely that the parents would have to sacrifice part of their income. This being the case, individuals with higher incomes would face a higher opportunity cost of being a parent than those with lower incomes, and thus the higher-income individuals may be more inclined to terminate a pregnancy.

[17] The reader is again referred to Freeman (1999) for a survey of research on crime rates.

[18] These arguments would likely be more appropriate for property crimes and less so for violent crimes. Our data are for total recorded crime and thus combine these two subcategories.

regression results help us decide if one has greater credibility than the other. Data on wealth for the British police force areas are, unfortunately, unavailable. Thus, as a proxy for wealth, we will use a measure called CARS, equal to the number of registered motor vehicles per 1,000 people.[19]

Another likely determinant of criminal activity is the presence of police. Other things being equal, the greater the number of police, the greater the likelihood that a criminal would be caught. Given the negative consequences of being caught (e.g., fines or imprisonment), we would expect a lower crime rate as police presence increases. One complication, however, is that communities may increase the number of police as a response to rising crime rates. This would seem to reverse the causality: Crime rates determine police presence. In order to avoid this problem of bidirectional causality, we can use the previous year's (or "lagged") value for police presence (POLICE) as our X variable.[20]

Finally, because most crime is committed by individuals in their late teens to early 20s, it may be important to consider the proportion of the local population that falls into this age band. That is, police force areas with a higher concentration of individuals in this age band may expect to have greater crime rates, other things being equal. In order to consider this possibility, we include the variable "%pop15_24," which is equal to the percentage of the population in a police force area that falls into the age band of 15 to 24 years.

Adding these two variables to our model yields the following sample regression function for crime:

$$Y_i = a + b_1 X_{1i} + b_2 X_{2i} + b_3 X_{3i} + b_4 X_{4i} + e_i, \tag{4.13}$$

where Y_i is, as before, the number of recorded crimes per 1,000 people for the year 2004 (CRIME). The variables X_{1i}, X_{2i}, X_{3i}, and X_{4i} represent the male unemployment rate (UNEM), registered motor vehicles per 1,000 people (CARS), lagged (i.e., 2003) police per 1,000 people (POLICE), and the percentage of the population aged 15 to 24 years (%pop15_24), respectively. Table 4.4 presents the OLS results (using Excel).

Using the estimated coefficients from Table 4.4, we have the following predicted sample regression function:

---

[19] Witt, Clarke, and Fielding (1999) use this proxy for wealth in their research on British crime rates.

[20] Previous research on crime has used this approach (e.g., see Donohue & Levitt, 2001).

Table 4.4

SUMMARY OUTPUT					
Regression Statistics					
Multiple R	0.793				
R Square	0.629				
Adjusted R Square	0.589				
Standard Error	11.496				
Observations	42				
ANOVA					
	df	SS	MS	F	Significance F
Regression	4	8302.645	2075.661	15.705	0.000
Residual	37	4890.130	132.166		
Total	41	13192.775			
	Coefficients	Standard Error	t stat	P value	
Intercept	0.309	36.312	0.009	0.993	
UNEM	5.352	2.703	1.980	0.055	
CARS	−0.052	0.036	−1.442	0.158	
POLICE	−4.204	7.546	−0.557	0.581	
%pop 15_24	7.941	2.176	3.649	0.001	

$$\hat{Y}_i = 0.309 + 5.352\ X_{1i} - 0.052\ X_{2i} - 4.204\ X_{3i} + 7.941\ X_{4i}, \qquad (4.14a)$$

or, using variable labels,

$$\widehat{CRIME}_i = 0.309 + 5.352\ (UNEM_i) - 0.052\ (CARS_i)$$
$$- 4.204\ (POLICE_i) + 7.941\ (\%pop\ 15\_24_i). \quad (4.14b)$$

Examining the R^2 reported in Table 4.4, we see that the model as a whole explains approximately 63% of the variation in crime rates across the 42 British police force areas in 2004. The adjusted R^2 is now reported as 0.589, which is larger than the 0.424 value we had from the model without CARS, POLICE, and %pop15_24, as reported in Table 3.4. In other words, the model shown in Equation 4.13 clearly outperforms the model discussed in Chapter 3, which included only UNEM.

Turning to the estimated coefficients, we see that *UNEM* has the predicted positive coefficient and that it is statistically different from zero at an acceptable level of significance, given its *P* value of 0.055. The estimated coefficient of 5.352 tells us that, all else being equal, a 1 percentage point increase in the unemployment rate tends to increase crime by 5.352 crimes per 1,000 people. The estimated coefficient for *CARS* is negative and thus agrees with the first hypothesis put forward above that greater wealth reduces crime. The *P* value for this estimated coefficient is 0.158, which means that this variable is statistically significant at about the 15% level of significance. Interpreting its estimated coefficient, we see that an increase of one car per 1,000 people reduces crime on average by 0.052 crimes per 1,000 people. In this case, however, the *P* value is greater than 10%, and if our chosen significance level was indeed 10%, then we would not have a meaningful interpretation for this estimated coefficient. This case brings us back to the issue raised earlier with our election model. Namely, how small does the *P* value need to be before there is a meaningful interpretation of an estimated coefficient? Ultimately, as noted before, the decision is up to the researcher (or those reading the research) as to whether a *P* value is small enough.[21]

As for the coefficient to *POLICE*, we have a value of –4.204 with a corresponding *P* value of 0.581. Although the negative coefficient is in agreement with our hypothesized relationship, the *P* value is much too large, and any interpretation of the estimated coefficient would be meaningless.

Finally, the coefficient to *%pop15_24* is 7.941 with a *P* value of 0.001. The positive value for the estimated coefficient does support the hypothesis that, other things being equal, police force areas with a greater proportion of the population in the age band of 15 to 24 years tend to experience greater crime rates. The estimated coefficient implies that a 1 percentage point increase in *%pop15_24* leads to an increase of 7.941 crimes per 1,000 people on average.

Further Considerations for the Multiple Regression Model

For each of our examples, we have successfully improved our ability to predict the behavior of the dependent variable by building a better, albeit more

---

[21] Although there are differences of opinion among researchers as to how small the *P* value needs to be before a meaningful interpretation of an estimated coefficient can be made, most would not proceed with an interpretation for *P* values greater than 10%.

complicated, multiple regression model. There are, however, two additional concerns that arise in the context of the multiple regression model.

The first concern has to do with the limitation of our data set and the ability to add X variables to our model. The limitation is that the number of X variables we include in our model must be less than the number of observations we have in our sample. To illustrate this restriction, consider our baseball example. We expanded the model to include two additional X variables (*SLUGGING* and *FIELDING*), and this new multiple regression model outperformed the two-variable model we had before. Given this improvement, we could consider adding other variables that may be important in explaining player salaries. For example, we could consider a player's height and weight, or a player's on-base percentage. In fact, there may be many other variables we could consider using in our model. Each time we add another X variable to our model, however, we pay a price in terms of degrees of freedom.[22] For each X variable we add to our model, we must calculate another coefficient, leaving fewer remaining degrees of freedom to perform other tasks, such as hypothesis testing. Thus, given that our data set has a limited amount of information, this puts a limit on the number of tasks we can perform.

The second concern has to do with the relationship (if any) between the X variables. Simply put, the OLS method will not tolerate any *perfect linear* relationship among the X variables in our model. That is, in the case of the multiple regression model, we now add to our list of assumptions outlined in Chapter 2 the following: We assume that there does not exist any perfect linear relationship between the independent (X) variables. That is, we assume that there is no perfect **multicollinearity**.[23] To understand this point, consider our baseball example. Suppose we wanted to include a player's age (years and months) as an independent variable with the hypothesis that older players may be rewarded for their experience and the leadership that they bring to the team. In addition, we can consider when a player was born (year and month) as an independent variable with the hypothesis that players from different generations may have different expectations on how they should be paid for playing baseball. Although these two X variables seem to capture different effects (the "experience factor" and the "generation difference"), they are, in fact, perfectly

---

[22] See footnote 22 in Chapter 2.

[23] Lesser degrees of multicollinearity, which is the case where two or more X variables are less than perfectly linearly related, are not necessarily a problem. We will have more to say about this case in Chapter 7. Furthermore, perfect *nonlinear* relationships are not ruled out, as we will discuss in Chapter 5.

redundant. That is, if we know when a player was born, then we know his age. These two variables are perfectly linearly related: Age equals current year and month minus birth year and month. In this case, the OLS method cannot distinguish any separate effects of these two variables because they contain the exact same information.[24] The solution is that only one of these two variables can remain in our model; the other must be dropped.

Summing Up

The two-variable model, although instructive, is insufficient in most cases, and a multiple regression model will be required.[25] We have seen in this chapter that by including relevant variables in our four examples, the estimated multiple regressions outperformed their two-variable counterparts, using the adjusted R^2 as our measure of improvement. The next chapter continues with the development of the multiple regression model by considering not the number but the various *types* and *forms* of X and Y variables we can consider.

PROBLEMS

4.1 Using the data in Table A4 of Appendix A,[26] reestimate the model shown in Equation 4.11, but now include the variable *EDUC* as an independent variable. Using your output, answer the following questions:

   a. What is the interpretation of the estimated coefficient to *EDUC*?
   b. Does this model, as a whole, outperform the one without *EDUC*? Explain.
   c. Is the coefficient to *EDUC* statistically different from zero at the 5% level of significance (95% level of confidence)?

---

[24] In fact, any attempt to estimate a model that has a perfectly multicollinear relationship will generally cause the software program to return an error message.

[25] In fact, if we estimate only a two-variable model, and in so doing exclude other relevant variable(s), then we have committed a model specification error. In this case, we cannot be sure that the OLS estimated model is BLUE (see the discussion on the CLRM assumptions in Chapter 2). We explore this issue in greater detail in Chapter 7.

[26] Note that these data are available for downloading off the Internet at www.cbe.csueastbay.edu/~lkahane/

4.2 Using the output from Table 4.2, test whether the coefficient to *GROWTH* is statistically different from 1.0 at the 10% significance (90% confidence) level. (Hint: Use Equation 3.6b to answer this question.)

4.3 Using Equation 4.7b, predict the salary of a MLB player who has 10 years of experience, a slugging average of 38.0, and a fielding percentage of 97.5.

4.4 Returning to our model of wages as described in Problem 3.1, suppose we now add experience to the equation. That is, we have

$$Y_i = \alpha + \beta_1 X_{1i} + \beta_2 X_{2i} + u_i,$$
where: Y_i is hourly wage
X_{1i} is years of education
X_{2i} is years of work experience.

  a. Use SPSS or Excel (or another program) to perform an OLS estimate of this multiple regression model and interpret the estimated coefficients.
  b. Test whether the estimated values for β_1 and β_2 are statistically different from zero at the 5% level of significance.

4.5 Recall our model of SUV prices in Question 2.3. Suppose we now add engine size as an independent variable to our model, giving us

$$Y_i = \alpha + \beta_1 X_{1i} + \beta_2 X_{2i} + u_i,$$
where: Y_i is *MSRP*
X_{1i} is horsepower
X_{2i} is engine size (in liters).

  a. Use SPSS or Excel to calculate the OLS estimate of this model and interpret the results. Are both estimated slope coefficients statistically different from zero at the 5% level of significance? Explain.
  b. Given that the R^2 from the model without engine size is 0.695 and with an adjusted R^2 is 0.686, does the model with engine size produce a better fit? Explain.

4.6 Recall our model that has college GPA as a function of SAT scores (see Problem 2.4 from Chapter 2). Suppose we now consider adding the variable *HSRANK*, which is the individual's rank in his or her high school graduating class.

  a. What sign do we expect for the coefficient to the new variable *HSRANK*? Explain.
  b. Estimate the new model with *HSRANK* and determine if the estimated coefficient to this new variable is statistically different from zero at the 5% level of significance.
  c. Does the model with *HSRANK* outperform the one without it? Explain.

5

Nonlinear and Logarithmic Models, and Dummy and Interaction Variables

In the previous chapter, we built multiple regression models for our four examples. In each case, new independent (X) variables were introduced that we hypothesized were important in explaining the dependent variable (Y). In all of the examples, the new X variables were continuous measures, and they entered our model linearly (i.e., with the power of 1). There are, however, other *types* of variables we can consider that may be desirable under certain circumstances. Four types that we will discuss in this chapter are nonlinear X variables; logarithmic models where the natural log of X and/or Y is considered; **dummy variables** that denote "categories"; and **interaction variables,** which show how two variables may interact with each other. We begin with nonlinear X variables.

Nonlinear Independent Variables: The Quadratic Model

In Chapter 1, where we introduced our baseball example, we hypothesized that a player's salary may increase with the number of years he has played in MLB (see Equation 1.2b). The theory is simply that a player's skills improve the longer he plays in the major leagues, and as a result, he is rewarded with increased pay. Although this may be true, it may also be the case that the reward for time on the job is not constant throughout a player's career. That is, a player may witness larger salary increases in the early years, but smaller increases in the later years. This may be the case because in the beginning of a player's career, experience is very important as he "learns the ropes" and improves rapidly. Later in a player's career, additional experience may improve his performance, but to a lesser degree because he is already quite experienced.[1] Mathematically, this would imply a nonlinear function, such as

$$Y = \alpha + \beta_1 X + \beta_2 X^2. \tag{5.1}$$

The function shown in Equation 5.1 is called a quadratic, and if β_1 is positive and β_2 is negative, Y will increase as X increases, but at a decreasing rate. This kind of function would produce a graph like the one shown in Figure 5.1.[2]

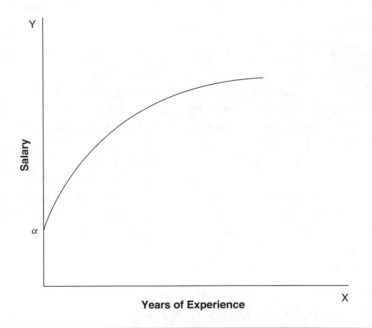

Figure 5.1

---

[1] This is analogous to the "learning curve." In the beginning of a new activity, a participant learns very quickly about performing the activity. Later, additional experience teaches the participant little about performing the activity.

[2] If both β_1 and β_2 are positive, the function will be increasing but at an increasing rate.

As we see in Figure 5.1, salary increases with years of experience, but at a decreasing rate. Thus, all that is needed to allow for such a nonlinear relationship in our regression model is to create a new variable that is equal to the square of *YEARS*.[3] This new variable can now be included with the other *X* variables we had in our sample regression function, as shown in Equation 4.5. This gives us a new sample regression function:

$$Y_i = a + b_1 X_{1i} + b_2 X_{2i} + b_3 X_{3i} + b_4 X_{1i}^2 + e_i, \qquad (5.2)$$

where the *X* variables are the same as before: X_{1i} is years of MLB experience, X_{2i} is a player's career slugging average, and X_{3i} is a player's fielding percentage. Notice that we have now added X_{1i}^2 to the list of independent variables. Before going any further, it should be pointed out that including the square of an existing *X* variable as an additional independent variable does not violate the assumption made in Chapter 4 of no perfect multicollinearity. As noted before, this assumption rules out perfect linear relationships, but not perfect nonlinear relationships.[4]

Using Excel to calculate the OLS estimates for a, b_1, b_2, b_3, and b_4, we obtain the results shown in Table 5.1.

We see in Table 5.1 that the R^2 is about 0.633. This tells us that our model explains about 63.3% of the variation in salaries. Comparing the results shown in Table 5.1 to those in Table 4.1, we see that the adjusted R^2 has substantially increased with the inclusion of years of MLB experience squared (shown as *YEARS SQUARED* in Table 5.1). Furthermore, the *P* value for the coefficient to *YEARS SQUARED* is approximately 0.019,

---

[3] This is easily accomplished in both SPSS and Excel. In SPSS, the "Transform" item on the main menu bar is chosen, then "Compute" is chosen. At the next dialog box, the "Target Variable" is the name to be given to the new variable (e.g., *YEARSSQ*, for *YEARS* squared). The equation is typed in the "Numeric Expression" box to create the new variable. For example, we would type *YEARS**2 to create the square of *YEARS*, and then select "OK." As for Excel, one would simply create a new column of data headed with, say, *YEARSSQ*. In the first entry below this label, we could type the equation, =(cell address)^2, where "cell address" would be the location of the first element below *YEARS*, and hit Enter. This would create the square of the first observation's value for *YEARS* and put below the label *YEARSSQ*. Once this is done, a "copy," "paste" command can be used to copy the newly created equation to all the cells below it for the entire sample.

[4] See footnote 23 of Chapter 4. Note that although including a variable and its square as independent variables does not violate the no perfect multicollinearity assumption, it may lead to problems of high multicollinearity. This issue is discussed briefly in Chapter 7.

Table 5.1

SUMMARY OUTPUT					
Regression Statistics					
Multiple R	0.796				
R Square	0.633				
Adjusted R Square	0.578				
Standard Error	3.598				
Observations	32				
ANOVA					
	df	SS	MS	F	Significance F
Regression	4	602.471	150.618	11.635	0.000
Residual	27	349.529	12.946		
Total	41	952.000			
	Coefficients	Standard Error	t stat	P value	
Intercept	−51.767	57.124	−0.906	0.373	
YEARS	2.136	0.754	2.832	0.009	
SLUGGING	0.284	0.127	2.230	0.034	
FIELDING	0.360	0.568	0.635	0.531	
YEARS SQUARED	−0.086	0.035	−2.494	0.019	

which tells us that the b_4 is statistically different from zero at a very small significance level (i.e., high confidence level). In sum, inclusion of YEARS SQUARED has improved our model. Using the value of the estimated coefficients from Table 5.1, the predicted equation, after rounding, is

$$\hat{Y}_i = -51.767 + 2.136X_{1i} + 0.284X_{2i} + 0.360X_{3i} - 0.086X_{1i}^2, \quad (5.3a)$$

or

$$\widehat{SALARY}_i = -51.767 + 2.136 \, (YEARS_i) + 0.284 \, (SLUGGING_i) \\ + 0.360 \, (FIELDING_i) - 0.086 \, (YEARS_i^2) \quad (5.3b)$$

We see that (ignoring the constant term) all of the coefficients in Equation 5.3b have the expected signs. SLUGGING is positive and significantly different from zero at about the 3.4% significance level. The variable FIELDING, however, is not statistically significant, a result that we found in our earlier regression (see Table 4.1).

The coefficients to *YEARS* and *YEARS SQUARED* are both statistically different from zero at a very low level of significance (i.e., high level of confidence). The combined effect of *YEARS* and *YEARS SQUARED* supports the hypothesis described earlier that *SALARY* tends to increase, but at a declining rate, as a player's years in MLB increase. As an example, consider a player with 2 years of MLB experience. We can use the results shown in Equation 5.3a to calculate the estimated increase in his salary for an additional year of experience. To do so, we first plug into Equation 5.3a the values of 2 for X_{1i} and 4 for X_{1i}^2, multiply these values by the estimated coefficients for b_1 and b_4, and then add these results together. This is then repeated for X_{1i} equal to 3 and X_{1i}^2 equal to 9. The difference between these two values is the gain in salary due to a third year of experience. Performing these calculations, we find that the expected increase in pay to this player for an additional year of experience would be approximately $1.705 million, other things being constant. On the other hand, using a similar calculation, we find that a player with 5 years of MLB experience can expect a salary increase of about $1.189 million for an additional year of experience, other things being constant. As expected, salary increases at a decreasing rate with experience.

Including the square of *YEARS* in our model has clearly improved our model's overall performance. It should be noted that we are not restricted to adding only squared terms. In some cases, we may wish to add the square of a variable *and* its cube when we hypothesize more complicated nonlinear relationships.[5]

Logarithmic Functional Forms

Some nonlinear relationships can be partly "straightened out" by transforming existing variables. One common way of doing this is to work with natural logs of variables. For example, we can consider the simple two-variable model (just to illustrate this concept) we had before in Chapter 1 (see Equation 1.2b):

$$Y_i = \alpha + \beta X_i + u_i.$$

We can transform this equation by taking the natural log of the *Y* and *X* values, leaving us with

---

[5] Reciprocal relationships can also be incorporated. That is, we can include an *X* variable and its reciprocal, $1/X$.

$$\ln Y_i = \alpha + \beta \ln X_i + u_i, \tag{5.4}$$

where the "ln" stands for the natural log.[6] This functional form not only can help linearize a nonlinear relationship, but it also gives us a sometimes quite useful interpretation for the coefficient to the $\ln X_i$ variable. In this case, where we use the natural log of both the Y_i and X_i values (sometimes called a "double-log" functional form), the coefficient β tells us the percentage change in Y for a 1% change in X, all else being equal.[7] Other versions of logarithmic functional forms take the natural log of one variable, but not the other (sometimes referred to as a "semi-log" model). For example,

$$\ln Y_i = \alpha + \beta X_i + u_i. \tag{5.5}$$

Here we take the natural log of the dependent variable, Y, but the independent variable, X, enters the equation linearly. In this case, the interpretation of β is the proportionate change in Y for a one-unit change in X, all else being equal. Or, if we multiply β by 100, that is, $\beta \times 100$, then the interpretation is the percentage change in Y for a one-unit change in X, again all else being equal. Finally, we can have Y entering the model linearly but using the natural log of X:

$$Y_i = \alpha + \beta \ln X_i + u_i. \tag{5.6}$$

For this case, the interpretation of β is the following: the change in Y for a proportionate change in X. Alternatively, if we multiply β by 0.01 (effectively dividing β by 100), the interpretation becomes the change in Y for a 1% change in X, ceteris paribus.[8]

In order to illustrate the logarithmic functional form, we can reconsider our British crime example. Using a variant of Equation 5.5, we can write Equation 4.13 as the following:

$$\ln Y_i = a + b_1 X_{1i} + b_2 X_{2i} + b_3 X_{3i} + b_4 X_{4i} + e_i, \tag{5.7}$$

where the only difference is that we now employ $\ln Y_i$, the natural log of the number of recorded crimes per 1,000 people for the year 2004, as our

---

[6] Note that both Excel and SPSS can compute natural logs of variables. See Appendix B for details. Also note that one cannot compute natural logs for nonpositive numbers, and so this will limit our ability to use the natural log transformation for some variables.

[7] Economists call this measure, the percentage change in Y for a 1% change in X, the "elasticity" of Y with respect to X.

[8] Gujarati (2003), pp. 175–191, or Wooldridge (2006), pp. 197–204, provide good discussions on various functional forms.

dependent variable. The variables X_{1i}, X_{2i}, X_{3i}, and X_{4i} are as they were before: the male unemployment rate, the number of registered motor vehicles per 1,000 people, lagged police per 1,000 people, and the percentage of the population aged 15 to 24 years, respectively. The resulting OLS estimation, using Excel, is presented in Table 5.2.

Using the estimated coefficients from Table 5.2, we can write the predicted sample regression function as

$$\ln \hat{Y}_i = 3.399 + 0.063X_{1i} - 0.001X_{2i} - 0.060X_{3i} + 0.098X_{4i}, \quad (5.8a)$$

or, using variable labels,

$$\widehat{LnCRIME}_i = 3.399 + 0.063 \ (UNEM_i) - 0.001 \ (CARS_i)$$
$$- 0.060 \ (POLICE_i) + 0.098 \ (\%pop \ 15\_24_i). \quad (5.8b)$$

Table 5.2

SUMMARY OUTPUT					
Regression Statistics					
Multiple R	0.795				
R Square	0.632				
Adjusted R Square	0.592				
Standard Error	0.137				
Observations	42				
ANOVA					
	df	SS	MS	F	Significance F
Regression	4	1.199	0.300	15.871	0.000
Residual	37	0.699	0.019		
Total	41	1.898			
	Coefficients	Standard Error	t stat	P value	
Intercept	3.399	0.434	7.831	0.000	
UNEM	0.063	0.032	1.961	0.057	
CARS	−0.001	0.000	−1.502	0.142	
POLICE	−0.060	0.090	−0.667	0.509	
%pop15_24	0.098	0.026	3.784	0.001	

According to the P value reported in Table 5.2, the coefficient to $UNEM$, the male unemployment rate, is statistically different from zero at approximately the 5.7% level of significance. Multiplying the estimated coefficient of 0.063 by 100 gives us 6.3. Thus, we can say that, other things being equal, a 1 percentage point increase in the unemployment rate increases the number of crimes per 1,000 people by about 6.3%, on average. The coefficient to $CARS$ has a P value of 0.142, meaning that the coefficient is different from zero at about the 14.2% level of significance. Although this is somewhat of a large P value, we can, for instructive purposes, interpret the estimated coefficient. Multiplying the estimated value of –0.001 by 100 yields the value –0.100. Thus, for an increase of one car per 1,000 people, the crime rate falls on average by approximately one tenth of 1%, all else being equal. Turning to $POLICE$, its P value of 0.509 tells us that the estimated coefficient is not statistically different from zero at an acceptable level of significance, and thus there is no meaningful interpretation of this coefficient.[9] Finally, the coefficient to the $\%pop15\_24$ is positive and significant at less than the 1% level of significance. Multiplying the estimated coefficient of 0.098 by 100 gives us 9.8. Thus, for every 1 percentage point increase of the percentage of the population aged 15 to 24, the crime rate is expected to increase by 9.8%, all else being equal.

Dummy Independent Variables

In some cases, one or more of our independent variables may not be a continuous measure. For example, we can consider our presidential election model. One factor that we have not considered is whether the incumbent party candidate is, in fact, the incumbent himself. An example would be Bill Clinton, who was the incumbent party candidate in 1996 when he ran for reelection.[10] We can contemplate how being the incumbent affects the percentage of two-party votes received by the incumbent party candidate. It would seem likely that, other things being equal (including growth of the economy and inflation), the incumbent would have an advantage over another candidate simply because he

---

[9] Recall that we had a similar conclusion for the insignificance of $POLICE$ as reported in Table 4.4. We shall see in Chapter 6, however, that when we increase our sample to include multiple years of data, that the estimated coefficient to the $POLICE$ variable is negative and significant.

[10] In contrast to this scenario, George H. W. Bush was the incumbent party candidate in the 1988 election, but he was not the incumbent.

is better known to the voters. That is, other things being equal, incumbent candidates would, on average, receive a larger percentage of the two-party votes. We can test this hypothesis by *creating* a dummy variable that indicates whether the incumbent party candidate is indeed the president running for reelection.[11] In order to facilitate a graphical representation of dummy variable effects, we can consider our earlier two-variable sample regression model shown in Equation 1.6, but now including a dummy variable to indicate whether the incumbent party candidate is, in fact, the incumbent:

$$Y_t = a + b_1 X_{1t} + b_3 X_{3t} + e_t, \qquad (5.9a)$$

where X_{3t} takes the value of 1 if the incumbent party candidate is the president running for reelection, 0 otherwise (we have excluded $b_2 X_{2t}$ for the moment so that our graph will be two-dimensional; it will be added back later). Thus, the coefficient b_3 would represent the effect on the Y_t, if any, from being the incumbent. Note that in the case where the incumbent party candidate is *not* the incumbent, then X_{3t} would be zero and the predicted portion of Equation 5.9a would be

$$\hat{Y}_t = a + b_1 X_{1t}. \qquad (5.9b)$$

However, if the incumbent party candidate is, in fact, the incumbent, then X_{3t} would be equal to 1 and the predicted portion of Equation 5.9a becomes

$$\hat{Y}_t = a + b_1 X_{1t} + b_3. \qquad (5.9c)$$

As we can see, the only difference between Equations 5.9b and 5.9c is that the latter includes b_3. Or, in other words, the intercept value for Equation 5.9b is a, whereas in Equation 5.9c, it is $a + b_3$. Graphically, these two equations are simply parallel lines with different intercept values. Figure 5.2 shows an example of this kind.

Notice that the line for incumbent party candidates who are, in fact, incumbents is shifted up by the value b_3. This shift represents the advantage of being an incumbent over nonincumbents for any given level of economic growth (i.e., for all values of X_{1t}).

---

[11] Dummy variables are sometimes called "indicator," "categorical," or "binary" variables.

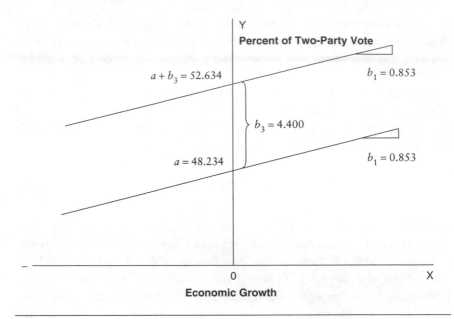

Figure 5.2

Using OLS to estimate the sample regression function shown in Equation 5.9a yields the following estimated relationship[12:]

$$\widehat{VOTE}_t = 48.234 + 0.853 \, (GROWTH_t) + 4.400 \, (INCUMBENT_t). \quad (5.9d)$$

According to the above estimated equation, given the same level of growth in the economy, incumbents enjoy about a 4.4 percentage point advantage over nonincumbents. That is, in terms of Figure 5.2, the sample regression line for incumbents would be shifted vertically upward by about 4.4 percentage points above the sample regression line for nonincumbents.

Adding back to this model the variable for inflation, X_{2t}, we now have

$$Y_t = a + b_1 X_{1t} + b_2 X_{2t} + b_3 X_{3t} + e_t. \quad (5.10)$$

In this case, we would have a three-dimensional graph (which would be difficult to draw and hence is not attempted). The interpretation of the coefficient b_3, however, would be similar to that of the simpler case discussed above. Namely, given the same level of economic growth *and* inflation, b_3 represents the added votes that an incumbent candidate is expected to receive as compared to nonincumbents.

---

[12] The reader is invited to verify this regression result.

It should be noted that X_{3t} is not a continuous measure, such as growth, which can theoretically take on any value. This variable takes on only the values of 1 or 0.[13] Reviewing Table A3, we see the column headed *INCUMBENT*. The values for this column indicate if the incumbent ran for reelection. A value of 1 indicates yes, 0 indicates no. The treatment for this variable, however, is no different from the treatment for any other X variable in our model. Using SPSS, we simply include this dummy variable on the list of independent variables and perform the OLS estimation as usual. Estimating Equation 5.10, we have the results shown in Table 5.3.

Table 5.3

Model Summary

Model	R	R Square	Adjusted R Square	Std. Error of the Estimate
1	.816[a]	.665	.613	4.2453

a. Predictors: (Constant), *INCUMBENT, INFLATION, GROWTH*

ANOVA[b]

Model		Sum of Squares	df	Mean Square	F	Sig.
1	Regression	681.182	3	227.061	12.599	.000[a]
	Residual	342.430	19	18.023		
	Total	1023.612	22			

a. Predictors: (Constant), *INCUMBENT, INFLATION, GROWTH*

b. Dependent Variable: *VOTE*

Coefficients[a]

Model		Unstandardized Coefficients		Standardized Coefficients	t	Sig.
		B	Std. Error	Beta		
1	(Constant)	50.502	2.127		23.740	.000
	GROWTH	.683	.196	.564	3.480	.003
	INFLATION	−.463	.306	−.245	−1.511	.147
	INCUMBENT	4.342	1.864	.310	2.330	.031

a. Dependent Variable: *VOTE*

---

[13] It is possible to use other numbers to represent categories, but using 1 and 0 makes the interpretation of our results easier and more intuitive.

Starting with the model summary, we see that R^2 is 0.665, meaning that about 66.5% of the variation in Y is explained by our model. As for the adjusted R^2, it is now 0.613, whereas in the model without the dummy variable INCUMBENT, it was 0.527 (see Table 4.2). Thus, based on the adjusted R^2, this model performs better. The F statistic and the associated Sig. value (shown in the ANOVA panel) indicate that the regression as a whole is statistically significant at a very high level of confidence (i.e., small level of significance).[14]

The estimated coefficients for all of the X variables have the predicted signs. Using these values, we have the following estimated sample regression function:

$$\hat{Y}_t = 50.502 + 0.683X_{1t} - 0.463X_{2t} + 4.342X_{3t}. \qquad (5.11a)$$

Rewriting using variable names, we have

$$\widehat{VOTES}_t = 50.502 + 0.683\,(GROWTH_t) - 0.463$$
$$(INFLATION_t) + 4.342\,(INCUMBENT_t). \qquad (5.11b)$$

Checking the significance of each estimated coefficient, we see that the Sig. values for the constant and GROWTH indicate that they are significantly different from zero at better than the 1% significance (or 99% confidence) level. INFLATION, with a Sig. value of 0.147, is statistically different from zero at the 14.7% significance (or 85.3% confidence) level— a somewhat weak result. Concerning our dummy variable, INCUMBENT, it has a Sig. value of 0.031, indicating that it is statistically different from zero at the 3.1% significance (or 96.9% confidence) level. Thus, in sum, the results give strong support for the hypothesis that GROWTH and INCUM-BENT are important in explaining VOTES, and moderate support that INFLATION is an important determinant for VOTES as well.

The interpretation of the estimated coefficients for the constant, GROWTH, and INFLATION are similar to what they were before. That is, all else being equal, if GROWTH, INFLATION, and INCUMBENT are all zero, then the constant term implies that, on average, the incumbent party candidate is expected to win about 50.502% of the two-party votes. The coefficient for GROWTH suggests that, on average, a 1 percentage point increase in the growth of the economy prior to the election will increase the percentage of two-party votes that the incumbent party candidate wins by

---

[14] This test is somewhat trivial in light of the fact that the regression without INCUM-BENT was statistically significant, and by adding this dummy variable, our model is strengthened.

approximately 0.683 percentage points, all else being equal. If *INFLATION* rises by 1 percentage point, all else held constant, the regression results imply that the incumbent party candidate will lose about 0.463 percentage points of the two-party votes. Finally, the coefficient to our dummy variable, *INCUMBENT*, is shown as 4.342. This suggests that, controlling for growth and inflation, if the incumbent party candidate is, in fact, the incumbent (i.e., $X_{3t} = 1$), then he is expected to receive about 4.342 percentage points more of the two-party votes than someone who is the incumbent party candidate but who is not the incumbent (i.e., $X_{3t} = 0$). In other words, all else being equal, if the president runs for reelection, he has a considerable advantage over someone from the same party running for his first term as president.[15]

Dummy variables are widely used in regression analysis.[16] For example, in research projects where a data set has observations on both males and females, one may wish to create a dummy variable to control for gender differences (e.g., a dummy variable that takes the value of 1 if the individual is a female, 0 if a male). Or we can consider the effects of education by creating a dummy variable that is 1 for a high school graduate, 0 otherwise.

In the above example, we created a variable that indicated whether something was true where there were only two possibilities: either the incumbent party candidate was the incumbent or he was not the incumbent. In some cases, there may be more than two possible categories. For example, in our analysis of salary paid to baseball players, we could consider whether a player's salary depends on his race. In this case, we can consider three categories for a player's race: white (including Asian), black, or non-black Hispanic. In order to cover these three categories, however, we need to create only two dummy variables. One dummy variable takes the value of 1 if the player is black, 0 otherwise.[17] The second dummy variable takes the value of 1 if the player is a non-black Hispanic, 0 otherwise. If both of these dummy variables equal zero, then it must be the case that the player is white. This example demonstrates an important rule regarding dummy variables: *If we have m categories for which we wish to control, we need only m – 1 dummy variables.* This is true because if the value of all m – 1 dummy variables is 0, then it must be the case that the observation belongs to the

---

[15] The reason for this advantage may be due to the fact that the president typically has much more exposure to voters through the media than other candidates and can use this exposure to his benefit.

[16] For a more extensive discussion on the use of dummy variables, see Hardy (1993). It is also possible that the dependent (Y) variable could be a dummy variable. This topic, however, is beyond the scope of this book, and the reader is referred to Aldrich and Nelson (1984) or Wooldridge (2006).

[17] In this example, in the event that a player is both black and Hispanic, he is classified as black.

excluded category. In fact, if we tried to include m dummy variables in our model, we would end up violating the regression model assumption of *no perfect multicollinearity* (see Chapter 4) because our model would contain redundant information and software programs would return an error message.

In addition to race, we can also consider whether salaries differ between leagues. That is, is salary higher or lower in the National League as compared to the American League? Given that we have two categories, we can control for league effects by creating one dummy variable that takes on the value of 1 if a player is in the National League, 0 otherwise (i.e., if a player is in the American League).

Incorporating the two dummy variables for black and non-black Hispanic players and the dummy variable for the National League into our model, the sample regression function becomes

$$Y_i = a + b_1 X_{1i} + b_2 X_{2i} + b_3 X_{3i}$$
$$+ b_4 X_{1i}^2 + b_5 X_{5i} + b_6 X_{6i} + b_7 X_{7i} + e_i, \qquad (5.12a)$$

where X_{5i} takes the value of 1 if the player is black, 0 otherwise. The variable X_{6i} takes the value of 1 if the player is a non-black Hispanic, 0 otherwise. And X_{7i} is equal to 1 if the player is in the National League, 0 otherwise. In this example, our "base category" for race would be players who are white. For white players, X_{5i} and X_{6i} are both zero, and thus the terms $b_5 X_{5i}$ and $b_6 X_{6i}$ in Equation 5.12a drop out, leaving the following sample regression function:

$$Y_i = a + b_1 X_{1i} + b_2 X_{2i} + b_3 X_{3i} + b_4 X_{1i}^2 + b_7 X_{7i} + e_i. \qquad (5.12b)$$

If a player is black, then X_{5i} is 1, giving us the following sample regression function:

$$Y_i = a + b_1 X_{1i} + b_2 X_{2i} + b_3 X_{3i} + b_4 X_{1i}^2 + b_5(1) + b_7 X_{7i} + e_i. \qquad (5.12c)$$

Notice that the only difference between Equation 5.12b and Equation 5.12c is that the latter includes b_5. Thus, the expected effect of being a black player is to increase (or decrease) a player's salary above (or below) a white player's salary by the amount b_5, other things being equal. If a player is Hispanic, then X_{6i} will be 1, giving us the following sample regression function:

$$Y_i = a + b_1 X_{1i} + b_2 X_{2i} + b_3 X_{3i} + b_4 X_{1i}^2 + b_6(1) + b_7 X_{7i} + e_i. \qquad (5.12d)$$

In this case, the value of b_6 would represent the difference in salary (positive or negative) for non-black Hispanic players as compared to our base case of white players, all else being equal. As in the case for our voting model, notice that the dummy variables simply alter the intercept of the model shown in Equation 5.11a. That is, in the case of a white player, the intercept is simply a because $b_5 X_{5i}$ and $b_6 X_{6i}$ drop out of the equation. In the case of a black player, b_5 remains in the sample regression function. This is simply a number (whatever b_5 turns out to be) that adjusts the intercept a upward or downward, depending on the sign of b_5. Similarly for the case of non-black Hispanics, b_6 remains in the sample regression function and adjusts the intercept a upward or downward, depending on the sign of b_6. As for the dummy variable for the National League, the analysis is similar. If a player is in the National League, then the term $X_{7i} = 1$ and the term b_7 is added to the intercept and will adjust it upward or downward, depending on the value of b_7. The value of b_7 thus reflects the pay differential (if any) for National League players as compared to the base case, which is the American League, other things being equal.

Using the data shown in Table A1 and SPSS to estimate the model shown in Equation 5.12a, we obtain the results shown in Table 5.4.

Table 5.4 reports an R^2 of 0.708, meaning that our model explains about 70.8% of the variation in player salaries. Comparing the adjusted R^2 here to that of Table 5.1, we see that there is an increase from 0.578 to 0.623, respectively. Thus, based on the adjusted R^2, this model outperforms the earlier one. The F statistic and associated Sig. value indicate that, overall, our model is statistically significant. Using the estimated coefficients shown in Table 5.4, we can write our predicted equation as

$$\widehat{SALARY}_i = -58.016 + 2.087\,(YEARS_i) + 0.212\,(SLUGGING_i)$$
$$+ 0.457\,(FIELDING_i) - 0.083\,(YEARS_i^2) + 3.275\,(BLACK_i)$$
$$- 0.378\,(HISPANIC_i) - 2.00\,(LEAGUE_i). \tag{5.12e}$$

Focusing on the coefficients for b_5 and b_6, the first is the coefficient to BLACK, which is positive, indicating that, other things being equal, black players tend to earn more than whites. Specifically, a black player is expected to earn about \$3.275 million more than a white player (our base category) with equal ability (i.e., with the same number of YEARS, YEARS SQUARED, SLUGGING, FIELDING, and LEAGUE values). As for non-black Hispanics, they tend to earn about \$0.378 million less than white players with equal values for the other independent variables. Finally, the dummy variable for LEAGUE suggests that players in the National League earn, on average, about \$2 million less than American Leaguers, all else being equal. With regard to the coefficients to HISPANIC and LEAGUE, however, *they are not statistically*

Table 5.4

Model Summary

Model	R	R Square	Adjusted R Square	Std. Error of the Estimate
1	.842[a]	.708	.623	3.40084

a. Predictors: (Constant), *LEAGUE, FIELDING, YEARS SQUARED, HISPANIC, BLACK, SLUGGING, YEARS*

ANOVA[b]

Model		Sum of Squares	df	Mean Square	F	Sig.
1	Regression	674.428	7	96.347	8.330	.000[a]
	Residual	277.576	24	11.566		
	Total	952.005	31			

a. Predictors: (Constant), *LEAGUE, FIELDING, YEARS SQUARED, HISPANIC, BLACK, SLUGGING, YEARS*

b. Dependent Variable: *SALARY*

Coefficients[a]

Model		Unstandardized Coefficients		Standardized Coefficients	t	Sig.
		B	Std. Error	Beta		
1	(Constant)	−58.016	54.881		−1.057	.301
	YEARS	2.087	.715	1.869	2.920	.008
	YEARS SQUARED	−.083	.033	−1.503	−2.521	.019
	SLUGGING	.212	.124	.276	1.704	.101
	FIELDING	.457	.547	.098	.837	.411
	BLACK	3.275	1.566	.260	2.091	.047
	HISPANIC	−.378	1.582	−.029	−.239	.813
	LEAGUE	−2.000	1.342	−.174	−1.490	.149

a. Dependent Variable: *SALARY*

different from zero at a credible significance level, judging by the Sig. values shown. Remember, however, that this conclusion is based on the sample used in this regression. A different (perhaps larger) sample might produce different results.[18] In any case, as pointed out in Chapter 4, in practice, when estimated coefficients are not statistically different from zero at a credible significance

---

[18] One should not read too much into these results because they are presented mostly for the purpose of understanding the concept of dummy variables and how to interpret their coefficients. The sample of MLB players used in this discussion is actually quite small and is not likely to be a good representation of the population of MLB players.

level (e.g., 10% or smaller), it is best to not provide any interpretation of the estimated coefficients because they are statistically meaningless. The interpretation of the estimated coefficients for *HISPANIC* and *LEAGUE* are given here simply to illustrate the meaning of the dummy variable coefficients.

Interaction Variables

Our voting model above, which included a dummy variable for whether or not the incumbent party candidate was actually the incumbent, implicitly assumed that the only difference between incumbents and nonincumbents is the intercept term (see Equation 5.9a). Another possibility, however, is that there may be differences in the slope coefficients between incumbents and nonincumbents. For example, it may be the case that as the economy grows, an incumbent may be rewarded with votes at a greater *rate* than nonincumbents. The reasoning may be that voters consider the actual incumbent as more responsible for the growth in the country than simply a candidate who is not the current president, but only belongs to the same party as the president.

In order to capture this effect, consider the following sample regression function (again, we will temporarily exclude the variable for inflation in order to facilitate a graphical representation):

$$Y_t = a + b_1 X_{1t} + b_4(X_{1t}{}^* X_{3t}) + e_t, \qquad (5.13a)$$

where Y_t, X_{1t}, and X_{3t} are as they were in Equation 5.9a, namely, the percentage of two-party votes won by the incumbent party candidate, the real growth rate, and a dummy variable for whether or not the incumbent party candidate is actually the incumbent, respectively. In this case, the dummy variable for incumbency does not enter into the equation separately, as in Equation 5.9a; rather, it is being multiplied by, or "interacted" with, the variable for growth. This interaction effect captures the difference in the *rate* of votes gained due to economic growth between incumbent and nonincumbent candidates. To see this, consider how Equation 5.13a changes for incumbents versus nonincumbents. That is, suppose the incumbent party candidate is not the incumbent (e.g., Al Gore, who was the incumbent party candidate for the 2000 election but was not the incumbent president), then the predicted relationship for Equation 5.13a becomes

$$\hat{Y}_t = a + b_1 X_{1t} + b_4(X_{1t}{}^*0) = a + b_1 X_{1t}. \qquad (5.13b)$$

We can compare this to the case where the incumbent party candidate is, in fact, the incumbent (e.g., Bill Clinton running for reelection in 1996):

$$\hat{Y}_t = a + b_1X_{1t} + b_4(X_{1t}{}^*1) = a + b_1X_{1t} + b_4X_{1t}$$
$$= a + (b_1 + b_4)X_{1t}. \tag{5.13c}$$

Comparing Equations 5.13b and 5.13c, we see that both have the same intercept, a, but the coefficients to variable X_{1t} differ. For nonincumbents, the coefficient to $GROWTH$ is b_1, whereas for incumbents, it is $(b_1 + b_4)$. These cases are shown graphically in Figure 5.3.

Before estimating Equation 5.13a, we can first bring back the variable $INFLATION$ (X_{2t}) into our model (and in doing so reduce the risk of mis-specifying the model), giving us

$$Y_t = a + b_1X_{1t} + b_2X_{2t} + b_4(X_{1t}{}^*X_{3t}) + e_t. \tag{5.14a}$$

Using SPSS to estimate this equation produces the results shown in Table 5.5. We can now write the estimated regression as

$$\widehat{VOTES}_t = 54.012 + 0.439\ (GROWTH_t) - 0.617\ (INFLATION_t)$$
$$+ 0.297\ (GROWTH{}^*INCUMBENT_t). \tag{5.14b}$$

Before interpreting the coefficients to this regression, it should be pointed out that, other than the intercept, none of the estimated coefficients is statistically different from zero at reasonable levels of significance (e.g., 10% or less). This is an interesting, if not surprising, result, given that the regression without the interaction effect (see Table 5.3) showed that both $GROWTH$ and $INCUMBENT$ were statistically significant factors in determining $VOTES$. The reason for the loss of significance for these two variables is likely due to extreme multicollinearity, a subject we take up in greater detail in Chapter 7.[19] For the purposes of understanding how to interpret models with interaction effects, we shall proceed with examining the estimated coefficients, but again, *the reader is reminded that these results have little meaning given the lack of significance of the estimated coefficients.*

The intercept, which in fact is statistically significant in this regression, predicts that the percentage of the two-party vote received by the incumbent party candidate is, on average, about 54%, when $INFLATION$ and $GROWTH$ are zero. The coefficient to $INFLATION$, –0.617, suggests that, other things being

---

[19] For now, suffice it to say that when new variables are added to a regression model, and when these new variables are highly correlated to ones already in the model, then this correlation reduces the importance of one or both of the correlated variables. In our present case, we would expect the new variable, $GROWTH{}^*INCUMBENT$, to be highly correlated to the variable $GROWTH$, which was in our model before. It is often the case that models that include interaction effects frequently suffer from extreme multicollinearity.

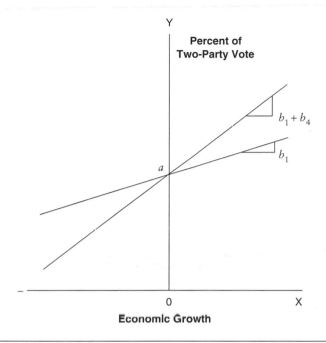

Figure 5.3

equal (i.e., *GROWTH*), the incumbent party candidate will receive about 0.617 percentage points less of the two-party vote when inflation increases by 1 percentage point. Finally, the effect of a 1 percentage point increase in *GROWTH*, holding other things constant (i.e., *INFLATION*) will increase the percentage of the two-party vote by 0.439 percentage points for nonincumbents and by (0.439 + 0.297) = .736 percentage points for incumbents.

It should be noted that we need not consider the dummy variable (additive) form of our model (i.e., Equation 5.10) separately from our interaction effect (multiplicative) form (i.e., Equation 5.14a). Indeed, we may consider both cases together in a single model and, in doing so, allow for differences in both intercepts and slopes. That is, we may estimate the following relationship:

$$Y_t = a + b_1 X_{1t} + b_2 X_{2t} + b_3 X_{3t} + b_4 (X_{1t} * X_{3t}) + e_t. \qquad (5.15)$$

The estimation of this model is left as an exercise for the reader (see Problem 5.3).[20]

---

[20] A note of caution, however: Models that include both dummy variables *and* interaction effects using the same dummy variables are even more likely to suffer from extreme multicollinearity than models that just contain one or the other.

Table 5.5

Model Summary

Model	R	R Square	Adjusted R Square	Std. Error of the Estimate
1	.761[a]	.579	.513	4.7625

a. Predictors: (Constant), *GROWTH*INCUMBENT, INFLATION, GROWTH*

ANOVA[b]

Model		Sum of Squares	df	Mean Square	F	Sig.
1	Regression	592.668	3	197.556	8.710	.001[a]
	Residual	430.945	19	22.681		
	Total	1023.612	22			

a. Predictors: (Constant), *GROWTH*INCUMBENT, INFLATION, GROWTH*

b. Dependent Variable: *VOTE*

Coefficients[a]

Model		Unstandardized Coefficients		Standardized Coefficients	t	Sig.
		B	Std. Error	Beta		
1	(Constant)	54.012	2.193		24.625	.000
	GROWTH	.439	.469	.362	.935	.361
	INFLATION	−.617	.407	−.326	−1.517	.146
	GROWTH*INCUMBENT	.297	.463	.210	.641	.529

a. Dependent Variable: *VOTE*

Interaction effects can also be used to consider subcategories in models with several dummy variables. For example, we can return to our baseball player salary model shown in Equation 5.12a. As we saw earlier, based on our regression analysis of our 32-player sample, there is some evidence that there is a difference in salaries in MLB between black and white players, other things being equal. But what about the subcategory of players who are both black *and* in the National League? Our dummy variable *BLACK* captures the effect of being a black player (whether a National League player or American League player), whereas the dummy *LEAGUE* controls only for league effects (whether a black player or not). These two variables, however, do not allow us to consider the subcategory of black National Leaguers. It may be the case, for example, that black players who are also in the National League have a salary differential as compared to other players. One method of capturing this subcategory is to create an interaction variable. This is done by simply multiplying the dummy variable *BLACK* times *LEAGUE*. That is, we create a new variable that is the product of X_{5i} and X_{7i}. Note that this new variable will be equal to 1 only if *BLACK* equals 1 (indicating a black player) *and LEAGUE* equals 1 (indicating a National League player). In terms of our sample regression function, we can write it as follows:

$$Y_i = a + b_1X_{1i} + b_2X_{2i} + b_3X_{3i} + b_4X_{1i}^2 + b_8(X_{5i} * X_{7i}) + e_i. \quad (5.16a)$$

Note that for simplicity, we have left out the separate dummy variables for *BLACK* (X_{5i}), *HISPANIC* (X_{6i}), and NATIONAL *LEAGUE* (X_{7i}).[21] If a player is black and plays in the National League, then X_{5i} and X_{7i} will be equal to 1, giving us

$$Y_i = a + b_1X_{1i} + b_2X_{2i} + b_3X_{3i} + b_4X_{1i}^2 + b_8(1*1) + e_i, \quad (5.16b)$$

where b_8 captures the effect on salary for players who are *both* black and in the National League as compared to all other players.

The Excel output provided in Table 5.6 shows the OLS estimate of Equation 5.16a. As we can see, judging by the adjusted R^2, the overall performance of this model has been slightly reduced in comparison to the model without the interaction effect, shown in Table 5.1.

Using the regression results, we can write the predicted equation as follows (after rounding to three decimal places):

$$\widehat{SALARY}_i = -50.956 + 2.140\ (YEARS_i) + 0.282\ (SLUGGING_i)$$
$$+ 0.352\ (FIELDING_i) - 0.086\ (YEARS_i^2)$$
$$+ 0.318\ (BLACK_i * LEAGUE_i). \quad (5.16c)$$

As can be seen in Table 5.6, the coefficient to (*BLACK**NATIONAL *LEAGUE*) is not statistically different from zero at an acceptable level of significance. Nevertheless, it is instructive to interpret its coefficient. The estimated value for b_8 is 0.318, meaning that other things being equal, black players who are also in the National League earn on average about \$0.318 million dollars (or \$318,000) more than other players. (Note that "other players" now includes white players, non-black Hispanic players, and black players not in the National League.) But once again, these results are not reliable, given the large P value for the coefficient to *BLACK**NL shown in Table 5.6.

---

[21] Including separate dummy variables for *BLACK* and NL would likely introduce severe multicollinearity (see footnotes 19 and 20).

Table 5.6

SUMMARY OUTPUT					
Regression Statistics					
Multiple R	0.796				
R Square	0.633				
Adjusted R Square	0.563				
Standard Error	3.665				
Observations	32				
ANOVA					
	df	SS	MS	F	Significance F
Regression	5	602.819	120.564	8.977	0.000
Residual	26	349.181	13.430		
Total	31	952.000			
	Coefficients	Standard Error	t stat	P value	
Intercept	−50.956	58.400	−0.873	0.391	
YEARS	2.140	0.769	2.785	0.010	
SLUGGING	0.282	0.130	2.166	0.040	
FIELDING	0.352	0.581	0.607	0.549	
YEARS SQUARED	−0.086	0.035	−2.452	0.021	
BLACK*NL	0.318	1.973	0.161	0.873	

Summing Up

We have seen in this chapter that a variety of types and forms of variables are possible. Nonlinear independent variables can be incorporated into our regression models to allow for increasing or decreasing effects of independent variables on the dependent variable. We also saw how various logarithmic forms can be used to consider *relative* relationships. In cases where one or more independent variables are not continuous, but are instead categorical, we can create dummy variables to control for categorical effects. Finally, we saw how interaction effects can be used to consider, among other things, the possible effects of membership in subcategories of groups on the dependent variable.

PROBLEMS

5.1 In Equation 5.2, the *level* of MLB player salaries is our dependent variable. The coefficients to the variables included in our model (i.e., b_1, b_2, b_3, and b_4) show how a player's salary increases (i.e., number of dollars increase) for a one-unit increase in the related X variable. Economic theories of labor, however, suggest that wage earners tend to be rewarded with *relative* increases in salary (i.e., percentage increases) and not dollar increases. One way of estimating such a relationship is to use the *natural log* of salaries, instead of actual salaries, for the dependent variable. Furthermore, by carrying out this natural log transformation, the nonlinear relationship we had before (as seen in Figure 5.1) may be (at least to some degree) "straightened out," leaving us with something close to a linear relationship. That is, consider the following sample regression function (not including the dummy variables for race):

$$\ln Y_i = a + b_1 X_{1i} + b_2 X_{2i} + b_3 X_{3i} + e_i,$$

where the natural log of salaries ($\ln Y_i$) is shown as a simple linear function of years of MLB experience (X_{1i}), slugging average (X_{2i}), and fielding percentage (X_{3i}). In this case, the OLS-produced estimates of b_1, b_2, and b_3 show the *relative* change in salary for a one-unit change in the associated Xs. Multiplying the coefficient by 100 thus gives the estimated *percentage* change in salary for a one-unit change in the Xs. For example, if the OLS estimate for b_1 is equal to 0.10, then $b_1*100 = 10$; thus, if YEARS increases by 1, then salary is expected to increase by 10%. Using the data in Table A1, do the following:

  a. Use SPSS or Excel (or an equivalent program) to calculate the natural log of SALARY and estimate the above regression using OLS.
  b. Interpret the estimated coefficients to the X variables.

5.2 Two other factors that may affect the abortion rate in a state is whether or not the state provides public funds that can be used for abortions and whether or not there are laws, such as required parental consent, that may restrict access to abortion services. In order to control for these potential factors, two dummy variables are included in Table A4: FUNDS, which equals 1 if a state provides public funds for abortions, 0 otherwise; and LAWS, whether a state enforces laws that may restrict access to abortions.

  a. Reestimate Equation 4.11, adding FUNDS and LAWS as independent variables, and interpret the values of the coefficients for these two variables.
  b. Does this model outperform the one without FUNDS and LAWS? Explain.
  c. Are the coefficients to FUNDS and LAWS statistically different from zero at the 5% significance (95% confidence) level?

5.3 Models can be estimated that allow for differences in intercepts (using a dummy variable) *and* slopes (using an interaction effect). Such a model is shown in Equation 5.15. Estimate this model using OLS and interpret the results. (Note that some of the estimated coefficients will turn out not to be statistically different from zero. As a matter of practice, interpret these coefficients, but with the understanding that their values are not reliable results.)

5.4 Returning to Problem 4.4, which models wage as a function of education and experience, we can build on this model by considering various categorical variables. Specifically, we can consider the effects of gender, marital status, and race. Reviewing Table A6, we see the columns headed *"FEMALE," "MARRIED,"* and *"BLACK/HISPANIC."* These three dummy variables indicate whether the particular individual is female, married, or either black or Hispanic; in each case, a 1 indicates "yes" and a 0 indicates "no."

    a. Given these definitions for *FEMALE*, *MARRIED*, and *BLACK/HISPANIC*, what is the base category?

    b. Estimate the sample regression model with WAGE as the dependent variable and *EDUC*, *EXPER*, *FEMALE*, *MARRIED*, and *BLACK/HISPANIC* as the independent variables, and interpret the estimated coefficients. Which coefficients are statistically different from zero at the 10% level of significance?

5.5 Building on our model from Problem 4.6 of Chapter 4, estimate college GPA as a function of SAT, *HSRANK*, and now adding *FEMALE*.

    a. Does this model outperform the one without *FEMALE*? Is the coefficient to *FEMALE* statistically different from zero at the 5% level of significance? Explain.

    b. Interpret the estimated coefficient to *FEMALE*.

    c. Now add the variable *ATHLETE* to the regression and check if it is a significant determining factor of GPA.

    d. Finally, to consider a particular subgroup, female athletes, create a new variable equal to the product of *ATHLETE* and *FEMALE*. Include this new interaction effect in the regression and check whether female athletes have significantly different GPAs. How would you interpret the coefficient to the interaction effect (regardless of its significance)?

6

Time Variables and Panel Data

A Simple Introduction

I n the preceding chapters, we have considered various examples, most of which have one thing in common: They used **cross-sectional data sets** (the presidential elections example being an exception). That is, the previous examples used samples of data that were related to one point in time. For example, the baseball example considers a sample of players' salaries for the 2006 season. With cross-sectional data, time is held fixed and we consider variation across "space" (e.g., across baseball players) to identify the effects of X variables on a Y variable. We can, however, consider other types of data sets and relationships. One possibility is to fix space and allow time to change. For example, we could choose a single baseball player (thus fixing space) and follow his salary (Y) across time. This is an example of a **time series data set.**

A third type of data set is a combination of the other two. For example, we could choose a sample of baseball players and follow this group of players' salaries (Y) and performance (Xs) across several years. Visually, this would amount to "stacking" one year's sample on top of another, creating what is commonly called a **panel data set.**[1] Panel data sets are very rich data

[1] This kind of data set is sometimes called a "longitudinal" data set. Another closely related data structure is called a "pooled" or "pooled cross-sectional" data set where we have cross sections of data collected over a period of years; however, each year's cross section is a different sample. For example, we could randomly select a sample of baseball players for the 2006 season and combine that with a new, randomly selected sample of players for the 2005 season, do the same for the 2004 season, and so on.

sets in that they contain variation across both time *and* space to help identify the effects of various X variables on some Y variable. Along with this richness, however, comes complexity with regard to the regression methods necessary so that full advantage can be taken of the variation across time and space. We will pursue a very simple approach in this chapter. We begin our inclusion of time, however, with a simple example of estimating a time trend.

Time as an Independent Variable

When dealing with a time series data set, in some cases we may want to consider the effect time itself has on our dependent variable. That is, we may want to consider whether our dependent variable follows a **trend** (upward or downward) as time passes. As an example, we can consider a variation on our baseball example. Instead of considering the salary of our sample of 32 players for the year 2006, we can consider the average wage of *all* MLB players *over* the years. Many people believe that Major League Baseball salaries, on average, have been increasing (i.e., following an upward trend) from year to year. This hypothesis can be tested by collecting data on average baseball salaries over the years and then *creating* a **time index**, which is simply a variable that keeps track of time periods. For example, we can consider the following linear model:

$$Y_t = \alpha + \beta t + u_t, \tag{6.1}$$

where Y_t is the average salary paid to players in year t, and this is shown as a linear function of t itself.[2] In this case, β represents the increase in the average player's salary from one year to another. The corresponding sample regression function for Equation 6.1 would be

$$Y_t = a + bt + e_t. \tag{6.2a}$$

The OLS method can be used to estimate the equation shown in Equation 6.2a, and it will be BLUE as long as the CLRM regression model assumptions are satisfied (see Chapter 2).[3]

---

[2] It should be made clear that we are now considering the average salary paid to all MLB players in a particular year.

[3] In this type of analysis, the regression model assumption of "no autocorrelation" (see Chapter 2, CLRM Assumption 3) frequently will be violated, and the OLS results are not strictly valid. In this case, other methods of estimating the regression model are necessary. This issue is touched on in Chapter 7.

In order to illustrate this task of fitting a trend to a time series of data, consider the data on average baseball salaries shown in Table A2 in Appendix A. The data show real average player salaries (in thousands of 2000 dollars) for the years 1969 through 2006.[4] The time index we will use, which will serve as our independent variable, will be the column for *TIME* shown in the table. Using Excel to calculate the OLS regression for Equation 6.2a, we obtain the results shown in Table 6.1.

The R^2 of 0.919 tells us that about 91.9% in the variation in salaries over these years can be explained by our model. Using the values for the intercept and the coefficient to *TIME*, we can write the estimated sample regression function as

$$\hat{Y}_t = -370.43 + 68.015t. \qquad (6.2b)$$

Table 6.1

SUMMARY OUTPUT					
Regression Statistics					
Multiple *R*	0.959				
R Square	0.919				
Adjusted *R* Square	0.916				
Standard Error	227.875				
Observations	38				
ANOVA					
	df	SS	MS	F	Significance F
Regression	1	21138784.665	21138784.665	407.085	0.000
Residual	36	1869379.647	51927.212		
Total	37	23008164.312			
	Coefficients	Standard Error	t stat	P value	
Intercept	−370.430	75.416	−4.912	0.000	
Time	68.015	3.371	20.176	0.000	

---

[4] What is meant by "real average salaries" is that the average salary figures are adjusted for inflation by using the Consumer Price Index (CPI), where the base year is 2000. The CPI data are available at the U.S. Department of Labor Bureau of Labor Statistics Web site: http://www.bls.gov/cpi/

As we can see, the intercept has no reasonable interpretation. Technically, it tells us that if $t = 0$, then expected salary is –$370,430. This unrealistic result is due (in part) to the fact that our data for time do not actually go back to t equal to zero. The coefficient to our time index tells us, on average, how salaries have increased from one year to the next. The value for b, whose P value shows that the coefficient is statistically different from zero at a very small level of significance (i.e., a very high level of confidence), suggests that salaries increased on average by about $68,015 each year. Given Equation 6.2b, we can now use it to **forecast** salaries for future years. For example, suppose we wanted to forecast average baseball salaries for the year 2007. All we need to do is plug the value for $t = 39$ (the value of the time index for 2007) into Equation 6.2b for t. Doing so, we obtain

$$\hat{Y}_{39} = -370.43 + 68.015(39) = 2282.155. \qquad (6.2c)$$

Thus, forecasted average salaries for the year 2007 are about $2.28 million.[5]

The model shown in Equation 6.2a is a simple linear trend. In many cases, however, *nonlinear* trends may better reflect the behavior of a time series. Indeed, many believe that baseball salaries have not only increased over the years but that they have increased at an *increasing rate*. If this is true, then a linear trend is not the appropriate functional form for our forecasting equation, and we will need to estimate a nonlinear trend.[6] A simple way of determining whether a linear or nonlinear trend is appropriate is to plot the data and check it visually. Figure 6.1 shows the plot of average baseball salaries over the years 1969 to 2006. Also included in this plot is the estimated trend line (i.e., the sample regression function) from Equation 6.2b.[7]

We can clearly see in Figure 6.1 that the linear trend is a poor representation of the data. In fact, average salaries do appear to increase at an increasing rate over time; thus, a nonlinear trend is warranted. In order to fit a nonlinear trend to the data, we can use a quadratic functional form for our sample regression function, such as

$$Y_t = a + b_1 t + b_2 t^2 + e_t. \qquad (6.3a)$$

---

[5] Again, these salaries are inflation adjusted to be in 2000 dollars.

[6] If we estimate a linear model when the data clearly follow a nonlinear trend, then we are committing a "specification error," the results of which may invalidate our estimated sample regression function. See Gujarati (2003) for more details.

[7] Excel's chart function includes an option that allows a trend line to be plotted to a set of data points in the chart. This is simply the OLS regression line we found in Equation 6.2b. The equation displayed on the graph and the R^2, which are part of Excel's chart options, are the same as we found earlier (see Table 6.1).

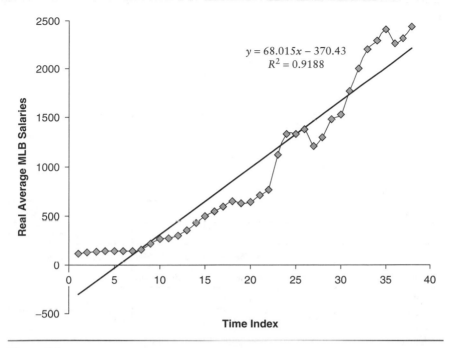

$$y = 68.015x - 370.43$$
$$R^2 = 0.9188$$

Figure 6.1

In order to estimate the sample regression function shown in Equation 6.3a, we first create another independent variable, which is simply the squared value of the time index ("*TIME SQ.*"). We can then use Excel to calculate the OLS values for a, b_1, and b_2 in Equation 6.3a. Doing so yields the results shown in Table 6.2.

The output shown in Table 6.2 indicates that, overall, our model is performing quite well. The R^2 of approximately 0.980 tells us that 98% of the variation in salaries over the years is explained by our model.[8] The very large F statistic indicates that our regression is significant at a very small significance (high confidence) level. As for the estimated coefficients, we can see that the coefficient to *TIME* is no longer statistically significant at a reasonable significance level, whereas *TIME SQ.* is highly significant. The loss in significance for *TIME* is an interesting development, and one that we will explore further in Chapter 7.[9] Furthermore, the adjusted R^2 has increased from 0.916 for the linear trend to 0.979 for the quadratic trend, providing empirical support for the nonlinear trend over the linear trend. The intercept

---

[8] It is not uncommon to obtain a very high R^2 in trend analyses of this type.

[9] Essentially, we have a case of high multicollinearity, where the introduction of a new X variable (*TIME SQ.*) that is highly correlated to an existing X variable (*TIME*) reduces the significance of the latter.

Table 6.2

SUMMARY OUTPUT					
Regression Statistics					
Multiple R	0.990				
R Square	0.980				
Adjusted R Square	0.979				
Standard Error	113.448				
Observations	38				
ANOVA					
	df	SS	MS	F	Significance F
Regression	2	22557695.199	11278847.599	876.330	0.000
Residual	35	450469.113	12870.546		
Total	37	23008164.312			
	Coefficients	Standard Error	t stat	P value	
Intercept	97.177	58.250	1.668	0.104	
TIME	−2.126	6.888	−0.309	0.759	
TIME SQ.	1.798	0.171	10.500	0.000	

is positive, which is more appealing than the negative value that we found for our simple linear trend, but it still has no useful interpretation because *TIME* and *TIME SQ.* never have zero values in our data set. The coefficient for b_1 is negative and for b_2 is positive. These together will produce a "J" shaped nonlinear trend with the trend declining in the beginning but increasing at an increasing rate later.[10] Using the calculated values for b_1 and b_2 from Table 6.2, we can write the estimated nonlinear trend (i.e., the sample regression function) as

$$\hat{Y}_t = 97.177 - 2.126t + 1.798t^2 \qquad (6.3b)$$

[10] If both b_1 and b_2 are positive, the function would increase at an increasing rate, and it will not decline anywhere. Here, given that b_1 is negative and b_2 is positive, we have a small decline in the beginning of the trend, but it later increases at an increasing rate.

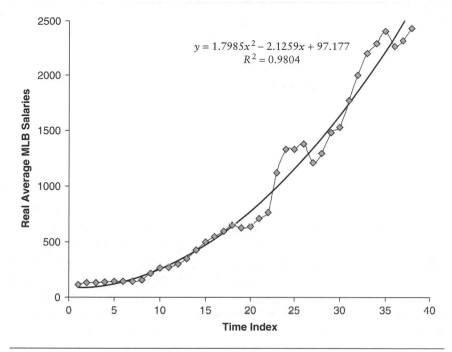

Figure 6.2

Figure 6.2 provides a plot of the data along with the nonlinear trend.[11] It is evident that this model provides a better fit than the simple linear trend.

Using Equation 6.3b, we can again forecast expected average salaries for the year 2007 by simply plugging in this value for t:

$$\hat{Y}_{39} = 97.177 - 2.126\,(39) + 1.798\,(39)^2 = 2749.021. \qquad (6.3c)$$

Thus, the result in Equation 6.3c forecasts an average salary for baseball players of approximately \$2.75 million for the 2007 season.[12]

In addition to quadratic trends like the one considered above, we can consider higher-ordered polynomials. Furthermore, following the discussion in the previous chapter, another useful functional form is the semi-log (see Equation 5.5), where we have the natural log of Y as the dependent variable

---

[11] Note that the equation for the nonlinear trend embedded in Figure 6.2 is the same as shown in Equation 6.3b, except for some rounding.

[12] Not bad work if you can get it!

and the time index as the independent variable. An example of this kind is left as an exercise for the reader (see Problem 6.1).[13]

Panel Data: A Simple Introduction

Recall our British crime example employed in Chapter 4, where we used data for 42 police force areas for the year 2004 to estimate crime rates as a function of male unemployment rates, the number of registered motor vehicles per 1,000, police presence (lagged one period), and the percentage of the population aged 15 to 24 years (see Equation 4.13). There are, in fact, data available for these four variables for other years. For example, data are available for these measures for police force areas for the years 1996 through 2004.[14] The question that arises is, how can we make use of these additional years of cross-sectional data? One possibility would be to run nine separate regressions, one for each year. This approach, however, would not make very good use of the available data because each regression would be based on a sample of 42 observations. A better use of the data would be to pool the nine cross sections of data, thus creating a much larger sample size of 378 observations (9 years × 42 police force areas). By pooling the data, we gain several advantages. First, larger data sets generally produce better (more precise) estimates of population parameters. Second, with a greater number of observations, we have the ability to estimate richer models containing more X variables (assuming data on other X variables are available) without the fear of depleting our degrees of freedom. Third, pooling cross sections over time allows for variation in our Y and X variables across both time *and* space, which may better identify the effects of the X variables on Y. That is, in our crime example, by having multiple cross sections, we can now consider how crime differs across regions as well as how crime for all regions tends to change from one period to the next.

We begin with the easiest attempt to extend our previous example, which used only 2004 data, by simply "stacking" the additional 8 years of data on

---

[13] It should be noted that it is common for time series models to contain more than just a time index on the right-hand side. For example, we could consider a model such as $Y_t = a + b_{1t} + b_2 X_t + e_t$, where X_t is an explanatory measure that varies across time. Although seemingly simple, models like this can have serious complications (e.g., a problem called "spurious regression") that make applying simple OLS estimation inappropriate. This discussion is beyond the scope of this book, and the reader is referred to Diebold (2004) for details.

[14] Indeed, data are available for even earlier years.

Table 6.3

Model Summary

Model	R	R Square	Adjusted R Square	Std. Error of the Estimate
1	.757[a]	.573	.568	15.5791858

a. Predictors: (Constant), %pop15_24, UNEM, CARS, POLICE

ANOVA[b]

Model		Sum of Squares	df	Mean Square	F	Sig.
1	Regression	121393.5	4	30348.386	125.039	.000[a]
	Residual	90531.21	373	242.711		
	Total	211924.8	377			

a. Predictors: (Constant), %pop15_24, UNEM, CARS, POLICE

b. Dependent Variable: CRIME

Coefficients[a]

Model		Unstandardized Coefficients		Standardized Coefficients		
		B	Std. Error	Beta	t	Sig.
1	(Constant)	−76.212	13.908		−5.480	.000
	UNEM	2.358	.498	.230	4.739	.000
	CARS	−.038	.016	−.115	−2.441	.015
	POLICE	4.185	2.702	.077	1.549	.122
	%pop15_24	12.992	1.010	.536	12.861	.000

a. Dependent Variable: CRIME

top of our 2004 data. This pooled data set is now much larger than the single cross section of data we had before. We can then estimate the same regression we had in Equation 4.13.[15] Doing so yields the following estimated regression (see Table 6.3 for the SPSS output):

$$\widehat{CRIME}_{it} = -76.212 + 2.358\ (UNEM_{it}) - 0.038\ (CARS_{it})$$
$$+ 4.185\ (POLICE_{it}) + 12.992\ (\%\text{pop } 15\_24_{it}). \tag{6.4}$$

---

[15] The data used for this regression are not included in Appendix A because of their size. They are available online at www.cbe.csueastbay.edu/~lkahane

Comparing this sample regression to that reported in Equation 4.14b, we see that the results are quite different. The estimated coefficients have changed considerably, with the most remarkable result being that the coefficient to *POLICE* is positive, although only significant at the 12% level. Clearly, this is not the expected relationship. Adding to this is the fact that the R^2 is smaller for the pooled regression, with a value of 0.573, than it was for the single cross section for 2004, which had a value of 0.629.

Why has this new regression failed to give us better results? The answer has to do with the fact that by simply stacking the additional years' cross sections on top of the 2004 cross section and running the same regression as before, we fail to consider two important factors that may affect crime in our pooled sample. First, given that we are observing crime rates across a period of years, it may be important to consider year-specific events or changes that may affect the crime rates of all 42 police force areas. For example, changes in the law or sentence lengths may have an impact on the crime rates for all police force areas. In order to control for this possibility, we can create year dummies and include them as explanatory variables in our regression model. Given that we have 9 years' worth of data, we need to create eight year dummies, "yr_t," where t ranges from 2 to 9 (why not nine dummies?).[16] Thus, for example, we can let "yr_2" be the dummy variable that has the value of 1 if the observation is from 1997 (the second year of our nine), 0 otherwise. Similarly, we can let "yr_3" take the value of 1 if the observation comes from 1998 (our third year), 0 otherwise. Continuing in the same way, we can construct dummies yr_4 through yr_9 to cover the years 1999 to 2004. Note that by excluding a dummy for 1996, we are making this our base year and as such the interpretation of the coefficients to the year dummies will be in comparison to 1996 crime rates.

A second factor that the simple pooled regression fails to consider is the fact that there may be certain unique, time-invariant characteristics of each police force area. For example, some police force areas may be less densely populated than others. Or perhaps there are differences in the proportion of the population that is male versus female. We could try to include such measures, but it may be difficult to obtain the necessary data. One way of controlling for time-invariant characteristics is to create a new set of dummy variables, pfa_is, one for each police force area (excluding one, which will serve as our base category). For example, we can create the dummy pfa_2, which takes the value of 1 if our observation is for the police force area "Bedfordshire" (our second of the 42 police force areas; see Table A7), 0

---

[16] The answer is because if we have 9 categories (i.e., years), then we need $9 - 1 = 8$ dummies (see Chapter 5).

otherwise. The dummy pfa_3 would take the value of 1 if the observation is for "Cambridgeshire," 0 otherwise, and so on. Thus, rewriting our sample regression function, we would have

$$Y_{it} = a + b_1 X_{1it} + b_2 X_{2it} + b_3 X_{3it} + b_4 X_{4it} + \delta_2 yr_2 + \delta_3 yr_3 + \delta_4 yr_4. \ldots$$
$$+ \delta_9 yr_9 + \gamma_2 pfa_2 + \gamma_3 pfa_3 + \gamma_4 pfa_4. \ldots \gamma_{42} pfa_{42} + e_{it}, \qquad (6.5a)$$

or, we can write this more compactly as

$$Y_{it} = a + b_1 X_{1it} + b_2 X_{2it} + b_3 X_{3it} + b_4 X_{4it} + \sum_{t=2}^{9} \delta_t yr_t + \sum_{i=2}^{42} \gamma_i pfa_i + e_{it}. \quad (6.5b)$$

There are several things to notice in Equation 6.5b. First, our dependent variable, Y; the X variables; and the residual term now have two subscripts, i and t. This is done to recognize that we are dealing with panel data where observations on Y, the Xs, and the resulting residuals vary across time and police force area. Thus, the value for Y_{11} indicates that this observation is for the crime rate from police force area 1 (i.e., "Avon & Somerset") for year 1 (i.e., 1996); similarly for the X variables and residuals. The second thing to notice is that the year dummies have only one subscript, t. This is because the year dummies are included to control for year-specific effects that we assume affect crime nationwide (i.e., they are not region-specific). The third thing to notice is that the police force area dummies also have only one subscript, i. This is because these dummies are designed to capture region-specific characteristics that do not vary across time. In fact, these region-specific components are frequently called **fixed effects** because they are assumed to be fixed across time, and the regression shown in Equation 6.5b is often referred to as a fixed effects model.[17] Fourth, notice that by adding the year and police force area dummies, we have increased the number of coefficients to be estimated, from 5 (a plus 4 bs) to 54 (a plus 4 bs plus 8 δs plus 41 γs)! This would not be possible with a single cross section of data, which has 42 observations (because we would deplete all the degrees of freedom), but it is possible now that we have a total of 378 observations.

---

[17] This method of modeling fixed effects is sometimes called the "least-square dummy variable" approach, or LSDV for short. The LSDV approach has limitations because it requires the estimation of a large number of time-invariant coefficients, equal to one less than the number of cross-sectional units ($42 - 1 = 41$, in our case), which may leave few degrees of freedom remaining. The reader should note that there are a variety of other approaches to modeling fixed effects that conserve the degrees of freedom. See Wooldridge (2006) for details.

Finally, it should be noted that if the fixed effects (i.e., the *pfa* dummies) are not included in our pooled regression model, then we run the risk of violating one of our CLRM assumptions discussed in Chapter 4. Namely, by excluding the fixed effects, we may violate Assumption 4: The independent variables (X_{it}s) are uncorrelated with the error term, u_{it}. To see how this may be the case, suppose a particular police force area, say, "Dorset," has a very high proportion of the population that is female in comparison to other police force areas. Given that the majority of crimes are committed by males, then Dorset may choose to have fewer police per 1,000 people than other areas. By not taking into account this specific aspect of Dorset (i.e., its relatively high proportion of females), then it would appear that crime rates are *lower* when there are fewer police per 1,000, which is the opposite of what we expect. Or, conversely, that crime rates increase when we have more police per 1,000 people. Indeed, this is what we found when we simply pooled our nine cross sections of data without controlling for the fixed effects (see the results in Table 6.3). Essentially, what occurs when we exclude the fixed effects is that they become part of the error term (which would then contain both the u_{it} and the fixed effects), and this leads to a "corrupted" (or, more formally, a biased) estimate for the coefficient to police per 1,000 people variable.[18]

When it comes to estimating the sample regression shown in Equation 6.5b, we can apply OLS to this model. Doing so gives us the output (using SPSS[19]) shown in Table 6.4.

The table is quite lengthy because we now are estimating 54 coefficients.[20] As Table 6.4 reports, the R^2 is now quite large, at 0.944, in comparison to Table 6.3, which had an R^2 of 0.573 when the year and police force area dummies are excluded. This new, higher R^2 should not be too surprising because our model now controls for year effects and fixed effects for all observations. Turning to the year effects, although not all of them are statistically different from zero at a reasonable significance level, the year dummies do display a particular pattern. Note that the excluded year, 1996, is our base year. The estimated coefficients to yr_2 (1997) through yr_5 (2000)

---

[18] Indeed, it will lead to biased estimates of the other coefficients in the model as well. For a more detailed discussion of the fixed effects model (and the consequence of excluding the effects), see Wooldridge (2006).

[19] Note that Excel's standard regression routine will not accept more than 16 variables, and so we must use SPSS for this regression.

[20] It is quite common to exclude the separate fixed effects coefficients from the output table, leaving only the estimated coefficient for the Xs and year dummies.

are all negative, indicating that crime apparently was dropping in Britain generally during this period *in comparison to the base year of 1996*. From that point forward, the year dummies are all positive, indicating a general increase in crime nationwide from 2001 to 2004 in comparison to 1996.

The estimated coefficients to the police force area dummies (the *pfas*) are statistically significant in most cases and have varying signs. Recall that the omitted pfa_1, which is for Avon & Somerset, is our base category here. Thus, if we consider, say, the coefficient to pfa_2 (Bedfordshire), it is negative and significant at about the 0.1% level, which indicates that, controlling for other things (e.g., unemployment, the number of registered motor vehicles per 1,000 people, etc.), time-invariant characteristics of Bedfordshire tend to leave it with about 9.5 fewer crimes per 1,000 people than the base case, Avon & Somerset.

The estimated coefficients to X variables (the bs in Equation 6.5b) are typically our greatest concern. The values reported in Table 6.4 are considerably

Table 6.4

Model Summary

Model	R	R Square	Adjusted R Square	Std. Error of the Estimate
1	.972[a]	.944	.935	6.0459828

a. Predictors: (Constant), pfa42, yr9, pfa41, pfa40, pfa39, pfa38, pfa37, pfa36, pfa35, pfa34, pfa33, pfa32, pfa31, pfa30, pfa29, pfa28, pfa27, pfa26, yr8, pfa25, pfa24, pfa23, pfa22, pfa21, pfa20, pfa19, pfa18, yr7, pfa17, pfa16, pfa15, pfa14, pfa13, pfa12, yr5, pfa11, pfa10, pfa9, yr4, pfa8, pfa7, pfa6, yr3, pfa5, pfa4, yr2, pfa2, yr6, pfa3, *CARS, UNEM, %pop15_24, POLICE*

ANOVA[b]

Model		Sum of Squares	df	Mean Square	F	Sig.
1	Regression	200081.3	53	3775.119	103.275	.000[a]
	Residual	11843.47	324	36.554		
	Total	211924.8	377			

a. Predictors: (Constant), pfa42, yr9, pfa41, pfa40, pfa39, pfa38, pfa37, pfa36, pfa35, pfa34, pfa33, pfa32, pfa31, pfa30, pfa29, pfa28, pfa27, pfa26, yr8, pfa25, pfa24, pfa23, pfa22, pfa21, pfa20, pfa19, pfa18, yr7, pfa17, pfa16, pfa15, pfa14, pfa13, pfa12, yr5, pfa11, pfa10, pfa9, yr4, pfa8, pfa7, pfa6, yr3, pfa5, pfa4, yr2, pfa2, yr6, pfa3, *CARS, UNEM, %pop15_24, POLICE*

b. Dependent Variable: CRIME

(Continued)

Table 6.4 (Continued)

Coefficients[a]

Model		Unstandardized Coefficients		Standardized Coefficients	t	Sig.
		B	Std. Error	Beta		
1	(Constant)	106.841	22.840		4.678	.000
	UNEM	2.503	.646	.244	3.872	.000
	CARS	.001	.012	.002	.047	.963
	POLICE	-8.742	3.813	-.161	-2.293	.023
	%pop15_24	-.390	1.699	-.016	-.230	.819
	yr2	-3.350	2.040	-.044	-1.642	.102
	yr3	-3.925	2.651	-.052	-1.480	.140
	yr4	-3.080	2.851	-.041	-1.081	.281
	yr5	-4.000	3.150	-.053	-1.270	.205
	yr6	2.303	3.238	.031	.711	.477
	yr7	8.749	3.211	.116	2.725	.007
	yr8	9.455	3.156	.125	2.996	.003
	yr9	5.268	3.396	.070	1.551	.122
	pfa2	-9.505	2.931	-.061	-3.243	.001
	pfa3	-6.042	3.322	-.039	-1.819	.070
	pfa4	-29.811	3.373	-.192	-8.838	.000
	pfa5	16.015	5.039	.103	3.178	.002
	pfa6	-26.348	4.228	-.170	-6.232	.000
	pfa7	-20.538	3.274	-.132	-6.273	.000
	pfa8	-40.350	3.280	-.260	-12.303	.000
	pfa9	-28.844	3.978	-.186	-7.251	.000
	pfa10	-22.700	3.595	-.146	-6.314	.000
	pfa11	-58.387	3.071	-.376	-19.011	.000
	pfa12	-42.252	3.375	-.272	-12.520	.000
	pfa13	-10.832	3.664	-.070	-2.957	.003
	pfa14	37.403	4.077	.241	9.174	.000
	pfa15	-17.377	3.589	-.112	-4.842	.000
	pfa16	-22.021	3.007	-.142	-7.324	.000
	pfa17	-32.704	3.966	-.211	-8.246	.000
	pfa18	29.391	3.493	.189	8.414	.000
	pfa19	-24.074	3.108	-.155	-7.746	.000
	pfa20	-13.996	3.024	-.090	-4.629	.000
	pfa21	-7.581	3.735	-.049	-2.030	.043
	pfa22	-28.792	3.833	-.185	-7.512	.000
	pfa23	28.478	7.495	.183	3.800	.000
	pfa24	3.298	5.586	.021	.590	.555
	pfa25	-29.877	3.609	-.192	-8.278	.000
	pfa26	-6.785	3.066	-.044	-2.213	.028
	pfa27	-5.353	4.548	-.034	-1.177	.240
	pfa28	32.614	3.652	.210	8.929	.000
	pfa29	-32.641	3.212	-.210	-10.161	.000
	pfa30	-26.656	3.353	-.172	-7.951	.000
	pfa31	-6.521	2.947	-.042	-2.213	.028
	pfa32	-40.359	3.666	-.260	-11.008	.000
	pfa33	-47.244	4.403	-.304	-10.731	.000
	pfa34	-20.412	3.860	-.131	-5.289	.000
	pfa35	1.600	3.997	.010	.400	.689
	pfa36	2.049	3.881	.013	.528	.598
	pfa37	-10.751	3.494	-.069	-3.077	.002
	pfa38	-20.846	3.665	-.134	-5.688	.000
	pfa39	-37.518	4.736	-.242	-7.921	.000
	pfa40	-30.942	3.693	-.199	-8.377	.000
	pfa41	13.856	5.067	.089	2.735	.007
	pfa42	24.471	4.009	.158	6.104	.000

a. Dependent Variable: CRIME

different from those shown in Table 6.3. Whereas the coefficient to *UNEM* has not changed much, the coefficients to *CARS*, *POLICE*, and *%pop15_24* are quite different. The coefficient to *CARS* was negative and significant in the model without year and fixed effects, but it is now positive and statistically insignificant. Thus, differences across the years and police force areas in *CARS* appear to be picked up by the year and police force area dummies, leaving *CARS* somewhat redundant in the regression. The presence of police (lagged one period) had the wrong sign in the regression without year and police force area dummies, but it is negative and significant (at the 2% level of significance) when these dummies are included. The estimated coefficient implies, all else being equal, that an additional police officer per 1,000 people reduces crime by about 8.7 crimes per 1,000 people. Finally, the coefficient to *%pop15_24* is not statistically significant in the regression with year and area fixed effects.[21]

Summing Up

In this chapter, we have seen that when working with time series data, we can use time itself (or an index of time) as an independent variable. Doing so produces estimates of time trends (either linear or nonlinear) that can be used to carry out some simple forecasting for the dependent variable.

We also saw in this chapter how we can use multiple cross sections of data for various time periods to construct panel data sets. Working with panel data may be beneficial because they increase our sample size and also allow us to consider variation in our dependent and independent variables across time *and* space, something that is not possible with a single cross section of data.

PROBLEMS

6.1 Using the data on average MLB salaries over the period 1969 to 2006, estimate the following regression:

$$\ln Y_t = a + bt + e_t,$$

where: $\ln Y_t$ is the natural log of the average annual salaries
t is the time index (Time).

---

[21] As with *CARS*, that the variable *%pop15_24* is not statistically important in this regression is likely due to the fact that differences in the age breakdown of the population across time and police force areas is largely described by the year and area fixed effects.

Interpret the coefficient to the time index.

6.2 Time variables can be used in a regression along with other variables. Using the data in Table A3, reestimate Equation 5.105, adding a time index. (Note: You can create a time index based on the election year. For example, the election year 1916 can be $t = 1$, election year 1920 can be $t = 2$, and so on.) Compare your results to those in Table 5.3. Is the coefficient to the time index statistically different from zero at the 10% significance (90% confidence) level?

6.3 Consider the fixed effects model shown in Equation 6.5b. Reestimate the model excluding the year dummies (i.e., the yr_t variables) and compare your results to those shown in Table 6.4. Why do these new results differ from those in Table 6.4? Explain.

7

Some Common Problems in Regression Analysis

In Chapter 2, the regression model assumptions were introduced with a brief explanation about their significance. Later, in Chapter 4, we added the assumption of "no perfect multicollinearity." It was noted that if these assumptions are met, then OLS produces the best possible estimation of our model, or OLS is BLUE. This is clearly a powerful result.

It is often the case, however, that one or more of the regression model assumptions are not satisfied. In this case, OLS is typically *not* the best method for estimating our sample regression function. The purpose of this chapter is to briefly discuss some of the most common problems that occur in regression analysis and to map out directions for further study. The goal is to provide the reader with an intuitive understanding of the problem at hand and how it might be solved. The application of these proposed solutions is an advanced topic, and the reader is pointed to more advanced books on these subjects.

The Problem of High Multicollinearity

Recall from Chapter 4 that perfect multicollinearity is the case when one of our independent variables has a perfect linear relationship to one or more of the other independent variables in our model. If this occurs, then we have perfectly redundant information between these X variables and we are unable to use the least-squares method to estimate such a model.[1] Our solution to this problem is simple: Drop one of the redundant variables.

A related problem that is somewhat more difficult to solve is the case of *high multicollinearity*. This occurs when one of the independent variables has nearly a perfect linear relationship to one or more of the other X variables. The intuition as to why this may be problematic is not too difficult to grasp. Suppose we have one X variable that is not perfectly linearly related, but very closely related to one or more other X variables. If this is the case, then there is a considerable overlap in the information that these variables contain about the behavior of our dependent variable, Y. Because these X variables share much of the same explanatory power over Y, they rob each other of significance. This being the case, each variable on its own may appear to be statistically insignificant, yet together they may be highly significant. Put another way, if two or more X variables look very similar in their information about the behavior of Y, then the OLS procedure may not be able to distinguish the *unique* explanatory ability of one X variable from the others. The solution to such a problem may seem simple: Drop one of these *highly* (but not *perfectly*) redundant variables. The problem with this solution is that in dropping one of the variables, we may be compromising our theory behind our model. *It is important to understand that high multicollinearity does not signal a problem with our theory; rather, it is the inability of our data to clearly distinguish the separate yet subtle effects of two X variables.*

As an illustration of the problem of high multicollinearity, we can return to our example of presidential elections. In Chapter 4, we estimated a model showing the percentage of two-party votes received by the incumbent party candidate as a function of economic growth and inflation. This model is reproduced below:

$$Y_t = a + b_1 X_{1t} + b_2 X_{2t} + e_t, \qquad (7.1)$$

where X_{1t} is our measure of economic growth and X_{2t} is our measure of inflation. Later, in Chapter 5, we considered a voting model that added the interaction effect between growth and incumbency (see Equation 5.14a). This equation is reproduced below:

$$Y_t = a + b_1 X_{1t} + b_2 X_{2t} + b_4 (X_{1t} {}^* X_{3t}) + e_t, \qquad (7.2)$$

---

[1] Recall our example in Chapter 4 of considering the two independent variables, birth-date and age. These are perfectly redundant because knowing one, we can determine the other.

where $(X_{1t}*X_{3t})$ is our interaction effect for growth and incumbency (X_{3t}). Recall that when Equation 7.1 was estimated using OLS, we found that the estimated coefficient to GROWTH (b_1) was statistically different from zero at better than the 1% level of significance (see Table 4.2). When Equation 7.2 was estimated, the coefficient to GROWTH (b_1) was no longer statistically significant at a reasonable level of significance (see Table 5.5). For purposes of comparison, both regression results are shown in Table 7.1.

Thus, the addition of the interaction effect has led to the apparent loss in significance of a variable that previously was statistically significant. In this event, we should suspect a problem with high multicollinearity.[2] If we consider what kind of relationship we may have among the X variables, we would immediately suspect that perhaps growth and the interaction effect

Table 7.1a

Coefficients[a]

Model		Unstandardized Coefficients		Standardized Coefficients		
		B	Std. Error	Beta	t	Sig.
1	(Constant)	53.365	1.919		27.811	.000
	GROWTH	.705	.217	.581	3.250	.004
	INFLATION	−.478	.339	−.252	−1.411	.174

a. Dependent Variable: VOTE

Table 7.1b

Coefficients[a]

Model		Unstandardized Coefficients		Standardized Coefficients		
		B	Std. Error	Beta	t	Sig.
1	(Constant)	54.012	2.193		24.625	.000
	GROWTH	.439	.469	.362	.935	.361
	INFLATION	−.617	.407	−.326	−1.517	.146
	GROWTH*INCUMBENT	.297	.463	.210	.641	.529

a. Dependent Variable: VOTE

---

[2] This is one of several signs of high multicollinearity. There are others, such as unexpected signs on variables. For more details, see Gujarati (2003).

are closely related. One method of detecting whether we have a problem of high multicollinearity is to calculate the **correlation coefficient** between the two variables. The correlation coefficient is a measure showing the degree to which any two variables are linearly related. A correlation coefficient of 1 implies that two variables are perfectly, positively related. A correlation coefficient of –1 implies a perfect negative relationship. A value of 0 implies that the two variables are not linearly related.[3] In cases where two independent variables have a correlation coefficient of 0.8 or greater (in absolute terms), then this may signal a high multicollinearity problem. In our voting model, the correlation coefficient between growth (X_{1t}) and the interaction term ($X_{1t}{}^{*}X_{3t}$) is 0.843[4]; thus, high multicollinearity is apparently why the coefficient to $GROWTH$ (b_1) is not statistically different from zero in the model that includes both of these independent variables.[5]

Given evidence that high multicollinearity is present in our data, we may ask what it means for our OLS estimation method and what we can do to alleviate the problem. With regard to the first issue, the most important point to remember is that *in the presence of high multicollinearity, OLS is still BLUE.* That is, high multicollinearity is a nuisance, but it doesn't destroy any of the desirable properties of the ordinary least-squares method.

As for remedies for this problem, several methods are possible, but they often bring problems of their own.[6] The best solution to the problem of high multicollinearity is to try to increase the sample size of our data set. As noted earlier, multicollinearity does not signal a problem with our model. Rather, it reflects the inability of the OLS method to distinguish the subtle, separate effects of our X variables on Y, given our data set. In the case of our model shown in Equation 7.2, it may be that if we had a larger sample size, then the added information contained in this larger sample would enable OLS to distinguish the separate, subtle effects of our interaction term from the effects of

---

[3] Both Excel and SPSS are capable of calculating correlation coefficients for pairs of variables.

[4] The reader is invited to verify this correlation.

[5] Recall in Chapter 6 that we regressed real average MLB salaries on a time index. We later added a squared time index to create a quadratic function (see Equation 6.3a). When we added the squared term, the coefficient of the linear term became statistically insignificant (see Table 6.2). This is, in large part, due to high multicollinearity between t and t^2. Indeed, the correlation coefficient for t and t^2 is 0.970, which explains why the coefficient to t lost its significance when we added t^2.

[6] For example, we can use a method called "ridge regression," but this method brings with it other problems. See Judge, Hill, Griffiths, and Lee (1985) for a discussion of this potential remedy.

growth on its own. Of course, it may also be true that our interaction term is truly unimportant in explaining our dependent variable. In any event, given that presidential elections are relatively few and far between, it seems unlikely that we would be able to increase our sample size. Thus, in this case, given that the inclusion of the interaction term did not improve the overall performance of our regression model (the adjusted R^2 in fact dropped when the interaction term was added), we may drop the interaction term from the model.

Other potential cases of multicollinearity problems are not so clear-cut. For example, recall our crime model. In Chapter 4, we estimated a sample regression function showing crime as a function of UNEM, CARS, POLICE, and %pop15_24 (see Equation 4.13). The results, provided in Table 4.4, showed that the variable CARS was not statistically significant at a reasonable significance level. We may suspect that there is a problem with multicollinearity, and so to test for this possibility, we can compute pairwise correlations of CARS with the other three X variables. We can do this in Excel for the four X variables, producing the results shown in Table 7.2.[7]

Here we see a "correlation matrix," which shows correlation values for pairings of our four variables. Each cell in the correlation matrix shows the correlation between the row and column variables. Thus, the correlation between POLICE and CARS is −0.639. Notice that all variables are perfectly correlated with themselves, thus giving a value of 1 along the diagonal. Also note that the cells above the diagonal are blank. This is because the correlation between, say, POLICE and CARS is the same as between CARS and POLICE. Thus, all the cells above the diagonal would be redundant.

Reviewing the values in the correlation matrix, we see that the largest correlation, in absolute terms, between CARS and the other variables is 0.639

Table 7.2

	CARS	POLICE	%pop15_24	UNEM
CARS	1			
POLICE	−0.639	1		
%pop15_24	−0.519	0.620	1	
UNEM	−0.575	0.810	0.598	1

---

[7] To do this in Excel, we choose Tools on the main menu bar. We then select Data Analysis and then Correlation, and then provide the relevant Input Range.

(the case mentioned earlier for *POLICE* and *CARS*). This is below our cutoff of 0.8 noted earlier, and so we would not conclude on the basis of pairwise correlations that the variable *CARS* is suffering from high multicollinearity in our regression. Correlation coefficients between pairs of variables, however, are not capable of capturing more complex relationships between independent variables. For example, *CARS* may not be highly correlated with any single variable, but it may be linearly related to a *combination* of variables. This seems reasonable, especially with regard to *UNEM* and *%pop15_24,* as one's ability to purchase and register a car may be influenced by his or her employment status and age. This (potential) relationship among the *X* variables can be represented, in fact, as a regression function:

$$CARS_i = \alpha + \beta_1(UNEM_i) + \beta_1(\%pop15\_24_i) + \beta_2(POLICE_i) + u_i. \quad (7.3)$$

If there is indeed a statistically significant relationship between *CARS* and the other independent variables shown in Equation 7.3, then this suggests that there is an overlap among these variables in our original regression function, shown in Equation 4.13. Using our sample of data, we can estimate the sample regression function for Equation 7.3 and check to see if this **auxiliary regression** produces a reasonably high R^2 and a small Significance *F*, indicating a statistically significant regression. If it does, then this is evidence of high multicollinearity between *CARS* and the other three independent variables. Table 7.3 shows the results of this estimated auxiliary regression function.

Reviewing Table 7.3, we can see that the R^2 is approximately 0.437 and the Significance *F* is rounded to 0.000, indicating a statistically significant regression. Thus, there is evidence of multicollinearity between *CARS* and the remaining independent variables.[8] What can be done about this problem? As noted earlier, increasing the sample size may produce better results. One temptation is to drop one or more of the correlated *X* variables. Doing so, however, may lead to a violation of the CLRM Assumption 4 discussed in Chapter 2 by creating an omitted variable bias (a topic discussed in more detail later in this chapter). High multicollinearity is sometimes a difficult problem to solve. But it is worth noting again that OLS is still BLUE in the presence of high multicollinearity.

Nonconstant Error Variance

When working with cross-sectional data sets, a problem that frequently comes up **is nonconstant error variance.** This problem relates to the second regression

---

[8] There are other means for testing for multicollinearity (see, for example, Gujarati, 2003).

Table 7.3

SUMMARY OUTPUT					
Regression Statistics					
Multiple R	0.661				
R Square	0.437				
Adjusted R Square	0.393				
Standard Error	51.294				
Observations	42				
ANOVA					
	df	SS	MS	F	Significance F
Regression	3	77596.171	25865.390	9.831	0.000
Residual	38	99980.168	2631.057		
Total	41	177576.340			
	Coefficients	Standard Error	t stat	P value	
Intercept	770.548	103.074	7.476	0.000	
UNEM	−6.552	12.013	−0.545	0.589	
%pop15_24	−10.907	9.548	−1.142	0.260	
POLICE	−63.941	32.032	−1.996	0.053	

model assumption that was discussed in Chapter 2 and has to do with the spread, or "variance," of the population error terms, u_i, around the population regression function. Recall that we assumed that the error variance is constant throughout the regression line. In this case, the errors are said to be **homoscedastic**, meaning "constant variance." This was shown graphically in Figure 2.7, which is shown again in Figure 7.1a.

If the error variance is not constant throughout the population regression line, and thus violates our second regression model assumption, the errors are said to be **heteroscedastic**, meaning "nonconstant variance." A graphic example is where our observations tend to "funnel out" as we move out along the population regression function. An example is provided in Figure 7.1b. Alternatively, the observations may "funnel in," as shown in Figure 7.1c.

In order to understand the intuition as to why nonconstant error variance may occur, we can return to our example on abortion rates in the United States.

Recall our model as shown in Equation 4.11, where the abortion rate in state i is hypothesized to be a function of state i's religious makeup

(*RELIGION*), the average price of an abortion (*PRICE*), the average income (*INCOME*), and the frequency of antiabortion activities (as measured by *PICKET*). We can focus our attention on the variable *INCOME*. If we think of abortion services as simply a service that people can consume, we can consider the different purchasing behavior of people with high versus low incomes.[9] People with high income have greater freedom in choosing how to spend (or not spend) their money, and as such, we may witness greater variation in the way individuals consume. Thus, although abortion rates tend to be larger in higher-income states on average (see Table 4.3), there may also be a greater spread around the average, reflecting the fact that in some high-income states, individuals decide not to purchase abortion services, whereas in other high-income states, individuals choose to purchase this service. In low-income states, this story is reversed. That is, because individuals in these states have lower incomes, on average, they have less freedom in how they spend their income; this being the case, spending behavior would tend to have less variation. Graphically, we can represent this scenario in Figure 7.2 by considering, for the sake of this discussion, just two groups: high-income and low-income states.

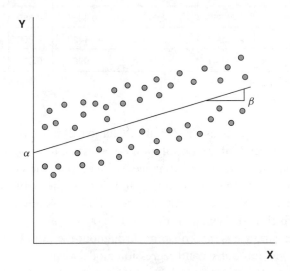

Figure 7.1a

---

[9] To reiterate what was noted in footnote 12 of Chapter 4, thinking of abortion services as simply another service that consumers can purchase is done for the purpose of facilitating our discussion and is not intended to trivialize this socially important subject.

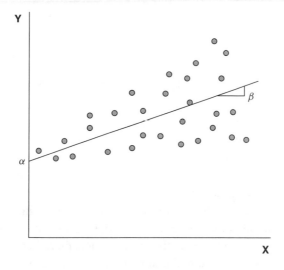

Figure 7.1b

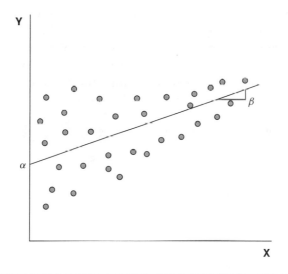

Figure 7.1c

We can let X_{HIGH} represent the value of income for high-income states and X_{LOW} represent the value of income for low-income states. The variable Y represents the abortion rate. The fact that our line slopes upward reflects the hypothesis that, *on average*, the abortion rate increases as income increases.

Considering high-income states, the heavy dot on the line may represent the average abortion rate for those states, with the actual values for individual states' abortion rates falling above or below the group's average. Similarly for the low-income states, the heavy dot on the line may represent this group's average abortion rate, with individual states' values falling above or below the group average. The key aspect of Figure 7.2 is that the individual observations for low-income states are more closely speckled around their group's mean, whereas individual observations from the high-income group are more broadly speckled around their mean. This reflects the point made earlier that those with larger incomes have greater choice of how to spend them, and thus we may witness greater variation in their purchases of abortion services, with the reverse being true for those with low incomes. Recalling that the vertical distance from an individual observation to the regression line is equal to the error term, then we can see that the sum of the squared errors for the low-income group is smaller than the sum of the squared errors of the high-income group. Or, using more formal language, the error variance increases (and is hence nonconstant) as incomes increase. This kind of behavior of the error variance may also be true at incomes between X_{HIGH} and X_{LOW}, thus producing the "funneling out" shape as shown in Figure 7.1b. In fact, Figure 7.3 plots our actual data on abortion rates and income levels for the 50 states. The graph of the data has a generally upward sloping relationship as our hypothesis predicts. The dots also appear to slightly funnel out as income gets larger, indicating potential nonconstant error variance.

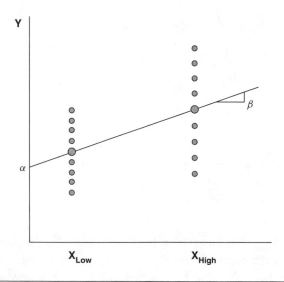

Figure 7.2

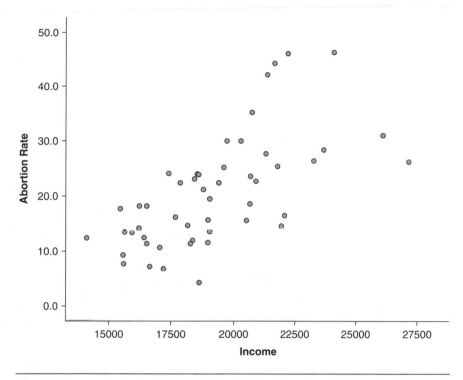

Figure 7.3

Another graphical way that is commonly used to detect heteroscedasticity is first to perform a least-squares regression and save the residuals from the regression.[10] Then, we create a plot with the squared residuals on the vertical axis and the variable we suspect may be the source of the heteroscedasticity, *INCOME*, on the horizontal axis.[11] If there is no pattern in the errors, (i.e., if the errors are homoscedastic), then the plot should show a fairly uniform horizontal band of dots. If it is true that the error variance increases as *INCOME* increases, then this plot should show the squared errors getting larger as *INCOME* increases. Figure 7.4 shows this graph, and as is evident, the squared residuals get larger as *INCOME* increases, indicating heteroscedasticity.[12]

---

[10] Both Excel and SPSS have the option to save the residuals from a regression.

[11] Squaring the errors will often make subtle patterns in the errors more obvious and easier to detect.

[12] There are many other tests for heteroscedasticity. See Gujarati (2003) for more details.

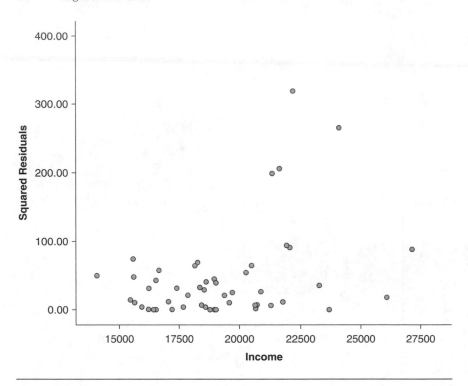

Figure 7.4

Given that heteroscedasticity is present, what does this mean for our OLS method? Unfortunately, it means that OLS is no longer BLUE. It is still a Linear Unbiased Estimator, but it is no longer the Best. Recall that Best meant that our method produced sample regression estimates of the intercept term, a, and the bs with the smallest variance. Or, in other words, the parameters are estimated with the greatest accuracy. Furthermore, in the presence of heteroscedasticity, the OLS-produced standard errors of the intercept and coefficients to the X variables are not valid. This means that the associated t statistics and P values for the a and bs in our model are not valid and we cannot legitimately perform hypothesis tests.

Given detection of heteroscedasticity and the problems it causes for OLS, we can now consider, briefly, a possible remedy. There are, in fact, a number of proposed solutions to this problem, but a common one is that of **weighted least-squares** (WLS). The details of this method are somewhat complicated, but the intuition behind this method is not too difficult to follow. Consider again Figure 7.2, where we have two income groups shown, states with low income (X_{LOW}) and states with high income (X_{HIGH}). Recall our general goal, which is to draw a sample of data from the population and use it to find a sample regression function that best fits the data. As can be seen in Figure 7.2, sample observations from the X_{LOW} group have a smaller variance because they are more tightly centered around the group's mean (the heavy dot), as compared to sample observations that are drawn from the X_{HIGH} group. Thus, on average, sample observations drawn from X_{LOW} are more reliable predictors of its group mean (because they tend to be closer to their heavy dot) than are observations from X_{HIGH} as predictors of their group mean. Weighted least-squares takes note of this difference, and when fitting a line to the data, WLS assigns greater weight to observations from the more reliable, low-variance group (X_{LOW} in this example) and less weight to the less reliable, high-variance group (X_{HIGH} in this case). Estimating a sample regression function in this way can produce results that are, in fact, BLUE.

As noted, details of performing a WLS estimation method are somewhat complicated, and the reader is referred to other sources for a complete discussion.[13] Some regression programs, such as SPSS, do include the WLS method, and the user must provide some information about how to reweight observations to take into account nonconstant error variance.[14] Table 7.4 provides the SPSS results of a WLS estimation that was performed for our model on state abortion rates.

In performing this WLS estimation, the data are reweighted by dividing all observations by the square root of INCOME (i.e., the variable SQRT-INC).[15] Notice in Table 7.4 that the WLS estimates for the coefficients to PRICE, INCOME, and PICKET have the same sign and are similar in size to the OLS results shown in Table 4.3. Also, as before, the coefficients to PRICE, INCOME, and PICKET are significantly different from zero at the 5% significance (95% confidence) level or better. The coefficient to the variable RELIGION is insignificant, as it was before. Thus, our results have not changed substantially, except that now they are valid.[16]

---

[13] See, for example, Gujarati (2003) or Greene (2003).

[14] Excel does not have a WLS routine provided as part of the program. An experienced user of Excel, however, could perform a WLS estimation with proper programming.

[15] This weighting variable was created using the Transform item on the main SPSS menu bar and then selecting Compute Variable. The newly created SQRTINC was then selected for use as the WLS Weight when running the linear regression. SPSS can also estimate a WLS regression by choosing Analyze on the main menu bar, then selecting Regression and then Weight Estimation. . . . In this case, the program experiments with various weighting schemes for the chosen Weight Variable and selects the one that performs the best. See Gujarati (2003) for a discussion on the choice of weighting schemes in performing the WLS.

[16] Using more formal language, our WLS results are BLUE *asymptotically* (i.e., for large samples).

Table 7.4

Model Summary

Model	R	R Square	Adjusted R Square	Std. Error of the Estimate
1	.731[a]	.535	.494	85.3389

a. Predictors: (Constant), *PICKET, PRICE, RELIGION, INCOME*

ANOVA[b,c]

Model		Sum of Squares	df	Mean Square	F	Sig.
1	Regression	377060.2	4	94265.059	12.944	.000[a]
	Residual	327723.1	45	7282.736		
	Total	704783.3	49			

a. Predictors: (Constant), *PICKET, PRICE, RELIGION, INCOME*

b. Dependent Variable: ABORTION

c. Weighted Least-Squares Regression—weighted by *SQRTINC*

Coefficients[a,b]

Model		Unstandardized Coefficients		Standardized Coefficients		
		B	Std. Error	Beta	t	Sig.
1	(Constant)	−5.015	9.224		−.544	.589
	RELIGION	.004	.086	.005	.052	.959
	PRICE	−.046	.022	−.220	−2.047	.047
	INCOME	.002	.000	.664	6.151	.000
	PICKET	−.116	.041	−.297	−2.805	.007

a. Dependent Variable: ABORTION

b. Weighted Least-Squares Regression—weighted by *SQRTINC*

Autocorrelated Errors

A common problem with time series data is autocorrelation. Recall that the third regression model assumption of Chapter 2 was that the error from one observation is not related to the error of another. However, if the errors are related, then we face the problem of autocorrelation. As with nonconstant error variance, the details of this problem are complex, but the intuition behind this problem is fairly easy to grasp.

Essentially, what the assumption of no autocorrelation means is that there is no systematic relationship among the population errors (i.e., the $u_i s$) in a time series regression. That is, if we know one period's error, it should tell us nothing about the next period's error. If this is not the case, and there is some systematic relationship among the errors, then our OLS method is no longer BLUE and other methods are needed.[17]

There are several reasons why there may be a systematic relationship, or pattern, in the errors. First, in time series data, it may be the case that any error in one period can carry over to subsequent periods because it may take several periods before any "shock" that caused the error is fully absorbed. For example, we may consider a model that estimates the price of a company's stock. Suppose the company suffers an unexpected financial setback. This may be reflected in a fall in the company's stock price that our model would not have predicted (because it was unexpected), and our error for this period would be negative (because the actual value of the stock price would be below our predicted value, other things being equal). But this fall in stock price may be spread over several periods, and the next period's error may also be negative. In other word, sometimes errors tend to have momentum such that an error in one period tends to carry over to subsequent periods.

Another common reason for patterns in the errors is model misspecification. That is, recall Figure 6.1, where a line is fitted to data that are apparently nonlinearly related. In this case, we see that the first group of observations falls above the linear regression function, and thus the observations all have positive errors. The next group of observations falls below the line and thus those observations all have negative errors. Thus, we clearly have a pattern in the errors in this case, as we would observe long strings of positive errors and long strings of negative errors.

Concerning the *types* of patterns in the errors, there are two basic patterns commonly observed. The first is the kind suggested in the above example, namely, that one period's error *tends* to have the same sign as the previous period's error. This is called "positive autocorrelation," and if we graphed the errors across time, they would generate a picture like the one shown in Figure 7.5a.

The second basic type of autocorrelation occurs when one period's error tends to have the opposite sign of the previous period's error. This type of pattern, called "negative autocorrelation," is shown in Figure 7.5b, which has a "sawtooth" look to it, indicating continual sign flips.

Several methods can be used to detect patterns in the errors.[18] A simple approach is to examine the errors visually from an OLS regression and

---

[17] If we use OLS when autocorrelation is present, then the estimated variance is likely to be biased and as such this makes our *t* statistics and *F* statistics invalid.

[18] The most common one is the Durbin-Watson test. See Gujarati (2003) for details about this test.

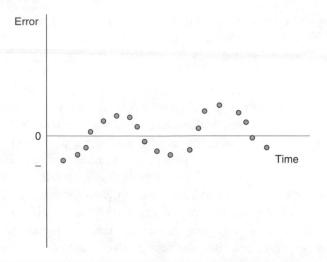

Figure 7.5a

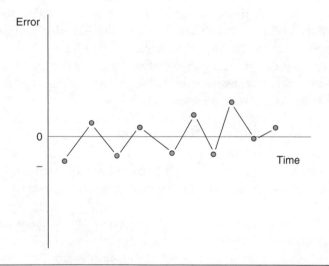

Figure 7.5b

see if there is, in fact, any distinguishable pattern. As an example, we can return to our model from Chapter 6 that looks at average player salaries in MLB over the years 1969 to 2006. Using our nonlinear model as shown in Equation 6.3a (so as to avoid any model misspecification bias), we can re-run this regression, save the errors, and analyze them. Table 7.5 provides a printout of the residuals.

Table 7.5

RESIDUAL OUTPUT

Observation	Predicted Real Salary	Residuals
1	96.850	19.973
2	100.119	29.986
3	106.986	27.072
4	117.449	23.010
5	131.510	10.366
6	149.167	−6.639
7	170.422	−27.459
8	195.273	−39.225
9	223.722	−7.694
10	255.767	7.905
11	291.410	−22.277
12	330.649	−30.199
13	373.485	−22.605
14	419.918	9.946
15	469.949	30.357
16	523.576	23.241
17	580.800	13.713
18	641.621	6.035
19	706.040	−79.109
20	774.055	−133.510
21	845.667	−132.869
22	920.876	−156.688
23	999.682	123.215
24	1082.085	251.737
25	1168.085	165.017
26	1257.682	121.186
27	1350.876	−140.613
28	1447.667	−153.003
29	1548.055	−67.627
30	1652.040	−124.150
31	1759.622	12.030
32	1870.801	127.233
33	1985.577	210.894
34	2103.949	183.956
35	2225.919	176.228
36	2351.486	−88.672
37	2480.650	−163.913
38	2613.410	−176.848

If we concentrate on the signs of the residuals, we can see an apparent pattern. There is a string of five positive residuals in a row, followed by a string of four negative. This pattern more or less repeats for all the residuals. The fact that we have long strings of positive and negative errors is a sign that we may have positive autocorrelation problems. If the errors were truly random and not related to each other, we would not expect to see such strings.[19] Another way to look for patterns in the residuals is to plot them in a graph. We have two ways of doing so. The first is to plot the residuals across time and look for apparent patterns in the plot. Figure 7.6a shows such a plot for the residuals shown in Table 7.5. As can be seen, the residuals follow a kind of wave pattern across time that is similar to the positive autocorrelation graph shown in Figure 7.5a.

The second graph we can create is to plot lagged period residuals on the horizontal axis and current period residuals on the vertical axis. In this case, if the residuals were truly random (i.e., one period's residual being unrelated to the previous period's residual), then the graph should have a more or less circular pattern of dots centered around the zero, zero point on the graph (i.e., where the two axes cross). If we have positive autocorrelation, as we suspect in this case, where one period's error seems to be followed by an error of the same sign (i.e., positive errors tend to be followed by positive errors, and negative errors tend to be followed by negative errors), then our graph would show a pattern of dots that slope upward (from left to right) and through the zero, zero point.[20] As seen in Figure 7.6b, the errors appear to follow a pattern consistent with positive autocorrelation.[21]

Given detection of positive autocorrelation, we can consider remedies to this problem. Details of common remedies are, in fact, quite complex, and

---

[19] If the errors are truly random and unrelated, we would expect the signs of the errors to be more random than what we observe in this example. That is, in this case, we see too few sign flips. Note that the pattern for negative autocorrelation tends to have *too many* sign flips, (i.e., errors that systematically oscillate between positive and negative values). There is, in fact, a formal test of autocorrelation, called the "runs test," that focuses on the signs of errors. See Geary (1970) for details.

[20] In the case of negative autocorrelation (i.e., where positive errors tend to be followed by negative errors, and negative errors tend to be followed by positive errors), the dots follow a pattern that slopes downward (from left to right) and goes through the zero axis.

[21] The Durbin-Watson test noted in footnote 18 confirms the presence of positive autocorrelation.

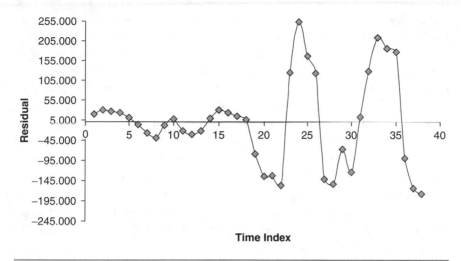

Figure 7.6a

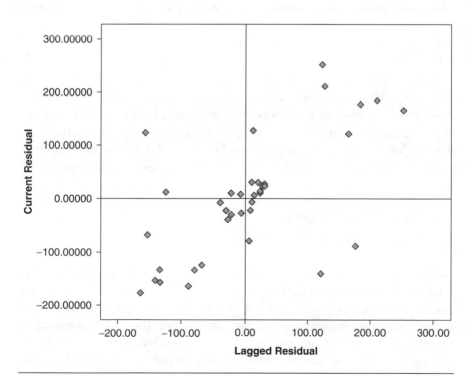

Figure 7.6b

the reader is encouraged to read more about this issue in more advanced books.[22] The basic idea behind these remedies is the following. Given that the errors have a pattern to them, this suggests that some systematic information in the errors is going unused in our OLS estimation method. One technique commonly used, called the **Prais-Winsten estimation** (Prais & Winsten, 1954), tries to discover the systematic component in the errors and then use this information to refine our estimates of the coefficients. In essence, we internalize the systematic information in the errors and, in so doing, produce a better fit for our data. The details regarding this technique are somewhat complicated and are beyond the scope of this book. As a means of comparison with our results in Equation 6.3b (which does not correct for autocorrelation), Equation 7.3 provides the estimated regression function for Equation 6.3b after applying the Prais-Winsten procedure to correct for autocorrelated errors:

$$\hat{Y}_t = 84.177 + 1.633t + 1.669t^2.$$

| t stat: | 0.815 | 0.134 | 5.551 | (7.3) |

| P value: | 0.421 | 0.894 | 0.000 |

Comparing these results to those shown in Table 6.2, we see some minor differences. The coefficient to t (Time) now has a positive sign, whereas it was negative before, but this is not important because in both cases, its coefficient is not statistically different from zero. As for t^2 (Time Sq.), its coefficient is now slightly smaller and it is (as it was before) highly significant. The main difference for these new results is that the t statistics and P values are valid.[23]

Omitted Variable Bias: Excluding Relevant Variables

Recall our crime model considered in Chapter 6, where we worked with multiple cross sections of data for various years. We noted that if we simply pooled the data and ignored the fact that we have multiple observations for each police force area, we run the risk of violating the CLRM assumption that the X variables are uncorrelated to the errors. We saw that without the fixed effects (i.e., the dummies for the pfas), we got an unexpected positive

---

[22] For example, Gujarati (2003) or Wooldridge (2006).

[23] To be more precise, the Prais-Winsten estimation will produce estimates that are BLUE and t statistics that are valid *asymptotically* (i.e., in large samples).

estimated coefficient for *POLICE*. When we added the fixed effects to the model, the estimated coefficient to *POLICE* became negative (as we would expect) and statistically significant. This is an example of "omitted variable bias," or the exclusion of a relevant variable.[24] We can be somewhat more specific about this issue. Suppose we consider a simple case where the so-called true population regression model is

$$Y_i = \alpha + \beta_1 X_{1i} + \beta_2 X_{2i} + u_i. \tag{7.4}$$

Thus, we have Y_i as a function of two explanatory variables, X_{1i} and X_{2i}. Suppose, due to ignorance or the unavailability of data, we estimated the following regression model:

$$Y_i = A + B_1 X_{1i} + v_i, \tag{7.5}$$

where A, B_1, and v_i are used in place of α, β, and u_i in order to keep it clear that Equation 7.4 is the correct specification and Equation 7.5 is the misspecified model. Note that the error term in Equation 7.5 now contains the effects of the omitted variable. That is, $v_i = u_i + \beta_2 X_{2i}$. If it is the case that X_{1i} and X_{2i} are correlated, then it is clear that in Equation 7.5, the error term v_i will be correlated with the included variable X_{1i}, thus violating CLRM Assumption 4 as discussed in Chapter 2, which will result in biased estimates for the coefficient to X_{1i}. In fact, Wooldridge (2006) summarizes the effects as shown in Table 7.6.

Table 7.6

	X_1 and X_2 positively correlated	X_1 and X_2 negatively correlated
Expected sign for $\beta_2 > 0$	B_1 positively biased	B_1 negatively biased
Expected sign for $\beta_2 < 0$	B_1 negatively biased	B_1 positively biased

Thus, if, for example, X_{1i} and X_{2i} are positively correlated and theory tells us that in the "true" model β_1 should be positive, then by estimating the model without X_{2i}, the estimated coefficient to X_{1i}, that is, B_1, will be larger than it should be (i.e., have a positive bias).[25]

---

[24] This is sometimes referred to as "underfitting a model" and is under the broader topic of "misspecification analysis."

[25] Table 7.6 is derived from Wooldridge's (2006) Table 3.2 (p. 97). Wooldridge provides a detailed derivation of the bias from omitted variables.

As an example of omitted variable bias, let us consider our crime model again. To keep things simple, we will consider just the year 2004, and we will model crime as being a function of the male unemployment rate (*UNEM*) and the percentage of the population aged 15 to 24 (*%pop15_24*). Estimating this regression, we find

$$\widehat{CRIME}_i = -40.445 + 5.472\ (UNEM_i) + 8.439\ (\%pop15\_24_i) \quad (7.6)$$

Both *UNEM* and *%pop15_24* are positive and significant at less than the 1% level of significance.[26]

If we now estimate the same regression but without the variable *%pop15_24*, we obtain the following results:

$$\widehat{CRIME}_i = 51.772 + 10.218\ (UNEM_i). \quad\quad (7.7)$$

Once again, the coefficient to unemployment is significant at less than the 1% level of significance. Notice, however, that the coefficient to *UNEM* is now almost twice the size of the case when *%pop15_24* is included! We clearly have a positive bias for the estimated coefficient to *UNEM*, and this is to be expected because *UNEM* and *%pop15_24* are positively correlated.[27] Note that this example and the information in Table 7.6 are for a simple case where the "true" model has only two *X* variables and we omit one that is correlated with the remaining *X* variable. In multiple regression models where the "true" model has more than two *X* variables and we omit one relevant variable that is correlated with one or more of the remaining *X* variables, the direction of the bias for the coefficients to the remaining *X* variables is difficult to ascertain.

Summing Up

The OLS estimation method is a powerful statistical technique for estimating regression functions. Its reliability, however, depends upon the CLRM assumptions being satisfied. In this chapter, we have noted examples where one of these key assumptions is violated. In the first case, we considered

---

[26] The reader is invited to verify this result and that for Equation 7.7.

[27] The correlation coefficient between *UNEM* and *%pop15_24* is approximately 0.60 for the year 2004.

multicollinearity. In the extreme scenario where one of the X variables is a perfect linear function of one or more of the other X variables, OLS cannot produce unique parameter estimates for all of the X variables. The solution was simple: Eliminate one of the redundant variables. In the less extreme case of high multicollinearity, *OLS is still BLUE*, but it may be difficult to discern the separate effects of some of the X variables on our outcome variable, Y.

We also considered two problems with the behavior of the error term, u— one where the errors suffered from heteroscedasticity (often a problem for cross-sectional data) and one where the errors were autocorrelated (a common problem for time series data). In both of these cases, OLS is not BLUE and we cannot reliably carry out hypothesis tests. When heteroscedasticity or autocorrelation is present, other estimation methods are necessary. Finally, we saw that when relevant variables are excluded from a regression, and when these excluded variables are correlated with the included variables, then the OLS-estimated coefficient for the included variables will be generally biased and hence unreliable. The best solution in this case is to include these relevant variables if at all possible.

PROBLEMS

7.1 One factor that may be important in determining a MLB player's salary is the number of games that he has played over his career. Players who play in a large number of games over their career are likely more important to their team, and hence should command a higher salary, than players who play in fewer games, all else being equal. Suppose a variable called *GAMES*, equal to the number of career games in which a player has appeared, is added to our model, shown in Equation 5.2. How might the inclusion of this variable cause a problem with high multicollinearity? Explain.

7.2 Recall our model, shown in Problem 4.5, for estimating *MSRP* prices for SUVs as a function of horsepower and engine size. Suppose we add to this model the following three independent variables:
CARGO = cargo space measured in cubic feet
MPG = miles per gallon, averaged between city and highway
CYLINDERS = number of cylinders in engine
The OLS estimate of this model produces the following estimated sample regression function:

$$\widehat{MSRP_i} = -21992.74 + 83.524\,(CARGO_i) - 406.398\,(MPG_i) - 9956.796\,(SIZE_i)$$
$$+ 7359.045\,(CYLINDERS_i) + 211.089\,(HORSEPOWER_i),$$

with $R^2 = 0.770$, Adjusted $R^2 = 0.734$.

Notice that *MPG* and *SIZE* have negative coefficients, implying that cars with greater gas mileage and larger engines are expected to have *lower* prices. This result seems counterintuitive. Additionally, *MPG* and *CARGO* are not statistically different from zero at the 10% level of significance. Thus, given the relatively high R^2, counterintuitive signs, and the insignificance of coefficients for variables we expect should be important, we seem to have a classic case of high multicollinearity. As a means of convincing us of this diagnosis, run auxiliary regressions for the five independent variables and report the estimated R^2 and Sig. F values.

7.3 One of the many ways of testing for nonconstant error variance is the **Glejser test** (Glejser, 1969). The intuition behind this test is easy to follow. Recall that with nonconstant error variance, or heteroscedasticity, the error variance is not uniform along the population regression line. For example, Figures 7.3 and 7.4 both indicate for our abortion example that the absolute size of the error tends to increase as *INCOME* increases. The Glejser test simply tries to show, using regression analysis, whether the absolute size of the error is a function of one (or more) of the independent variables. That is, for the abortion rate example, we may have

$$| e_i | = a + b_1 INCOME_i + w_i, \tag{7.8}$$

where $| e_i |$ is the absolute value of the error and it is shown to be a function of *INCOME*. The term w_i in Equation 7.8 represents an error term, indicating that the relationship between $| e_i |$ and *INCOME* (if any) would likely be imperfect. This hypothetical relationship in Equation 7.8 can be estimated using OLS by first estimating the equation shown in Equation 4.11 and saving the residuals from this regression. Next, the absolute value of the residuals can be computed and then used as the dependent variable in Equation 7.8 with *INCOME* as the independent variable. If the resulting OLS regression for Equation 7.8 shows that the coefficient to *INCOME* is statistically different from zero, then this provides evidence that heteroscedasticity is present. Using the data in Table A4, test for heteroscedasticity using the Glejser method and explain your results.

7.4 The presidential elections model shown in Equation 5.10 is estimated with a time series of data and as such is a candidate for autocorrelation problems. Estimate the model shown in Equation 5.10, plot the residuals from this regression, and visually inspect them for signs of autocorrelation. What are your conclusions?

7.5 Use the wage data set to estimate the regression where wage is a function of education (*EDUC*) and experience (*EXPER*). Now repeat the regression, excluding the variable for education. What happens to the estimated coefficient to *EXPER* when *EDUC* is removed? Why? (Hint: consider the correlation between *EXPER* and *EDUC*.)

8

Where to Go From Here

One of the goals of this book was to show the reader how the tools of regression analysis can be put to work on a wide scope of research topics and subject areas. Regression analysis is regularly applied to research in economics, political science, sociology, education, and the physical sciences, as well as other fields. It is a tool that can be applied in many creative ways. But it is also a tool that is often misused. Indeed, much of the criticism aimed at regression analysis can be traced to an irresponsible use of the methods discussed in this book. There are several things that a practitioner of regression analysis needs to bear in mind:

- Regression analysis is based on probability and statistical principles, and as such the *theory* of regression analysis is impeccable. The *application* of regression analysis, on the other hand, is in the hands of the researcher. If it is applied responsibly, it can be a powerful research tool. If it is applied irresponsibly, it can be very misleading.
- In most cases, regression analysis is incapable of *proving* anything. This is because research is typically carried out with *samples* of data. Sample results can be convincing and can *support* hypotheses, but proof beyond any doubt is beyond the ability of any sample of data.
- Computer programs that perform regression analysis simply obey the commands of the user. These programs are not capable of building theoretically sound models. This is the (often difficult) task of the researcher. A well-constructed model can provide us with valuable results. Applying regression analysis to a poorly constructed model can be misleading.
- Many of the examples used in this text were carried out with small-sized samples of data. This was done purposefully so that the reader could easily input

these data by hand into a program capable of performing OLS regressions. In general, samples should be as large as feasibly and reasonably possible. Larger samples generally provide more reliable estimates of population regression functions.

- The language of regression analysis is important. This book has at times used informal language in order to provide the reader with intuition. In the application of regression analysis, the researcher should endeavor to use formal language when appropriate. For example, when discussing a random variable, observations do not literally "bounce around" their mean, which was a phrase that was sometimes used in this book; rather, they have *variance*.

Other Topics in Regression Analysis

The methods used in this book are the most basic to regression analysis. There are quite literally dozens of other topics under regression analysis that can be pursued. Many of these topics have to do with the nature of the dependent variable. A few examples of specialized topics are offered below.

- Dummy Dependent Variables

We have already discussed dummy independent variables in Chapter 5. In some cases, however, it is the dependent variable that may be categorical. For example, we may wish to study the voting behavior of U.S. senators on a particular political issue. In this case, the dependent variable whose behavior we wish to explain would be the observed vote cast by a senator. For example, we may code a senator's vote as 1 equals a "yes" vote on the issue, 0 equals a "no" vote. We could then construct a model where we specify independent variables that we believe explain the likelihood (i.e., the *probability*) that a senator will vote, say, in favor of the issue. In this case, given that the dependent variable is a dummy, it is generally inappropriate to use our OLS method to estimate such a model. There are several appropriate estimation methods, such as the *Logit* and *Probit* estimation methods. See DeMaris (1992), Menard (1995a, 1995b), and Liao (1994) for a discussion of these types of models.

- Time Series Issues

In Chapter 6, we estimated some very simple models using time series data. The handling of time series data, however, can be quite complex. To go beyond simple trend estimation and to include X variables that are also time series themselves can lead to something called **"spurious regression"**[1] results. This occurs if we regress the time series variable X_t on another time series variable Y_t and obtain what appears to be a statistically significant relationship when, in fact, X_t has no true causal relationship with Y_t. See Wooldridge (2006) for a discussion on this topic.

- Panel Data Sets

In Chapter 6, we explored some simple ways of working with multiple cross sections of data across time, or panel data sets. There are, however, much more sophisticated methods that can be used to get the most out of these rich data sets. For an advanced discussion on methods of working with panel data, see Wooldridge (2002).

- Simultaneous Equations Methods

In some cases, to understand the behavior of a particular dependent variable, it must be considered in the context of a *system* of equations. That is, thus far, our sample regression models have considered the behavior of a dependent variable in a single equation. In many cases, a single dependent variable may be a component of two or more linked equations. For example, consider our abortion model. We have considered the demand for abortion as being a function of several independent variables, including the price of an abortion. Students of economics will recall, however, that the market price and the quantity of a good or service that is produced and consumed is determined by *both* supply and demand for the good or service. Thus, to fully understand demand for abortion, we should also consider supply simultaneously.[2] A discussion of special techniques for handling such *simultaneous equations* models can be found in Gujarati (2003) or Greene (2003).

Go Forward and Regress!

We have come a long way from our simple two-variable model that was introduced in Chapter 2. The multiple regression model we developed in

---

[1] See footnote 13 in Chapter 6.

[2] See Kahane (2000) and Medoff (1988) for a simultaneous equations approach to understanding the market for abortion services.

Chapter 4, together with the discussion in later chapters on various independent variable types, has left us with a powerful analytical tool that can be used to explore a great variety of topics. As this book comes to an end, the reader is encouraged to make use of the tools we have discussed. However, as the title of this book suggests, we have covered the basics of regression analysis and there is a great deal more to learn. Thus, the reader is also encouraged to continue to read and learn more about advanced regression analysis techniques such as those we have just noted above.[3] The discussion in this introductory-level book has provided the basic ideas and intuition of regression analysis, and the reader should now be well equipped to pursue more advanced topics in this field.

---

[3] There are a number of good books available that cover a broad range of topics from simple to advanced methods in regression analysis. These include the ones cited throughout this book such as Gujarati (2003), Greene (2003), and Wooldridge (2006). The bibliographies in these books list numerous other sources.

Appendix A

Data Sets for Examples in the Text

Table A1   MLB Data

Player	Salary (Millions $ 2006)	2006 Team	League (AL = 0, NL = 1)	Career 2005 MLB Years	Career 2005 Slugging	Career 2005 Fielding	Black (1 = yes, 0 = no)	Hispanic (1 = yes, 0 = no)
Abreu, Bobby	13.600	Philadelphia	1	10	51.2	98.3	1	0
Anderson, Garret	10.600	Los Angeles Angels	0	12	47.3	98.9	1	0
Biggio, Craig	4.000	Houston	1	18	43.7	99.2	0	0
Boone, Aaron	3.750	Cleveland	0	9	43.6	95.2	0	0
Byrd, Marlon	0.800	Washington	1	4	37.7	98.6	1	0
Chavez, Eric	9.500	Oakland	0	8	49.6	96.7	0	1
Crosby, Bubba	0.354	New York Yankees	0	3	30.1	98.9	0	0
Eckstein, David	3.333	St. Louis	1	5	36.2	98.1	0	0
Ford, Lew	0.425	Minnesota	0	3	42.4	97.7	0	0
Garciaparra, Nomar	6.000	Los Angeles Dodgers	1	10	54.4	97.2	0	0
Gibbons, Jay	4.200	Baltimore	0	5	46.6	99	0	0
Griffey, Ken Jr.	10.465	Cincinnati	1	17	56.1	98.6	1	0
Guerrero, Vladimir	13.500	Los Angeles Angels	0	10	58.7	96.3	1	0
Hernandez, Ramon	4.000	Baltimore	0	7	41.8	98.8	0	1
Jeter, Derek	20.600	New York Yankees	0	11	46.1	97.5	1	0
Jones, Chipper	12.333	Atlanta	1	13	53.8	95.7	0	0
Konerko, Paul	12.000	Chicago White Sox	0	9	48.8	99.5	0	0
Kotchman, Casey	0.340	Los Angeles Angels	0	2	38.4	99.5	0	0

Player	Salary (Millions $ 2006)	2006 Team	League (AL = 0, NL = 1)	Career 2005 MLB Years	Career 2005 Slugging	Career 2005 Fielding	Black (1 = yes, 0 = no)	Hispanic (1 = yes, 0 = no)
LeCroy, Matt	0.850	Washington	1	6	44.7	98.4	0	0
Lopez, Javy	9.000	Baltimore	0	14	49.8	99.2	0	1
Martinez, Victor	1.000	Cleveland	0	4	46.3	99.3	0	1
Melhuse, Adam	0.700	Oakland	0	6	42.4	99.3	0	0
Punto, Nick	0.690	Minnesota	0	5	32.1	97.9	0	0
Rodriguez, Ivan	10.616	Detroit	0	15	48.7	99.1	0	1
Rollins, Jimmy	5.000	Philadelphia	1	6	41.4	98.1	1	0
Sheffield, Gary	10.756	New York Yankees	0	18	52.7	96.3	1	0
Suzuki, Ichiro	12.500	Seattle	0	5	44.2	99.4	0	0
Sweeney, Mike	11.000	Kansas City	0	11	50.0	99	0	0
Taveras, Willy	0.400	Houston	1	2	34.1	98.9	0	1
Thome, Jim	14.167	Chicago White Sox	0	15	56.2	98.8	0	0
Vizquel, Omar	3.640	San Francisco	1	17	35.8	98.4	0	1
Wigginton, Ty	0.675	Tampa Bay	0	4	42.9	96.3	0	0

Variable definitions:
Salary = reported salary, in millions of dollars, the player earned for the 2006 MLB season.
League = 1 if the player was playing in the National League, 0 if in the American League.
Career 2005 MLB years = number of seasons through 2005 the player has played at least 130 at-bats.
Career 2005 slugging = the slugging average through 2005, calculated as the ratio (number of bases reached)/(number of at-bats)*100.
Career 2005 fielding = the fielding percentage through 2005, calculated as the ratio (assists + putouts)/(assists + putouts + errors)*100.
Black = 1 if a player is black, 0 otherwise.
Hispanic = 1 if a player is non-black Hispanic, 0 otherwise.

Table A2   MLB Yearly Average Salary Data

Year	Time	Real Salary (Thousands $ 2000)	Time Sq.	Salary ($Th)	CPI (2000)	Real Salary
1969	1	116.82321	1	24.909	4.69	116.82321
1970	2	130.10532	4	29.303	4.44	130.10532
1971	3	134.05775	9	31.543	4.25	134.05775
1972	4	140.45904	16	34.092	4.12	140.45904
1973	5	141.87608	25	36.566	3.88	141.87608
1974	6	142.52811	36	40.839	3.49	142.52811
1975	7	142.9632	49	44.676	3.2	142.9632
1976	8	156.04803	64	51.501	3.03	156.04803
1977	9	216.02744	81	76.066	2.84	216.02744
1978	10	263.67264	100	99.876	2.64	263.67264
1979	11	269.13246	121	113.558	2.37	269.13246
1980	12	300.45004	144	143.756	2.09	300.45004
1981	13	350.88039	169	185.651	1.89	350.88039
1982	14	429.86466	196	241.497	1.78	429.86466
1983	15	500.30562	225	289.194	1.73	500.30562
1984	16	546.81728	256	329.408	1.66	546.81728
1985	17	594.5136	289	371.571	1.6	594.5136
1986	18	647.6564	324	412.52	1.57	647.6564
1987	19	626.93008	361	412.454	1.52	626.93008
1988	20	640.54434	400	438.729	1.46	640.54434
1989	21	712.79756	441	512.804	1.39	712.79756
1990	22	764.1876	484	578.93	1.32	764.1876
1991	23	1122.89688	529	891.188	1.26	1122.89688
1992	24	1333.82184	576	1084.408	1.23	1333.82184

Year	Time	Real Salary (Thousands $ 2000)	Time Sq.	Salary ($Th)	CPI (2000)	Real Salary
1993	25	1333.10226	625	1120.254	1.19	1333.10226
1994	26	1378.86764	676	1188.679	1.16	1378.86764
1995	27	1210.26277	729	1071.029	1.13	1210.26277
1996	28	1294.6637	784	1176.967	1.1	1294.6637
1997	29	1480.42846	841	1383.578	1.07	1480.42846
1998	30	1527.89036	900	1441.406	1.06	1527.89036
1999	31	1771.6515	961	1720.05	1.03	1771.6515
2000	32	1998.034	1024	1998.034	1	1998.034
2001	33	2196.47091	1089	2264.403	0.97	2196.47091
2002	34	2287.9056	1156	2383.235	0.96	2287.9056
2003	35	2402.14744	1225	2555.476	0.94	2402.14744
2004	36	2262.81419	1296	2486.609	0.91	2262.81419
2005	37	2316.7364	1369	2632.655	0.88	2316.7364
2006	38	2436.5624	1444	2866.544	0.85	2436.5624

SOURCE: Rodney Fort's Web site: http://www.rodneyfort.com/SportsData/BizFrame.htm. Data were converted into real (2000) dollars using the Consumer Price Index (CPI). (See footnote 4 in Chapter 6.)

Table A3   Presidential Election Data

Year	Vote	Incumbent	Growth	Inflation
1916	51.7	1	2.2	4.3
1920	36.1	0	−11.5	16.5
1924	58.2	1	−3.9	5.2
1928	58.8	0	4.6	0.2
1932	40.8	1	−14.6	7.2
1936	62.5	1	11.7	2.5
1940	55	1	3.6	0.1
1944	53.8	1	4.4	5.6
1948	52.4	1	2.9	8.6
1952	44.6	0	0.8	2.3
1956	57.8	1	−1.4	1.9
1960	49.9	0	0.4	2
1964	61.3	1	5.1	1.3
1968	49.6	0	5.1	3.2
1972	61.8	1	6.1	4.8
1976	48.9	0	4	7.6
1980	44.7	1	−3.6	7.9
1984	59.2	1	5.6	5.3
1988	53.9	0	2.3	3
1992	46.5	1	2.2	3.3
1996	54.7	1	2.7	2.1
2000	50.3	0	1.6	1.7
2004	51.2	1	2.9	2
Mean:	52.335	0.65	1.44	4.29

Variable definitions:
Year = election year.
Votes = percentage of the two-party vote received by the incumbent party candidate.
Incumbent = 1 if the candidate is the incumbent, 0 otherwise.
Growth = growth rate, in percent, of real GDP over the three quarters prior to the election.
Inflation = inflation rate, in percent, over the 15 quarters prior to the election.

SOURCE: Ray C. Fair's Web site: http://fairmodel.econ.yale.edu/

Table A4   Abortion Data

State	Abortion	Religion	Price	Laws	Funds	Educ	Income	Picket
Alabama	18.20	36.40	272.00	1.00	.00	66.90	16522	89
Alaska	16.50	18.10	461.00	.00	1.00	86.60	22067	0
Arizona	24.10	29.30	249.00	.00	.00	78.70	17401	55
Arkansas	13.50	30.00	248.00	1.00	.00	66.30	15635	33
California	42.10	28.10	293.00	.00	1.00	76.20	21348	36
Colorado	23.60	21.20	309.00	.00	.00	84.40	20666	43
Connecticut	26.20	43.40	374.00	.00	1.00	79.20	27150	60
Delaware	35.20	19.80	247.00	.00	.00	77.50	20724	0
Florida	30.00	22.60	271.00	.00	.00	74.40	19711	37
Georgia	24.00	28.60	319.00	1.00	.00	70.90	18549	50
Hawaii	46.00	26.70	422.00	.00	1.00	80.10	22200	0
Idaho	7.20	36.80	303.00	.00	.00	79.70	16649	50
Illinois	25.40	37.10	272.00	.00	.00	76.20	21774	47
Indiana	12.00	16.50	288.00	1.00	.00	75.60	18366	67
Iowa	11.40	29.20	280.00	.00	.00	80.10	18275	50
Kansas	22.40	21.30	340.00	1.00	.00	81.30	19387	67
Kentucky	11.40	36.70	320.00	.00	.00	64.60	16528	75
Louisiana	13.40	50.90	228.00	1.00	.00	68.30	15931	60
Maine	14.70	22.40	328.00	.00	.00	78.80	18163	0
Maryland	26.40	22.80	264.00	.00	.00	78.40	23268	50

(Continued)

Table A4 (Continued)

State	Abortion	Religion	Price	Laws	Funds	Educ	Income	Picket
Massachusetts	28.40	50.10	330.00	1.00	1.00	80.00	23676	70
Michigan	25.20	28.00	352.00	1.00	.00	76.80	19586	28
Minnesota	15.60	44.60	270.00	1.00	.00	82.40	20503	67
Mississippi	12.40	38.00	256.00	.00	.00	64.30	14082	100
Missouri	11.60	32.20	348.00	1.00	.00	66.90	18970	50
Montana	18.20	26.90	329.00	.00	.00	81.00	16227	50
Nebraska	15.70	30.90	279.00	1.00	.00	81.80	18974	100
Nevada	44.20	23.50	275.00	.00	.00	78.80	21648	33
New Hampshire	14.60	27.80	372.00	.00	.00	82.20	21933	50
New Jersey	31.00	42.70	316.00	.00	1.00	76.70	26091	64
New Mexico	17.70	44.70	332.00	.00	.00	75.10	15458	20
New York	46.20	41.80	338.00	.00	1.00	74.80	24095	60
North Carolina	22.40	25.90	291.00	.00	1.00	70.00	17863	54
North Dakota	10.70	56.30	370.00	1.00	.00	76.70	17048	100
Ohio	19.50	24.70	298.00	1.00	.00	75.70	19040	60
Oklahoma	12.50	36.30	281.00	.00	.00	74.60	16420	75
Oregon	23.90	15.80	248.00	.00	1.00	81.50	18605	50
Pennsylvania	18.60	37.00	296.00	.00	.00	74.70	20642	82
Rhode Island	30.00	63.90	322.00	1.00	.00	72.00	20276	50
South Carolina	14.20	30.30	292.00	1.00	.00	68.30	16212	57

State	Abortion	Religion	Price	Laws	Funds	Educ	Income	Picket
South Dakota	6.80	38.90	400.00	.00	.00	66.30	17198	100
Tennessee	16.20	30.90	300.00	.00	.00	67.10	17674	43
Texas	23.10	41.80	257.00	.00	.00	72.10	18437	56
Utah	9.30	76.70	298.00	1.00	.00	85.10	15573	0
Vermont	21.20	26.60	276.00	.00	1.00	80.80	18792	50
Virginia	22.70	19.90	267.00	.00	.00	75.20	20883	38
Washington	27.70	17.80	270.00	.00	1.00	83.80	21289	24
West Virginia	7.70	9.80	251.00	.00	1.00	66.00	15598	50
Wisconsin	13.60	41.60	276.00	1.00	.00	78.60	19038	67
Wyoming	4.30	29.30	378.00	1.00	.00	83.00	18631	100
Mean	20.58	32.65	305.12	0.36	0.24	75.93	19215.52	52

Variable definitions:

Abortion = number of abortions per 1,000 women aged 15-44 in 1992.
Religion = percent of a state's population that is Catholic, Southern Baptist, Evangelical, or Mormon.
Price = average charged in 1993 in nonhospital facilities for an abortion at 10 weeks with local anesthesia (weighted by the number of abortions performed in 1992).
Laws = 1 if a state enforces a law that restricts a minor's access to abortion, 0 otherwise.
Funds = 1 if state funds are available for use to pay for an abortion under most circumstances, 0 otherwise.
Educ = percentage of a state's population that is 25 years or older with a high school degree (or equivalent), 1990.
Income = disposable income per capita, 1992.
Picket = the percentage of respondents who reported experiencing picketing with physical contact or blocking of patients.

SOURCE: Abortion-related and picketing data are from the Guttmacher Institute. Other data are from the *Statistical Abstract of the United States* (U.S. Bureau of the Census, 1993).

Table A5   Sport Utility Vehicle Data

Vehicle	MSRP	Cargo	MPG	Engine Size	Cylinders	Horsepower
Acura MDX	37740	81.5	20	3.5	6	253
BMW X3 4dr AWD 3.0i	36800	71.0	21	3.0	6	225
BMW X5 4dr 3.0i	43195	54.4	18	3.0	6	225
Buick Rendezvous CX	24990	108.9	21	3.5	6	196
Cadillac Escalade 4dr	54725	104.6	16	6.0	8	345
Chevrolet Trailblazer 4dr LS	25140	80.1	19	4.2	6	291
Chevrolet Equinox 4dr LS	21190	68.6	21.5	3.4	6	185
Dodge Durango 4dr SXT	29295	102.4	18.5	3.7	6	210
Ford Escape 4dr XLS Auto	20685	66.3	24	2.3	4	153
Ford Explorer 4dr XS	27175	85.8	18	4.0	6	210
GMC Envoy 4dr SLE 4wd	28990	80.1	18	4.2	6	291
Honda CRV 4dr LX 2wd	20945	72.0	26	2.4	4	156
Hummer H3 4dr	29500	55.7	18	3.5	5	220
Hyundai Santa Fe 4dr GLS 2wd	22295	77.7	22	2.7	6	170
Infiniti QX56 4dr 4wd	53550	91.7	15.5	5.8	8	315
Jeep Grand Cherokee Laredo 4wd	30080	67.4	19	3.7	6	210
Jeep Liberty Renegade 2wd	23790	69.0	20	3.7	6	210
KIA Sorento 4dr LX 4wd auto	25265	66.4	17.5	2.5	6	192
Land Rover Range Rover 4dr HSE	75750	71.0	16	4.4	8	305
Land Rover LR3 4dr	39000	90.3	16.5	4.0	6	216
Lexus LS 470	68090	90.4	15	4.7	8	275

Vehicle	MSRP	Cargo	MPG	Engine Size	Cylinders	Horsepower
Lincoln Navigator 4dr Ultimate 2wd	53175	104.8	15.5	5.4	8	300
Mazda Tribute 4Di manual 2wd	20705	66.8	26.5	2.3	4	153
Mercedes-Benz ML350	40525	72.4	18	3.5	6	268
Mercury Mariner Premier 4wd	27400	66.3	21	3.0	6	200
Isuzu Ascender 5 passenger	26644	80.1	19	4.2	6	291
Mitsubishi Endeavor LS 2wd	27224	76.4	20	3.8	6	225
Nissan Xterra X Auto 4wd	23455	65.7	18.5	4.0	6	265
Nissan Murano S AWD	29805	81.6	21.5	3.5	6	245
Pontiac Torrent AWD	23795	68.6	20.5	3.4	6	185
Porsche Cayenne Turbo S	112415	62.5	15.5	4.5	8	520
Saab 9-7X 4.2i	39240	80.1	18	4.2	6	290
Saturn VUE auto AWD	23645	63.8	22	3.5	6	250
Toyota 4Runner SR5 2wd	28240	75.1	20	4.0	6	236
Toyota Rav4 4wd	22305	73.0	25.5	2.4	4	166
Volkswagen Touareg	45420	71.0	16	4.2	8	310
Volvo XC90 2.5T	36770	84.9	20	2.5	5	208
Subaru Forrester X manual	22420	57.7	25.5	2.5	4	173

MSRP = manufacturer's suggested retail price for the 2006 base model.
Cargo = cargo space measured in cubic feet.
MPG = miles per gallon; averaged between city and highway.
Engine Size = size of engine in liters.
Cylinders = number of cylinders in engine.
Horsepower = engine horsepower.

SOURCE: Kelly Blue Book Web site: www.kbb.com

Table A6   Wage Data

Wage	Educ	Female	Married	Exper	Blk_Hisp
11	8	0	1	42	0
20.4	17	0	0	3	0
9.1	13	0	0	16	1
13.75	14	0	1	21	0
24.98	16	0	1	18	0
7.7	13	1	0	8	0
10	10	1	1	25	0
3.4	8	1	0	49	0
7.38	14	1	0	15	1
22	14	0	1	15	0
6.67	16	1	0	10	0
12	14	1	1	10	0
9.25	12	0	0	19	0
5	12	0	0	4	1
4.13	12	1	1	4	0
3.65	11	0	0	16	0
7	12	1	1	10	0
22.83	18	1	0	37	0
5	12	1	1	14	0
22.5	18	0	1	14	0
4.5	12	1	0	3	0
6	12	0	1	9	0
6.75	10	0	1	13	0
8.75	12	0	0	9	0
3.35	16	1	1	14	1
6	13	0	0	31	0
7.3	12	0	1	37	0
4.25	12	1	1	20	0
6.25	18	0	1	14	0
5.75	12	1	1	15	0
3.35	11	0	0	3	1
7.45	12	1	0	25	0

Wage	Educ	Female	Married	Exper	Blk_Hisp
3.43	12	0	0	2	1
4.35	8	1	1	37	1
5.85	18	0	1	12	0
8.5	12	1	0	16	0
7.5	12	1	1	27	1
3.35	12	1	1	10	1
4.22	8	1	1	39	0
5	12	1	1	39	0
9.6	12	1	1	14	0
12.57	12	0	1	12	0
12.5	13	1	1	16	0
8.89	16	1	1	22	0
6.25	9	0	0	30	0

Wage = hourly wage in dollars (1991 figures).
Educ = years of education.
Female = 1 if the individual is a female, 0 if male.
Married = 1 if the individual is married, 0 otherwise.
Exper = years of labor market experience.
Blk_Hisp = 1 if the individual is black or hispanic, 0 otherwise.

Table A7   British Crime Data for 2004

Area	Crime	Unem	Cars	Police	% pop15_24
Avon & Somerset	85.941	1.888	326.939	2.095	12.995
Bedfordshire	86.126	2.861	465.102	1.954	12.895
Cambridgeshire	83.575	1.969	494.055	1.906	13.376
Cheshire	79.805	4.022	567.128	2.158	11.676
Cleveland	113.711	5.782	393.259	2.871	13.591
Cumbria	73.302	2.682	485.400	2.356	11.055
Derbyshire	69.735	2.876	473.617	2.059	11.683
Devon & Cornwall	60.535	2.229	484.218	2.008	11.994
Dorset	65.535	1.429	521.688	2.033	11.294
Durham	66.293	2.956	414.201	2.807	13.117
Dyfed Powys	57.354	2.683	489.001	2.318	12.091
Essex	58.975	2.195	499.807	1.845	11.530
Gloucestershire	79.097	2.102	511.706	2.176	11.645
Greater Manchester	113.282	3.526	441.464	2.921	13.943
Gwent	81.303	3.668	313.344	2.426	12.253
Hampshire	79.701	1.788	508.839	2.063	13.256
Hertfordshire	84.142	1.813	523.659	1.899	11.332
Humberside	117.920	4.309	401.003	2.409	12.631
Kent	69.535	2.614	478.133	2.180	12.128
Lancashire	85.781	2.730	436.580	2.365	13.039
Leicestershire	82.338	3.096	475.094	2.286	14.215
Lincolnshire	68.328	2.031	493.485	1.858	11.537
London, City of	107.703	4.880	339.617	3.931	13.320
Merseyside	110.797	5.673	369.964	3.013	14.219
Norfolk	68.736	2.768	499.025	1.861	11.464
Northamptonshire	92.377	2.365	500.288	1.901	12.154
Northumbria	83.104	4.381	370.603	2.886	13.707
Nottinghamshire	122.511	3.116	417.643	2.357	14.399
North Wales	72.430	2.818	479.444	2.315	11.846
North Yorkshire	64.817	1.811	482.338	1.911	12.461
Staffordshire	83.224	2.407	485.064	2.120	12.488
Suffolk	60.549	2.593	517.603	1.855	11.248

Area	Crime	Unem	Cars	Police	% pop15_24
Surrey	55.155	1.240	572.673	1.816	11.282
Sussex	73.730	2.391	486.984	2.016	11.076
South Wales	91.927	3.469	503.310	2.695	14.445
South Yorkshire	97.540	3.737	399.165	2.510	13.767
Thames Valley	83.616	1.845	572.585	1.846	12.967
Warwickshire	73.585	2.069	522.824	1.926	11.912
Wiltshire	55.732	1.402	588.430	1.879	11.327
West Mercia	61.741	2.033	519.981	1.932	11.301
West Midlands	91.031	5.877	495.304	3.038	14.346
West Yorkshire	104.990	3.547	405.057	2.403	14.360

Area = police force area.
Crime = total crimes per 1,000 people.
Unem = male unemployment rate.
Cars = number of registered motor vehicles per 1,000 people.
Police = number of police officers per 1,000 people.
% pop15_24 = percentage of the population aged 15 to 24 years.

SOURCE: Various UK government publications.

Appendix B

Instructions for Using Excel and SPSS

The purpose of this appendix is to provide the reader with some basic instructions on how to use the programs Excel and SPSS to perform the regression analyses carried out in the text. This appendix assumes that the reader is somewhat familiar with using spreadsheet programs like Excel. For a more complete discussion on how to use Excel and SPSS, the reader is referred to the program manuals.[1]

For each program, we consider the following:

- How to input data, including inputting data by hand, reading data in from a data file, and saving data as a program file. (The instructions for reading data in from data files are given for the online data sets used in the examples in this book.[2] Data obtained from elsewhere may require different steps for reading into the programs, depending on their format.)
- How to transform variables into new variables.
- How to perform a simple least-squares regression, including how to save residuals from a regression.

Using Excel

Microsoft Excel is a spreadsheet program that is capable of doing simple least-squares regression analysis. Regression analysis, however, is not the primary intention of the program, and as such, performing OLS with Excel can at times be somewhat cumbersome as compared to other programs (e.g., SPSS).

---

[1] There are a number of books that describe how to use Excel and SPSS. See, for example, Berk and Carey (2000) for Excel and Einspruch (2005) for SPSS.

[2] Data are available at http://www.cbe.csueastbay.edu/~lkahane/

Inputting Data

By Hand. Data can be entered into Excel by typing in values directly. Data should be entered as columns where each column contains all observations on a single variable. In the first row of each column, there should be a variable name followed immediately by the associated data. Columns may contain non-numerical entries such as names, and so on. Figure B1 shows an example of how the baseball data set would look when properly entered into Excel.

(Variable definitions are as they were given in the text.)

Reading Data From a Data File. Rather than typing data in by hand, it is more convenient to read data from data files, if such files are available. Indeed, by reading data from a data file, there is less of a chance of incorrectly inputting data values than there is when doing so by hand.[3] Data files can be of a variety of formats. The most general format is the ASCII or "text" file. The online data available for use in this book's examples are text files, and the steps below describe how to read in these data. To read a data text file into Excel, it is assumed that the data have already been downloaded onto a computer disk and saved as a text file. Having done so, the following steps are carried out for reading the text data into Excel:

1. Launch Excel, then from the main tool bar menu, choose File, then Open and choose the appropriate location for Look In. Provide the appropriate File Name (e.g., baseball.txt), and under Files of Type select Text Files, then select Open.

2. The next screen shows Excel's Text Import Wizard (see Figure B2). Under Original Data Type choose Delimited (the default), then select Next.

3. At the next screen, select "tab" for Delimiters (the default) and for Text Qualifier select " (double quotation mark, again the default). Select Next.

4. At this screen, set the Data Format to General (the default) and then select Finish.

The data should now appear as they do in Figure B1. Before continuing, *you should save the data set* by going to File on the main menu bar. Select Save As. . . . Choose a location and file name and change the Save as Type to Microsoft Excel Workbook. Saving the file as a Microsoft Excel Workbook file will allow you to use the file at a later date without having to go through the steps noted above.

---

[3] In fact, data input errors are another source of stochastic error, e_i in our sample regression model.

PLAYER	SALARY	TEAM	LEAGUE	YEARS	SLUGGING	FIELDING	BLACK	HISPANIC
Abreu, Bobby	13.6	Philadelphia	1	10	51.2	98.3	1	0
Anderson, Garret	10.6	Los Angeles Angels	0	12	47.3	98.9	1	0
Biggio, Craig	4	Houston	1	18	43.7	99.2	0	0
Boone, Aaron	3.75	Cleveland	0	9	43.6	95.2	0	0
Byrd, Marlon	0.8	Washington	1	4	37.7	98.6	1	0
Chavez, Eric	9.5	Oakland	0	8	49.6	96.7	0	1
Crosby, Bubba	0.354	New York Yankees	0	3	30.1	98.9	0	0
Eckstein, David	3.333	St. Louis	1	5	36.2	98.1	0	0
Ford, Lew	0.425	Minnesota	0	3	42.4	97.7	0	0
Garciaparra, Nomar	6	Los Angeles Dodgers	1	10	54.4	97.2	0	0
Gibbons, Jay	4.2	Baltimore	0	5	46.6	99	0	0
Griffey, Ken Jr	10.465	Cincinnati	1	17	56.1	98.6	1	0
Guerrero, Vladimir	13.5	Los Angeles Angels	0	10	58.7	96.3	1	0
Hernandez, Ramon	4	Baltimore	0	7	41.8	98.8	0	1
Jeter, Derek	20.6	New York Yankees	0	11	46.1	97.5	1	0
Jones, Chipper	12.333	Atlanta	1	13	53.8	95.7	0	0
Konerko, Paul	12	Chicago White S	0	9	48.8	99.5	0	0
Kotchman, Casey	0.34	Los Angeles Angels	0	2	38.4	99.5	0	0
LeCroy, Matt	0.85	Washington	1	6	44.7	98.4	0	0
Lopez, Javy	9	Baltimore	0	14	49.8	99.2	0	1
Martinez, Victo	1	Cleveland	0	4	46.3	99.3	0	1
Melhuse, Adam	0.7	Oakland	0	6	42.4	99.3	0	0
Punto, Nick	0.69	Minnesota	0	5	32.1	97.9	0	0
Rodriguez, Ivan	10.616	Detroit	0	15	48.7	99.1	0	1
Rollins, Jimmy	5	Philadelphia	1	6	41.4	98.1	1	0
Sheffield, Gary	10.756	New York Yankees	0	18	52.7	96.3	1	0
Suzuki, Ichiro	12.5	Seattle	0	5	44.2	99.4	0	0
Sweeney, Mike	11	Kansas City	0	11	50	99	0	0
Taveras, Willy	0.4	Houston	1	2	34.1	98.9	0	1
Thome, Jim	14.167	Chicago White Sox	0	15	56.2	98.8	0	0
Vizquel, Omar	3.64	San Francisco	1	17	35.8	98.4	0	1
Wigginton, Ty	0.675	Tampa Bay	0	4	42.9	96.3	0	0

Figure B1

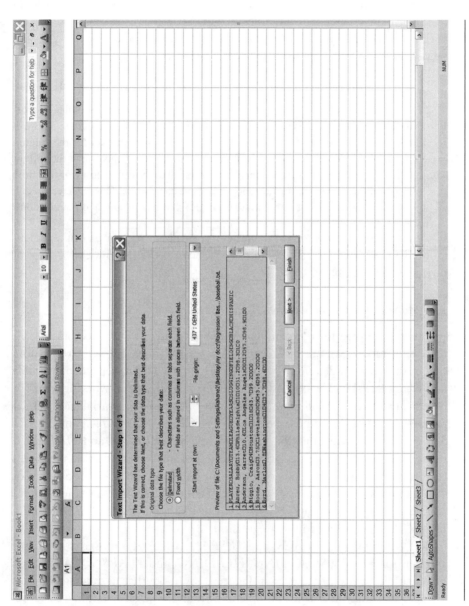

Figure B2

Transforming Variables

In many cases, we may wish to transform an existing variable into a new one. For example, in Chapter 5, we considered adding *YEARS* SQUARED to our list of independent variables in our MLB player salary model. This variable is created by calculating the square of the variable *YEARS*. This can be performed in Excel quite easily by following these steps:

1. Create a new column heading for the new variable (e.g., *YEARS* SQUARED).

2. In the cell immediately below this new heading, we may enter a formula. The formula should be typed literally as the following: =(E2*E2), then hit Enter. This will take the value shown in Cell E2 (which is the first entry of data for the column headed *YEARS*) and multiply it by itself and put the resulting value in the current cell. This formula can then be copied from this cell to the cells below (for the entire length of the data set) using the Copy and Paste commands. This will create a column of squared values for the variable *YEARS* that can be used in our regressions.

Other transformations can be made in a similar way, for example, calculating the natural log for a column of data. See Excel's help index for a list of formulas that can be used.

Performing a Least-Squares Regression

Having inputted the data and created the variables needed for our sample regression model, we are now ready to carry out a least-squares regression. Our first step is to determine which variable will be our dependent variable and which one(s) will be our independent variable(s). Again, working with our baseball example, we will have *SALARY* as our dependent variable. For independent variables, we can use *YEARS, SLUGGING, FIELDING,* and *YEARS* SQUARED (we will omit the variables for NL, *BLACK,* and *HISPANIC* for this example). Before performing the regression, one restriction of Excel's regression program is that all columns containing data for the independent or "*X*" variables must be next to each other. That is, we cannot have the columns arranged as shown in Figure B3a because the variables *BLACK* and *HISPANIC* are not included in the regression.

The columns with *BLACK* and *HISPANIC* must be moved so that the columns for *YEARS, SLUGGING, FIELDING,* and *YEARS* SQUARED can be alongside each other as seen in Figure B3b. (Note that in moving columns around, you must take care that formulas that are in cells continue to represent the proper equation. As columns are moved from one location to another, the cell formulas adjust cell addresses to the new relative location and thus the resulting equation may not be the one intended.)

Microsoft Excel - baseball.txt

	PLAYER	SALARY	TEAM	LEAGUE	YEARS	SLUGGING	FIELDING	BLACK	HISPANIC	YEARS SQUARED
2	Abreu, Bobby	13.6	Philadelphia	1	10	51.2	98.3	1	0	100
3	Anderson, Garret	10.6	Los Angeles Angels	0	12	47.3	98.9	1	0	144
4	Biggio, Craig	4	Houston	1	18	43.7	99.2	0	0	324
5	Boone, Aaron	3.75	Cleveland	0	9	43.6	95.2	0	0	81
6	Byrd, Marlon	0.8	Washington	1	4	37.7	98.6	1	0	16
7	Chavez, Eric	9.5	Oakland	0	8	49.6	96.7	0	1	64
8	Crosby, Bubba	0.354	New York Yankees	0	3	30.1	98.9	0	0	9
9	Eckstein, David	3.333	St. Louis	1	5	36.2	98.1	0	0	25
10	Ford, Lew	0.425	Minnesota	0	3	42.4	97.7	0	0	9
11	Garciaparra, Nomar	6	Los Angeles Dodgers	1	10	54.4	97.2	0	1	100
12	Gibbons, Jay	4.2	Baltimore	0	5	46.6	99	0	0	25
13	Griffey, Ken Jr	10.465	Cincinnati	1	17	56.1	98.6	1	0	289
14	Guerrero, Vladimir	13.5	Los Angeles Angels	0	10	58.7	96.3	1	1	100
15	Hernandez, Ramon	4	Baltimore	0	7	41.8	98.8	0	1	49
16	Jeter, Derek	20.6	New York Yankees	0	11	46.1	97.5	1	0	121
17	Jones, Chipper	12.333	Atlanta	1	13	53.9	95.7	0	0	169
18	Konerko, Paul	12	Chicago White S	0	9	48.3	99.5	0	0	81
19	Kotchman, Casey	0.34	Los Angeles Angels	0	2	38.4	99.5	0	0	4
20	LeCroy, Matt	0.85	Washington	1	6	44.7	98.4	0	0	36
21	Lopez, Javy	9	Baltimore	0	14	49.8	99.2	0	1	196
22	Martinez, Victo	0.7	Cleveland	0	4	46.3	99.3	0	1	16
23	Melhuse, Adam	0.7	Oakland	0	6	42.4	99.3	0	0	36
24	Punto, Nick	0.69	Minnesota	0	5	32.1	97.9	0	0	25
25	Rodriguez, Ivan	10.616	Detroit	0	15	48.7	99.1	0	1	225
26	Rollins, Jimmy	5	Philadelphia	1	6	41.4	98.1	1	0	36
27	Sheffield, Gary	10.756	New York Yankees	0	18	52.7	96.3	1	0	324
28	Suzuki, Ichiro	12.5	Seattle	0	5	44.2	99.4	0	0	25
29	Sweeney, Mike	11	Kansas City	0	11	50	99	0	0	121
30	Taveras, Willy	0.4	Houston	1	2	34.1	98.9	1	0	4
31	Thome, Jim	14.167	Chicago White Sox	0	15	56.2	98.8	0	0	225
32	Vizquel, Omar	3.64	San Francisco	1	17	35.8	98.4	0	1	289
33	Wigginton, Ty	0.675	Tampa Bay	0	4	42.9	96.3	0	0	16

Figure B3a

Microsoft Excel - baseball.txt

PLAYER	SALARY	TEAM	LEAGUE	YEARS	SLUGGING	FIELDING	YEARS SQUARRED	BLACK	HISPANIC
Abreu, Bobby	13.6	Philadelphia	1	10	51.2	98.3	100	1	0
Anderson, Garret	10.6	Los Angeles Angels	0	12	47.3	98.9	144	1	0
Biggio, Craig	4	Houston	1	18	43.7	99.2	324	0	0
Boone, Aaron	3.75	Cleveland	0	9	43.6	95.2	81	0	0
Byrd, Marlon	0.8	Washington	1	4	37.7	98.6	16	1	0
Chavez, Eric	9.5	Oakland	0	8	49.6	96.7	64	0	1
Crosby, Bubba	0.354	New York Yankees	0	3	30.1	98.9	9	0	0
Eckstein, David	3.333	St. Louis	1	5	36.2	98.1	25	0	0
Ford, Lew	0.425	Minnesota	0	3	42.4	97.7	9	0	0
Garciaparra, Nomar	6	Los Angeles Dodgers	1	10	54.4	97.2	100	0	0
Gibbons, Jay	4.2	Baltimore	0	5	46.6	99	25	0	0
Griffey, Ken Jr	10.465	Cincinnati	1	17	56.1	98.6	289	1	0
Guerrero, Vladimir	13.5	Los Angeles Angels	0	10	58.7	96.3	100	1	0
Hernandez, Ramon	4	Baltimore	0	7	41.8	98.8	49	0	1
Jeter, Derek	20.6	New York Yankees	0	11	46.1	97.5	121	1	0
Jones, Chipper	12.333	Atlanta	1	13	53.8	95.7	169	0	0
Konerko, Paul	12	Chicago White S	0	9	48.8	99.5	81	0	0
Kotchman, Casey	0.34	Los Angeles Angels	0	2	38.4	99.5	4	0	0
LeCroy, Matt	0.85	Washington	1	6	44.7	98.4	36	0	0
Lopez, Javy	9	Baltimore	0	14	49.8	99.2	196	0	1
Martinez, Victor	1	Cleveland	0	4	46.3	99.3	16	0	1
Melhuse, Adam	0.7	Oakland	0	6	42.4	99.3	36	0	0
Punto, Nick	0.69	Minnesota	0	5	32.1	97.9	25	0	0
Rodriguez, Ivan	10.616	Detroit	0	15	48.7	99.1	225	0	1
Rollins, Jimmy	5	Philadelphia	1	6	41.4	98.1	36	1	0
Sheffield, Gary	10.756	New York Yankees	0	18	52.7	96.3	324	1	0
Suzuki, Ichiro	12.5	Seattle	0	5	44.2	99.4	25	0	0
Sweeney, Mike	11	Kansas City	0	11	50	99	121	0	0
Taveras, Willy	0.4	Houston	1	2	34.1	98.9	4	0	1
Thome, Jim	14.167	Chicago White Sox	0	15	56.2	98.8	225	0	0
Vizquel, Omar	3.64	San Francisco	1	17	35.8	98.4	289	0	1
Wigginton, Ty	0.675	Tampa Bay	0	4	42.9	96.3	16	0	0

Figure B3b

Now, with our columns properly aligned, we are ready to perform a regression analysis. To do so, we follow these steps:

1. From the main menu bar, select Tools, then Data Analysis . . . , and then Regression.[4]

2. You will now be looking at the Regression screen. At this screen, you need to tell the program where the data for the dependent and independent variables are located. Click on the box for Input Y Range so that there is a blinking cursor there. Next, take the arrow to the column headed *SALARY* and starting with the cell containing the variable name *SALARY*, click and drag down this column, which will highlight it. As you do so, you should see the cell addresses for the location of the dependent variable appearing in the Input Y Range box. The location of the dependent variable data has now been completed.

3. Return to the Regression screen and click on the box for Input X Range, thus putting a blinking cursor there. Then take the arrow and now, starting with the cell containing the variable name *YEARS*, click and drag over to *YEARS SQUARED* and then down to the end of that column. Doing so should highlight the block that contains all the data for the independent variables, including the column headings. As this is done, the address of this block should appear in the Input X Range box. The location of the independent variable data has now been completed.

4. Next, check the box headed Labels; this tells the program that the first row of data contains the variable names (see Figure B4).

5. Under the Residuals option, check the box for Residuals; this will save our residuals from the regression for later use.

6. Select OK and the regression results are produced on a separate sheet.[5]

Using SPSS[6]

The program SPSS is better suited for regression analysis than Excel. Once data are read into SPSS, it is easier to transform the data and to perform

---

[4] Note that if you do not see Data Analysis under the Tools menu, this is likely because this particular module was not loaded during the installation of the Excel program. To load this module now, go to Tools, select Add-Ins . . . , and check the boxes for Analysis Toolpak and Analysis Toolpak–VBA. Doing this will load the module containing the Data Analysis features.

[5] Note that the regression results presented will differ somewhat from the ones shown in the text of this book. The results shown in the text were edited to simplify our discussion.

[6] These instructions are for SPSS version 15.0. Other versions may have slightly different steps required to perform the tasks described in this appendix.

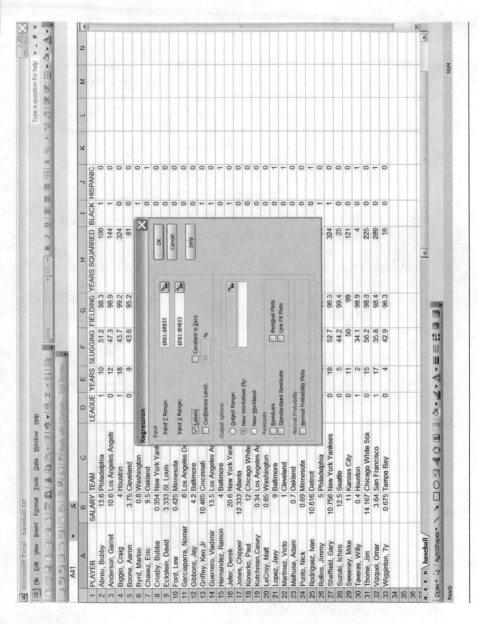

Figure B4

*Untitled2 [DataSet1] - SPSS Data Editor

File Edit View Data Transform Analyze Graphs Utilities Add-ons Window Help

1 : pfa   Avon and Somerset   Visible: 6 of 6 Variables

	pfa	crime	unem	cars	police	pctpop15_2	var	var	var	var	var	var	var
1	Avon and Somerset	85.94102	1.888	326.9390	2.095352	12.99454							
2	Bedfordshire	86.12634	2.861	465.1024	1.953642	12.89483							
3	Cambridgeshire	83.57501	1.969	494.0547	1.906002	13.37580							
4	Cheshire	79.80456	4.022	567.1277	2.157932	11.67640							
5	Cleveland	113.7105	5.782	393.2586	2.870537	13.59118							
6	Cumbria	73.30235	2.682	485.4001	2.356064	11.05497							
7	Derbyshire	69.73447	2.876	473.6172	2.055004	11.63301							
8	Devon and Cornwall	60.53487	2.229	484.2178	2.007869	11.99432							
9	Dorset	65.53541	1.429	521.6876	2.033171	11.29355							
10	Durham	66.29324	2.956	414.2005	2.807225	13.11723							
11	Dyfad Powys	57.35358	2.683	489.0014	2.317562	12.09053							
12	Essex	58.97536	2.195	499.8074	1.845125	11.53023							
13	Gloucestershire	79.09741	2.102	511.7057	2.175901	11.64455							
14	Greater Manchester	113.2824	3.526	441.4656	2.920585	13.94250							
15	Gwent	81.30255	3.368	313.3435	2.425716	12.25296							
16	Hampshire	79.70081	1.788	508.8393	2.062768	13.25562							
17	Hertfordshire	84.14193	1.313	523.6569	1.893318	11.33199							
18	Humberside	117.9200	4.309	401.0028	2.409256	12.63099							
19	Kent	69.53487	2.614	478.1327	2.180136	12.12817							
20	Lancashire	85.78089	2.730	436.5796	2.364959	13.03924							
21	Leicestershire	82.33845	3.096	475.0906	2.285897	14.21470							
22	Lincolnshire	68.32613	2.031	493.4948	1.857808	11.53675							
23	London, City of	107.7028	4.880	339.6166	3.931022	13.32014							
24	Merseyside	110.7973	5.673	369.9641	3.013438	14.21877							
25	Norfolk	68.73607	2.768	499.0251	1.861354	11.46356							
26	Northamptonshire	92.37668	2.365	500.2878	1.901354	12.15401							
27	Northumbria	83.10369	4.381	370.6030	2.885665	13.70667							
28	Nottinghamshire	122.5106	3.116	417.6430	2.356942	14.39892							
29	North Wales	72.42995	2.818	479.4440	2.315146	11.84581							
30	North Yorkshire	64.81695	1.811	482.3379	1.911222	12.46077							
31	Staffordshire	83.22387	2.407	485.0633	2.120114	12.48810							
32	Suffolk	60.54848	2.593	517.6027	1.855184	11.24762							
33	Surrey	55.15461	1.240	572.6733	1.815705	11.28186							
34	Sussex	73.72989	2.391	486.9838	2.016332	11.07580							
35	South Wales	91.92740	3.469	503.3095	2.694749	14.44527							
36	South Yorkshire	97.53989	3.737	399.1654	2.509822	13.76721							

Data View ∖ Variable View /

SPSS Processor is ready

Figure B5

regression analysis. In addition, SPSS is capable of performing more sophisticated regression techniques.

Inputting Data

By Hand. Launching the program brings you to the SPSS Data Editor. As with Excel, data should be entered as columns in which each column contains all observations on a single variable. Data can be simply typed in, and a column can contain non-numerical entries, such as player names. When a column is started, SPSS assigns the column a generic name (e.g., var000 . . .). To change the column name into something more understandable (e.g., crime), click on the tab at the bottom of the Data Editor screen called Variable View. At this screen, you can rename the column, giving it a Name (of no more than eight characters) and also a Label (which can have more than eight characters). This can be done for each column of data (see Figure B5 as an example).

Reading Data From a Data File. In order to read data from a data file, it is assumed that the text data file has been downloaded and saved on a disk.[7] As noted earlier, these instructions are for the data files that are available online, which have been saved as tab delimited text files.[8] Other data files may require different settings when reading them into SPSS. To read the text data file into SPSS, we follow these steps:

1. On the Data View page of the SPSS Data Editor, select File, then Read Text Data. Choose the appropriate location for Look In. Provide the appropriate File Name (e.g., crime04.txt), and under Files of Type select Text Files, then select Open.

2. The next screen is SPSS's "Text Import Wizard" (see Figure B6). On the first page of this wizard, you are asked, "Does your text file match a predefined format?" Select No (the default) and then select Next.

3. At the next page, you are asked, "How are your variables arranged?" Select Delimited (the default). The next question is, "Are variable names included at the top of your file?" Select Yes, and then select Next.

---

[7] It should be noted that SPSS has the ability to read various file formats, including files that have been saved as Excel files. For instructions on how to read files of different formats, see the held index in SPSS.

[8] See footnote 2 of this appendix.

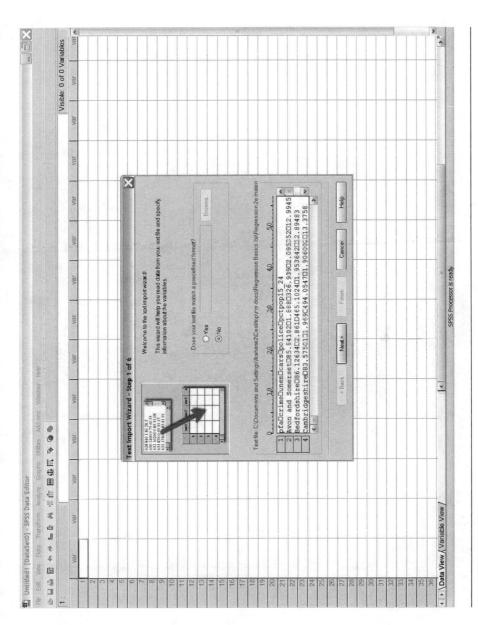

Figure B6

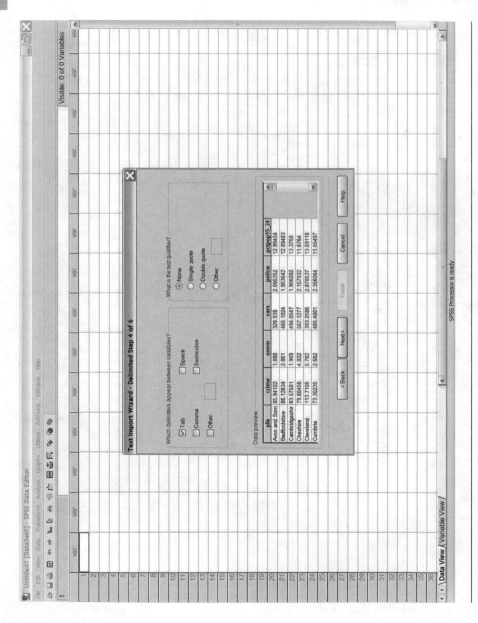

Figure B7

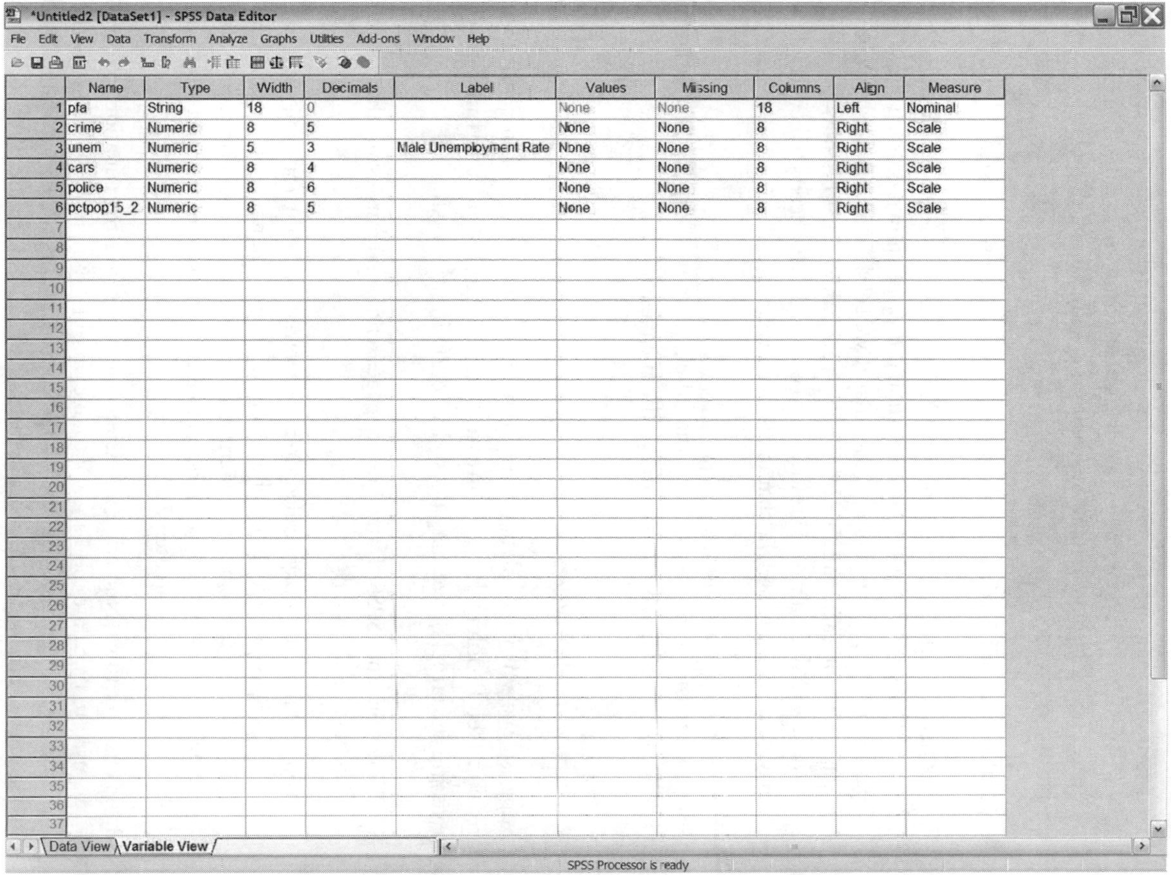
*Untitled2 [DataSet1] - SPSS Data Editor
File Edit View Data Transform Analyze Graphs Utilities Add-ons Window Help
Name Type Width Decimals Label Values Missing Columns Align Measure
1 pfa String 18 0 None None 18 Left Nominal
2 crime Numeric 8 5 None None 8 Right Scale
3 unem Numeric 5 3 Male Unemployment Rate None None 8 Right Scale
4 cars Numeric 8 4 None None 8 Right Scale
5 police Numeric 8 6 None None 8 Right Scale
6 pctpop15_2 Numeric 8 5 None None 8 Right Scale
Data View
Variable View
SPSS Processor is ready

Figure B8

4. On the third page of the Text Import Wizard, there is a series of questions, for which the default settings all can be used (i.e., the first case of data begins on line 2, each line represents a case, and we want to import all of the cases). Thus, we can simply select Next.

5. The fourth page of the Wizard asks, "Which delimiters appear between variables?" (see Figure B7). The default selections are Tab, Comma, and Space. *Un*select Comma and Space, leaving only Tab as the selection. Select Next.

6. No changes are needed on page 5 of the Wizard, so select Next.

7. The default settings on page 6 of the Wizard can be used (i.e., No and No), thus we may select Finish. The data should now be shown on the Data View page of the SPSS Data Editor. Note that if we select Variable View, we may add labels for each variable by simply typing them in. This may be useful because variable names are restricted to only eight characters, whereas labels may have more than eight characters (see Figure B8).

When regressions are performed, the labels (if they are given) are used in the results produced, which may make them easier to read.

Transforming Variables

Suppose we wish to calculate the natural log of *SALARY* for use in a regression (see Problem 5.1). To create a new variable that is a function of an existing variable(s), we may do so by following these steps:

1. While on the SPSS Data Editor page, choose Transform, then select Compute . . . .

2. You will next see a page called Compute Variable. At the top, you see a box titled Target Variable. In this box, you must type the name of the new variable you wish to create (e.g., lncrime for the natural log of crime; note that the name of this variable is restricted to 8 characters. You may add a variable label later as noted in Step 7 above.).

3. In the box titled Numeric Expression, you must give the equation that will be used to calculate the Target Variable. In our example, we would type the expression: ln(crime). The "ln" is the command for calculating the natural log of the variable that appears in the parentheses (see Figure B9). (Note that rather than typing "crime," we may instead highlight the variable shown in the list of variables on the left side of the box, and then click on the arrow button.)

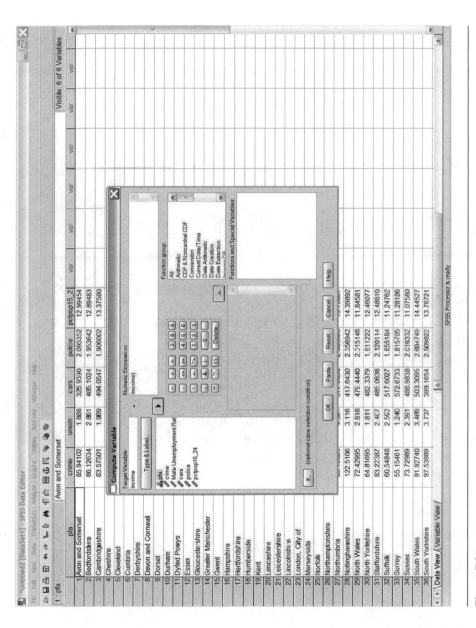

Figure B9

*Untitled2 [DataSet1] - SPSS Data Editor

File Edit View Data Transform Analyze Graphs Utilities Add-ons Window Help

1 : pfa

Analyze menu:
- Reports
- Descriptive Statistics
- Tables
- Compare Means
- General Linear Model
- Generalized Linear Models
- Mixed Models
- Correlate
- Regression
  - Linear...
  - Curve Estimation...
  - Binary Logistic...
  - Multinomial Logistic...
  - Ordinal...
  - Probit...
  - Nonlinear...
  - Weight Estimation...
  - 2-Stage Least Squares...
  - Optimal Scaling...
- Loglinear
- Classify
- Data Reduction
- Scale
- Nonparametric Tests
- Time Series
- Survival
- Multiple Response
- Missing Value Analysis...
- Quality Control
- ROC Curve...

	pfa			cars	police	pctpop15_2
1	Avon and Somerset	81.30255	888	326.9390	2.095352	12.99454
2	Bedfordshire	79.70081	861	465.1024	1.953642	12.89483
3	Cambridgeshire	84.14193	969	494.0547	1.906002	13.37580
4	Cheshire	117.9200	022	567.4277	2.457932	11.67640
5	Cleveland	69.53487	1.788	478.1327	537	13.59118
6	Cumbria	85.78009	2.730	436.5796	064	11.05497
7	Derbyshire	82.33845	3.096	475.0936	004	11.68301
8	Devon and Cornwall	68.32813	2.031	493.4848	869	11.99432
9	Dorset	107.7028	4.880	339.6166	171	11.29355
10	Durham	110.7973	5.673	369.9641	225	13.11723
11	Dyfed Powys	68.73607	2.768	499.0251	562	12.09053
12	Essex	92.37668	2.365	500.2876	125	11.53023
13	Gloucestershire	83.10369	4.381	370.6030	901	11.64455
14	Greater Manchester	122.5106	3.116	417.6430	585	13.94250
15	Gwent	3.668	313.3435		2.425716	12.25296
16	Hampshire	79.70081	1.788	508.8393	2.062768	13.25562
17	Hertfordshire	84.14193	1.813	523.6589	1.899318	11.33199
18	Humberside	117.9200	4.309	401.0028	2.409256	12.63099
19	Kent	69.53487	2.614	478.1327	2.180136	12.12817
20	Lancashire	85.78009	2.730	436.5796	2.364959	13.03924
21	Leicestershire	82.33845	3.096	475.0936	2.285897	14.21470
22	Lincolnshire	68.32813	2.031	493.4848	1.857808	11.53675
23	London, City of	107.7028	4.880	339.6166	3.931022	13.32014
24	Merseyside	110.7973	5.673	369.9641	3.013488	14.21877
25	Norfolk	68.73607	2.768	499.0251	1.861354	11.46356
26	Northamptonshire	92.37668	2.365	500.2876	1.901354	12.15401
27	Northumbria	83.10369	4.381	370.6030	2.885665	13.70667
28	Nottinghamshire	122.5106	3.116	417.6430	2.356942	14.39892
29	North Wales	72.42995	2.818	479.4440	2.315146	11.84581
30	North Yorkshire	64.81695	1.811	482.3379	1.911222	12.46077
31	Staffordshire	83.22387	2.407	485.0638	2.120114	12.48810
32	Suffolk	60.54848	2.593	517.6027	1.855184	11.24762
33	Surrey	55.15461	1.240	572.6733	1.815705	11.28186
34	Sussex	73.72989	2.391	486.9838	2.016332	11.07580
35	South Wales	91.92740	3.469	503.3095	2.694749	14.44527
36	South Yorkshire	97.53989	3.737	399.1654	2.509822	13.76721

▶ ▶ \ Data View \ Variable View /

Linear Regression

Visible: 6 of 6 Variables

SPSS Processor is ready

Figure B10

4. Finally, we select OK. The newly created variable is now shown as a new column of data on the SPSS Data Editor page.

Performing a Least-Squares Regression

Given that our data have been read into SPSS successfully and we have created the variables we need for our regression, we now follow these steps to perform a least-squares regression:

1. At the SPSS Data Editor page, choose Analyze, then Regression, then select Linear. . . (see Figure B10).

This brings us to the Linear Regression page. At this page, there are many selections we can make. We will use only the ones necessary to perform the simple least-squares regression used in this book, including saving the residuals from the regression.

2. From the list of variables shown on the left, we must select our dependent variable. We may choose, for this example, "crime." In order to select crime as our dependent variable, we may simply click on this variable shown in the variable list, thus highlighting it, and then click on the arrow button and the variable will appear in the Dependent box. (Note that to unselect a variable, we may click on the arrow button again. Furthermore, we may type variable names in boxes rather than using the arrow button.)

3. Our next task is to choose our independent variable(s). To do so, we may simply highlight the variables shown in our variable list and then click on the arrow button. Doing so, the variables are then placed in the box titled Independent(s), as seen in Figure B11.

4. In order to save the residuals from our regression, we select Save... shown at the bottom of the Linear Regression page. This brings us to the Linear Regression: Save page. Check the box for Unstandardized under Residuals and then select Continue.

5. Select OK. The regression is performed and the output is produced on an Output1 page in the SPSS Viewer.[9] (Note that you may toggle back and forth between the SPSS Viewer and the SPSS Data Editor by clicking on the appropriate buttons at the bottom of the page or by minimizing screens.)

---

[9] The output produced will be slightly different from that shown in this book. SPSS output provided in this book was edited to simplify our discussion.

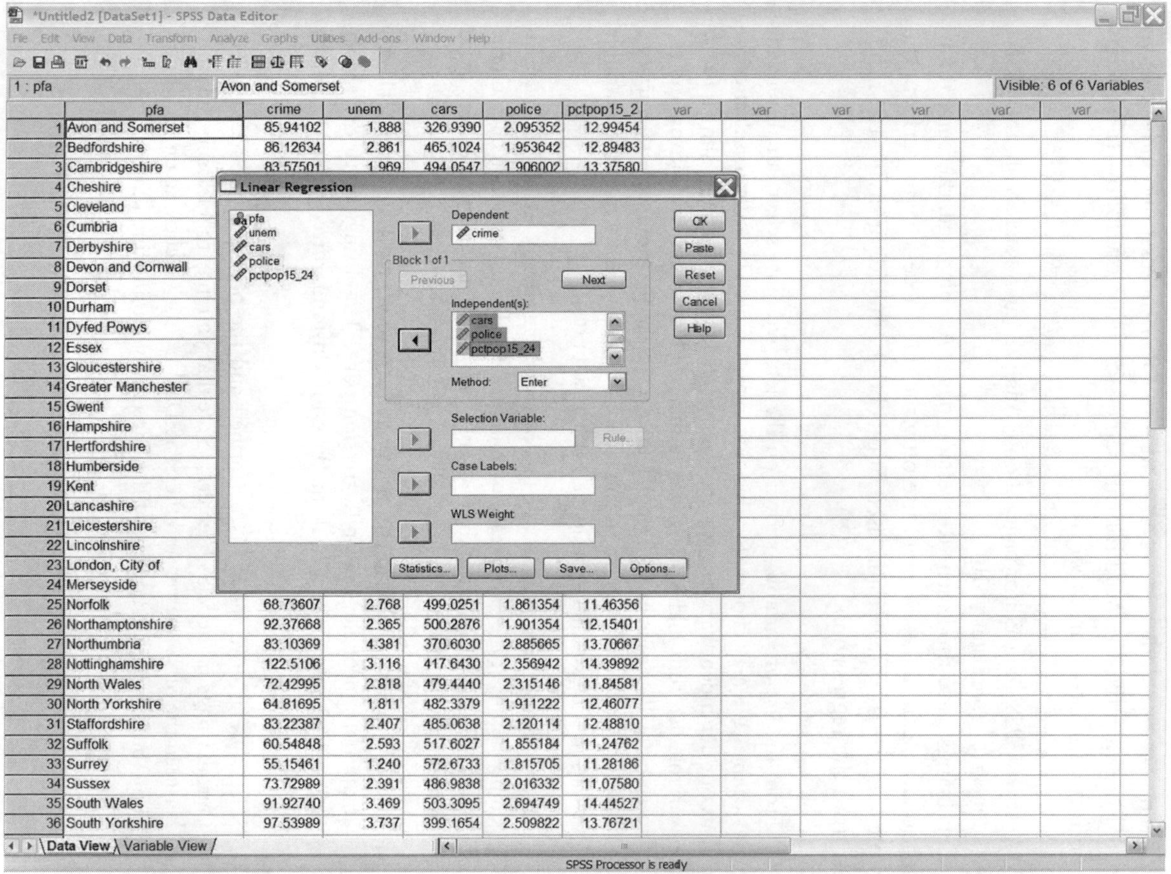

Figure B11

Appendix C

t Table

Table C1

	Confidence Level	50%	80%	90%	95%	98%	99%
df	Probability	0.5	0.2	0.1	0.05	0.02	0.01
1		1	3.078	6.314	12.706	31.821	63.657
2		0.816	1.886	2.92	4.303	6.965	9.925
3		0.765	1.638	2.353	3.182	4.541	5.841
4		0.741	1.533	2.132	2.776	3.747	4.604
5		0.727	1.476	2.015	2.571	3.365	4.032
6		0.718	1.44	1.943	2.447	3.143	3.707
7		0.711	1.415	1.895	2.365	2.998	3.499
8		0.706	1.397	1.86	2.306	2.896	3.355
9		0.703	1.383	1.833	2.262	2.821	3.25
10		0.7	1.372	1.812	2.228	2.764	3.169
11		0.697	1.363	1.796	2.201	2.718	3.106
12		0.695	1.356	1.782	2.179	2.681	3.055
13		0.694	1.35	1.771	2.16	2.65	3.012
14		0.692	1.345	1.761	2.145	2.624	2.977
15		0.691	1.341	1.753	2.131	2.602	2.947
16		0.69	1.337	1.746	2.12	2.583	2.921
17		0.689	1.333	1.74	2.11	2.567	2.898
18		0.688	1.33	1.734	2.101	2.552	2.878
19		0.688	1.328	1.729	2.093	2.539	2.861
20		0.687	1.325	1.725	2.086	2.528	2.845
21		0.686	1.323	1.721	2.08	2.518	2.831
22		0.686	1.321	1.717	2.074	2.508	2.819
23		0.685	1.319	1.714	2.069	2.5	2.807
24		0.685	1.318	1.711	2.064	2.492	2.797
25		0.684	1.316	1.708	2.06	2.485	2.787
26		0.684	1.315	1.706	2.056	2.479	2.779
27		0.684	1.314	1.703	2.052	2.473	2.771
28		0.683	1.313	1.701	2.048	2.467	2.763
29		0.683	1.311	1.699	2.045	2.462	2.756
30		0.683	1.31	1.697	2.042	2.457	2.75
40		0.681	1.303	1.684	2.021	2.423	2.704
50		0.679	1.299	1.676	2.009	2.403	2.678
60		0.679	1.296	1.671	2	2.39	2.66
70		0.678	1.294	1.667	1.994	2.381	2.648
80		0.678	1.292	1.664	1.99	2.374	2.639
90		0.677	1.291	1.662	1.987	2.368	2.632
100		0.677	1.29	1.66	1.984	2.364	2.626
infinity		0.674	1.282	1.645	1.96	2.326	2.576

NOTE: The values in the table are the *t* values for the given areas in both tails.

Appendix D

Answers to Problems

Chapter 1

1.1

a. The intercept, α, is the expected value of the dependent variable (Y) for the case when the independent variable (X) has a value of zero. In this example, the intercept is the expected wage for an individual with zero years of education. The expected sign for α, in this case, is a positive number indicating that someone with no education, but working, will earn a positive wage.

b. The coefficient to X, β, represents the average effect on Y for a one-unit increase in X. In this case, it shows how an individual's wage is expected to change for each additional year of education. We expect the sign for β to be positive, indicating that as an individual's education level increases, so should his or her wage, all else being equal.

c. Recall that the error term, u_i, captures all other effects that are not taken into account by our model. Thus, in this case, things that might affect an individual's wage, such as work experience, gender, race, and so on, may be present in the error term.

1.2

There are many factors that may affect the outcome of a presidential election besides the real growth rate. For example, other economic measures (e.g., inflation or unemployment) might have an impact on the number of votes that the incumbent party candidate receives. In addition, there could be advantages for presidents who run for reelection. These issues are taken up later in Chapters 4 and 5.

1.3

a. The parameter β represents the expected effect on Y for a one-unit increase in X, all else held constant. In this case, given that Y_i is a freshman college student's GPA and X_i is his or her SAT score, β is the expected increase in a student's GPA for a 1-point increase in his or her SAT score.

b. In this case, the error term captures other things that may affect a student's GPA, other than his or her SAT score. For example, things such as course load, age, gender, and involvement in extracurricular activities may have an influence on a student's GPA. (Some of these other factors are considered later in this book.) The error term may also capture any sort of measurement or recording errors on the Y and X variables.

Chapter 2

2.1

In order to answer this question, we can first calculate $\overline{X}$ and $\overline{Y}$, which are simply the average values of each variable. Adding the X column and dividing by the sample size of 5, we obtain $61/5 = 12.2$. Doing the same for the Y column, we obtain $50.5/5 = 10.1$. Using these values, we can now construct the following table:

X_i	Y_i	$(X_i - \overline{X})*(Y_i - \overline{Y})$	$(X_i - \overline{X})^2$
13	10.5	0.32	0.64
12	9.75	0.07	0.04
12	10.0	0.02	0.04
14	12.25	3.87	3.24
10	8.00	4.62	4.84
Sum: 61	50.5	8.9	8.8

Using the above table and Equation 2.3a, we have for b:

$$b = \frac{\sum_{i=1}^{n}(X_i - \overline{X})(Y_i - \overline{Y})}{\sum_{i=1}^{n}(X_i - \overline{X})^2} = \frac{8.9}{8.8} = 1.011.$$

And using Equation 2.3b for the intercept a:

$$a = \overline{Y} - b\overline{X} = 10.1 - (1.011 * 12.2) = -2.23.$$

Given these values for a and b, we can write the predicted equation as

$$\hat{Y}_i = -2.23 + 1.011\ X_i.$$

Thus, according to the predicted equation, if the value of X_i is zero, then the predicted value for the wage, Y_i, is approximately −$2.23 per hour. The interpretation of the intercept in this case is obviously meaningless because a negative wage is not possible. As for b, the coefficient to X_i, the value 1.011 tells us that each additional year of education tends to increase an individual's hourly wage by approximately $1.01 per hour, other things being equal.

2.2

Table A1 in Appendix A reports that Javy Lopez had 14 years of MLB experience by the end of 2005. Plugging this value into Equation 2.5b produces the following predicted salary:

$$\widehat{SALARY}_i = 0.765 + 0.656(14) = 9.949.$$

Comparing this prediction to Lopez's actual salary of $9.000 million, we find that the error in prediction is

$$e_i = Y_i - \hat{Y}_i = 9.000 - 9.949 = -0.949.$$

Thus, the OLS regression equation overpredicts Lopez's salary by approximately $0.949 million. This sizeable error is likely due to the fact that our two-variable regression model is overly simplistic as it does not take into account other important factors (such as his offensive and defensive abilities) that may explain Javy Lopez's salary. Chapter 4 introduces the "multiple regression model," which allows us to build more realistic models that include more than one X variable as a predictor for the dependent variable, Y.

2.3

a. The literal interpretation of the intercept, α, is the expected price for an SUV with zero horsepower. Obviously, however, this interpretation has no practical meaning because a vehicle with zero horsepower is not typically sold. As such, we have no meaningful expectation for the sign of α. The slope term, β, would show us the expected increase in SUV price for a one-unit increase in horsepower. Assuming that consumers would prefer more powerful cars, other things being equal, we would expect a positive value for β.

b. The SPSS results are shown in Table D1.

Table D1

Coefficients[a]

Model		Unstandardized Coefficients		Standardized Coefficients	t	Sig.
		B	Std. Error	Beta		
1	(Constant)	−18281.9	6150.555		−2.972	.005
	HORSEPOWER	222.815	24.609	.834	9.054	.000

a. Dependent Variable: MSRP

As noted, the intercept term has no reasonable interpretation. The coefficient for HORSEPOWER is 222.815, which tells us that, on average, an SUV's price increases by about $223 for a one-unit increase in horsepower, all else being equal.

2.4

a. The plot, created using Excel, is shown in Figure D1. As seen in the figure, there is no blatantly obvious relationship between GPA and SAT. The collection of points appears to slope upward slightly from left to right, indicating that GPA tends to increase as SAT score increases, other things being equal. This is a good example that illustrates that the naked eye is sometimes not capable of seeing subtle relationships between variables.

b. The OLS regression was performed using Excel, and the output appears in Table D2. We see under the column headed "Coefficients" that we have 0.672 for the intercept term and 0.002 for the coefficient to SAT. Thus, the intercept term tells us that if a student had an SAT score of zero, their predicted GPA would be 0.672. Once again, however, this is not meaningful as SAT scores are never equal to zero (the minimum possible score is 400, with a maximum possible of 1600 for the years covered by this data set). The estimated coefficient to SAT, 0.002, implies that for every 1-point increase in a student's SAT score,

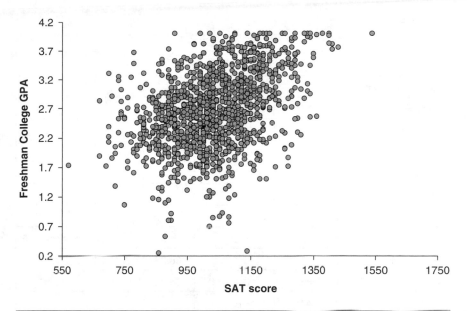

Figure D1

Table D2

SUMMARY OUTPUT				
	Coefficients	Standard Error	t stat	P value
Intercept	0.672	0.133	5.071	0.000
SAT	0.002	0.000	15.283	0.000

their freshman college gap increases by 0.002 GPA points. This is indeed a small effect, but a 1-point increase in a student's SAT score is rather small. For a 150-point increase in SAT (which is a little more than one standard deviation increase in SAT), our regression results would predict a 0.3-point increase in a student's GPA, which is a bit more substantial.

Chapter 3

3.1

The Excel output is shown in Table D3.

Table D3

SUMMARY OUTPUT					
Regression Statistics					
Multiple R	0.511				
R Square	0.261				
Adjusted R Square	0.244				
Standard Error	4.923				
Observations	45				
ANOVA					
	df	SS	MS	F	Significance F
Regression	1	368.233	368.233	15.192	0.000
Residual	43	1042.281	24.239		
Total	44	1410.514			
	Coefficients	Standard Error	t stat	P value	
Intercept	−5.127	3.611	−1.420	0.163	
EDUC	1.084	0.278	3.898	0.000	

The intercept term is approximately −5.13, meaning that a person with no education is expected to earn −$5.13 per hour. Obviously, this interpretation is not sensible. It should be noted that in the data set shown in Table A6, none of the observations has a zero value for education. Thus, even though our intercept term is technically required to define our sample regression line, it has no practical meaning in this case. The estimated coefficient to education (EDUC) is 1.08, indicating that as education increases by one year, an individual's hourly wage is expected to increase by about $1.08, other things being equal. The R^2 is reported as approximately 0.261, meaning that about 26.1% of the behavior (i.e., the variation) of Y is explained by our model; a rather poor fit.

3.2

a. Referring to Table D3, the estimated intercept term has a P value of approximately 0.163. Thus, because the P value is greater than the chosen level of significance for this test (i.e., 0.163 > 0.05), this means we cannot reject the hypothesis H_0: $\alpha = 0$. In other words, we cannot reject the hypothesis that the population's intercept term is equal to zero at the 5% significance (95% confidence) level.

b. Table D3 reports the *P* value for the coefficient to education as approximately 0.000 (rounding to three decimal places). Because this value is less than the chosen level of significance (i.e., 0.000 < 0.01), we can reject the hypothesis H_0: $\beta = 0$. That is, we can reject the hypothesis that the population's slope term is equal to zero at the 1% significance (99% confidence) level.

3.3

Table 3.4 reports the coefficient for *UNEM* as approximately 10.218 with an estimated standard error of about 1.829. Using these values and Equation 3.6b, where h in this case is 9, we have

$$t \text{ statistic} = \frac{b - h}{se(b)} = \frac{10.218 - 9}{1.829} = 0.666.$$

Given that we have 42 observations used in the regression, this means that there are 40 degrees of freedom left over (equal to the number of observations minus the number of estimated coefficients) for our hypothesis test. Viewing Table C1, we go down the column headed df (short for degrees of freedom) to row 40. We move across to the column headed 0.05 (given our significance level for the test is 5%) and find the *t* value 2.021. This is the value to which we compare the above *t* stat. Because the |*t* statistic| < *t* value (i.e., 0.666 < 2.021), this means that we cannot reject H_0: $\beta = 9$ at the 5% significance (95% confidence level). That is, we cannot reject the hypothesis that the population's true coefficient to *UNEM* is equal to 9.

3.4

The regression output is shown in Table D4.

The intercept is reported as 0.672 with a standard error of 0.133. Using Equation 3.6b, we have

$$t \text{ statistic} = \frac{b - h}{se(b)} = \frac{0.672 - 0.8}{0.133} = -0.962.$$

Our degrees of freedom in this case are 1200 − 2 = 1198. Looking at Table C1, we see that the values for "df" (the degrees of freedom) skip from

Table D4

Model Summary

Model	R	R Square	Adjusted R Square	Std. Error of the Estimate
1	.404[a]	.163	.162	.604

a. Predictors: (Constant), SAT

ANOVA[b]

Model		Sum of Squares	df	Mean Square	F	Sig.
1	Regression	85.078	1	85.078	233.567	.000[a]
	Residual	436.378	1198	.364		
	Total	521.456	1199			

a. Predictors: (Constant), SAT
b. Dependent Variable: GPA

Coefficients[a]

Model		Unstandardized Coefficients		Standardized Coefficients	t	Sig.
		B	Std. Error	Beta		
1	(Constant)	.672	.133		5.071	.000
	SAT	.002	.000	.404	15.283	.000

a. Dependent Variable: GPA

100 to infinity. We can also see that the t values change very little between 100 and infinity. Taking a more prudent view, we can use the t value for df equal to 100. Moving over to the column for the 95% confidence level (5% significance level), we see the value 1.984. Given that the absolute value of our t statistic is less than this t value (i.e., $|-0.962| < 1.984$), we cannot reject the hypothesis H_0: $\alpha = 0.8$.

Chapter 4

4.1

Table D5 shows the SPSS output of the regression shown in Equation 4.11, adding the variable EDUC (the percentage of a state's population that is 25 years or older with a high school degree or equivalent) as an independent variable.

Table D5

Model Summary

Model	R	R Square	Adjusted R Square	Std. Error of the Estimate
1	.751[a]	.564	.514	7.0123

a. Predictors: (Constant), *EDUC, RELIGION, PRICE, PICKET, INCOME*

ANOVA[b]

Model		Sum of Squares	df	Mean Square	F	Sig.
1	Regression	2794.014	5	558.803	11.364	.000[a]
	Residual	2163.612	44	49.173		
	Total	4957.626	49			

a. Predictors: (Constant), *EDUC, RELIGION, PRICE, PICKET, INCOME*

b. Dependent Variable: ABORTION

Coefficients[a]

Model		Unstandardized Coefficients		Standardized Coefficients	t	Sig.
		B	Std. Error	Beta		
1	(Constant)	12.553	14.816		.847	.401
	RELIGION	−.002	.082	−.002	−.021	.983
	PRICE	−.041	.022	−.197	−1.851	.071
	INCOME	.003	.000	.734	6.435	.000
	PICKET	−.126	.041	−.329	−3.084	.004
	EDUC	−.309	.197	−.182	−1.569	.124

a. Dependent Variable: ABORTION

a. The estimated coefficient for *EDUC* is −0.309, meaning that, from one state to another, as the percentage of a state's population that is 25 years or older with a high school degree (or equivalent) increases by 1 percentage point, the abortion rate tends to decrease by approximately 0.309, other things being equal.

b. Because the regression estimated in Table D5 has a different number of independent variables as compared to the one for Equation 4.11, the adjusted R^2 is the measure that we can use to compare the overall performance of the models. The adjusted R^2 for the model in Equation 4.11 is shown in Table 4.3 and is reported as 0.498. Table D5 reports an adjusted R^2 of 0.514. Thus, based on the adjusted R^2 measures, the model that includes *EDUC* is superior.

c. Reviewing the output shown in Table D5, the "Sig." value (analogous to Excel's "*P* value") for the coefficient to *EDUC* is 0.124. Given a significance level of 5%, because 0.124 > 0.05, we cannot reject the hypothesis that the population's coefficient to *EDUC* is truly zero. That is, we cannot reject the hypothesis that for the population data, *EDUC* has no effect on the abortion rate.

4.2

Table 4.2 shows the estimated coefficient for *GROWTH* to be 0.705 with a standard error of 0.217. Thus, using Equation 3.6b to calculate the appropriate t statistic, we find

$$t \text{ statistic} = \frac{b - h}{se(b)} = \frac{0.705 - 1.0}{0.217} = -1.359,$$

where h, the hypothesized value for the coefficient to *GROWTH*, is 1.0. Given a significance level of 10% and 20 degrees of freedom (23 observations minus 3 estimated parameters), the t value from Table C1 is shown as 1.725. Thus, because $|{-}1.359| < 1.725$, we cannot reject the hypothesis that the coefficient to *GROWTH* for the population's data is equal to 1.0.

4.3

Plugging in 10 for *YEARS*, 38.0 for *SLUGGING*, and 97.5 for *FIELDING* into Equation 4.7b, we find the predicted salary to be

$$\widehat{SALARY}_i = -30.913 + 0.298 (10) + 0.430 (38.0) + 0.157 (97.5) = 3.715.$$

That is, a player with 10 years of MLB experience, a career slugging average of 38.0, and a career fielding percentage of 97.5 is expected to make about \$3.7 million, according to our sample regression results.

4.4

a. The SPSS output for the regression is shown in Table D6.

Using the estimated coefficients provided, we can write the predicted equation, after rounding to two decimal places, as

Table D6

Model Summary

Model	R	R Square	Adjusted R Square	Std. Error of the Estimate
1	.553ª	.306	.273	4.8276

a. Predictors: (Constant), *EXPER, EDUC*

ANOVAᵇ

Model		Sum of Squares	df	Mean Square	F	Sig.
1	Regression	431.688	2	215.844	9.262	.000ª
	Residual	978.826	42	23.305		
	Total	1410.514	44			

a. Predictors: (Constant), *EXPER, EDUC*

b. Dependent Variable: WAGE

Coefficientsª

Model		Unstandardized Coefficients		t	Sig.
		B	Std. Error		
1	(Constant)	−9.399	4.386	−2.143	.038
	EDUC	1.263	.293	4.303	.000
	EXPER	.110	.067	1.650	.106

a. Dependent Variable: WAGE

$$\widehat{SALARY}_i = -9.40 + 1.26\,(EDUC_i) + 0.11\,(EXPER_i).$$

Interpreting our results, we see immediately that the intercept term, estimated as −9.40, is not sensible and warrants no interpretation. Again, the intercept is technically required to anchor our line, but given that $EDUC$ and $EXPER$ do not take on zero values in our data set, the intercept value is not meaningful. As for the coefficient to $EDUC$, the value of 1.26 suggests that on average, an additional year of education raises the hourly wage by $1.26, other things being equal. And for $EXPER$, the coefficient 0.11 implies that on average, an additional year of experience raises hourly wages by about 11 cents, all else being equal.

b. Observing the Sig. values shown in Table D6, we have 0.000 for *EDUC*; thus, we can reject the hypothesis H_0: $\beta_1 = 0$ at the 5% significance level (i.e., 0.000 < 0.05). As for *EXPER*, we have the Sig. value of 0.106; thus, we cannot reject the hypothesis H_0: $\beta_2 = 0$ at the 5% significance level (i.e., 0.106 > 0.05).

4.5

a. The Excel regression results are shown in Table D7.

As we can see, the negative coefficient to the intercept term has no sensible interpretation. The coefficient to horsepower, however, is positive as expected, and given its *P* value of approximately 0.000, it is statistically different from zero at the 5% level of significance (i.e., 0.000 < 0.05). The estimated coefficient is 244.212, implying that on average, one additional unit of horsepower increases the *MSRP* by about $244, all else being equal.

Regarding the engine size, the *P* value is about 0.429, indicating that this coefficient is *not* statistically different from zero at the 5% significance level (i.e., 0.429 > 0.05). Given that this coefficient is not statistically different from zero, any interpretation is meaningless. (Indeed, the negative value for this estimated coefficient is counterintuitive, but again, the coefficient is not statistically different from zero.)

b. Given that we have a different number of independent variables in the two models, the adjusted R^2 is the appropriate comparison (not the R^2). In the model with engine size, the adjusted R^2 is 0.683, which is smaller than the model without engine size (with an adjusted R^2 of 0.686), indicating that including engine size produces a worse fit.

4.6

a. We would expect that *HSRANK* would have a negative coefficient. This is because if someone is ranked number one in his or her class, then we would expect his or her freshman GPA to be, on average, greater than someone ranked number two in his or her class.

b. Table D8 reports the regression results using SPSS.

The negative coefficient supports our hypothesis in Part a. The estimated value of –0.003 implies that for every one-unit increase in *HSRANK*, the

Table D7

SUMMARY OUTPUT

Regression Statistics						
Multiple R	0.837					
R Square	0.700					
Adjusted R Square	0.683					
Standard Error	10383.083					
Observations	38					
ANOVA						
	df	SS	MS	F	Significance F	
Regression	2	8818600837.589	4409300418.795	40.899	0.000	
Residual	35	3773294680.227	107808419.435			
Total	37	12591895517.816				
	Coefficients	Standard Error	t Stat	P value		
Intercept	−15356.593	7182.197	−2.138	0.040		
HORSEPOWER	244.212	36.429	6.704	0.000		
ENGINE SIZE	−2204.770	2756.069	−0.800	0.429		

Table D8

Model Summary

Model	R	R Square	Adjusted R Square	Std. Error of the Estimate
1	.497[a]	.247	.245	.573

a. Predictors: (Constant), *HSRANK,* SAT

ANOVA[b]

Model		Sum of Squares	df	Mean Square	F	Sig.
1	Regression	128.576	2	64.288	195.869	.000[a]
	Residual	392.880	1197	.328		
	Total	521.456	1199			

a. Predictors: (Constant), *HSRANK,* SAT

b. Dependent Variable: GPA

Coefficients[a]

Model		Unstandardized Coefficients		Standardized Coefficients	t	Sig.
		B	Std. Error	Beta		
1	(Constant)	1.020	.129		7.885	.000
	SAT	.002	.000	.364	14.395	.000
	HSRANK	−.003	.000	−.291	−11.512	.000

a. Dependent Variable: GPA

student's GPA is expected to decrease by about 0.003 GPA units. The associated Sig. value for *HSRANK* is rounded to 0.000, and so we can conclude that it is statistically different from zero at the 5% level of significance (i.e., $0.000 < 0.05$).

c. The adjusted R^2 for the model with *HSRANK* is 0.245, whereas the model without *HSRANK* has an adjusted R^2 of 0.162. Thus, the model with *HSRANK* outperforms the one without it.

Chapter 5

5.1

a. The regression results are shown in Table D9.

Table D9

SUMMARY OUTPUT					
Regression Statistics					
Multiple R	0.813				
R Square	0.661				
Adjusted R Square	0.625				
Standard Error	0.821				
Observations	32				
ANOVA					
	df	SS	MS	F	Significance F
Regression	3	36.757	12.252	18.199	0.000
Residual	28	18.851	0.673		
Total	31	55.608			
	Coefficients	Standard Error	t stat	P value	
Intercept	−5.704	12.887	−0.443	0.661	
YEARS	0.112	0.036	3.069	0.005	
SLUGGING	0.093	0.026	3.622	0.001	
FIELDING	0.018	0.128	0.140	0.890	

The predicted equation is

$$\widehat{\ln SALARY_i} = -5.704 + 0.112\ (YEARS_i) + 0.093\ (SLUGGING_i) + 0.018\ (FIELDING_i)$$

b. The coefficient to *YEARS* (years of MLB experience) is shown as 0.112. Multiplying this by 100, we have 11.2, which means that an additional year of experience in MLB tends to increase salary by approximately 11.2%, other things being equal. The coefficient to *SLUGGING* (slugging average) is 0.093. Multiplying this coefficient by 100, we have 9.3; thus, an increase in the slugging average by one unit leads to approximately a 9.3% increase in salary, all else being equal. Finally, the coefficient to *FIELDING* (fielding percentage) is 0.018. This coefficient, however, is not statistically significant (it has a very large *P* value of 0.890), and thus any interpretation of its value would be meaningless.

Table D10

Model Summary

Model	R	R Square	Adjusted R Square	Std. Error of the Estimate
1	.746[a]	.557	.495	7.1501

a. Predictors: (Constant), *FUNDS, RELIGION, PRICE, PICKET, LAWS, INCOME*

ANOVA[b]

Model		Sum of Squares	df	Mean Square	F	Sig.
1	Regression	2759.306	6	459.884	8.996	.000[a]
	Residual	2198.319	43	51.124		
	Total	4957.626	49			

a. Predictors: (Constant), *FUNDS, RELIGION, PRICE, PICKET, LAWS, INCOME*

b. Dependent Variable: ABORTION

Coefficients[a]

Model		Unstandardized Coefficients		Standardized Coefficients		
		B	Std. Error	Beta	t	Sig.
1	(Constant)	−2.568	9.620		−.267	.791
	RELIGION	.026	.087	.033	.299	.766
	PRICE	−.047	.022	−.226	−2.092	.042
	INCOME	.002	.000	.603	5.042	.000
	PICKET	−.100	.041	−.262	−2.438	.019
	LAWS	−1.157	2.398	−.056	−.483	.632
	FUNDS	3.027	2.814	.130	1.076	.288

a. Dependent Variable: ABORTION

5.2

a. Table D10 shows the SPSS regression results.

The coefficient to *FUNDS* is 3.027, meaning that states that provide public funds for abortion services tend to have an abortion rate that is 3.027 higher than states that do not provide public funds for these services, all else being equal. Similarly, the coefficient to *LAWS* is −1.157, suggesting that states with laws that restrict access to abortion services (such as parental consent laws) and that are enforced tend to have an abortion rate that is 1.157 *less* than states that either do not have such laws or do not enforce them, other things being equal. (Note that these interpretations are provided while ignoring the issue of statistical significance. See Part C below.)

b. Because the model estimated in this problem has a greater number of X variables as compared to the one estimated for Equation 4.11, the *adjusted* R^2 should be used to compare these models. Table 4.3 reports an adjusted R^2 of 0.498, whereas the adjusted R^2 for the regression shown in Table D10 is 0.495; thus, by this measure, the model that includes the dummy variables does not outperform the original one. (Note that the R^2 for the present regression is 0.557, which is larger than the one shown in Table 4.3, reported as 0.539. Thus, this problem provides a good demonstration of the point raised in Chapter 4 that the R^2 may increase even if we add X variables to our model that are apparently not statistically important. This example illustrates why the adjusted R^2 should be used for comparing models that have a different number of X variables.)

c. Noting that the "Sig." values for the estimated coefficients for *LAWS* and *FUNDS* (shown as 0.632 and 0.288, respectively), are both larger than our significance level (i.e., 0.05), we cannot reject the hypothesis that they are statistically equal to zero. (This is not surprising, given our answer to Part *b* above.) In this light, the interpretations provided in Part a have little meaning.

5.3

The OLS results are shown in Table D11.

We can see from the output that, with the exception of the intercept and the coefficient to *INCUMBENT*, all of the P values are quite large, and thus we could not reject the hypothesis that the population coefficients are zero for the other variables. As a matter of practice, though, we can interpret all of the estimated coefficients. Starting with the intercept, we find that if all other variables took on a zero value (i.e., zero growth and inflation, and a nonincumbent), the incumbent party candidate is expected to receive 50.631% of the two-party vote. The effects of economic growth on Votes has two sources—the direct effect, shown as the coefficient to *GROWTH*, 0.645, and the coefficient for the interaction effect between *GROWTH* and *INCUMBENT*, 0.044. Thus, if the economy grows by 1 percentage point, then the incumbent party candidate is expected to gain about 0.645% of the two-party vote. However, if the incumbent party candidate is also, in fact, the incumbent, then the effects of a 1 percentage point increase in growth is equal to the sum of the *GROWTH* coefficient and the coefficient for the

Table D11

SUMMARY OUTPUT					
Regression Statistics					
Multiple *R*	0.816				
R Square	0.666				
Adjusted *R* Square	0.591				
Standard Error	4.360				
Observations	23				
ANOVA					
	df	SS	MS	F	Significance F
Regression	4	681.369	170.342	8.959	0.000
Residual	18	342.243	19.014		
Total	22	1023.612			
	Coefficients	Standard Error	t stat	P value	
Intercept	50.631	2.546	19.885	0.000	
GROWTH	0.645	0.440	1.465	0.160	
INFLATION	−0.484	0.377	−1.282	0.216	
INCUMBENT	4.290	1.986	2.160	0.045	
GROWTH* INCUMBENT	0.044	0.440	0.099	0.922	

interaction of GROWTH and INCUMBENT; thus, we have 0.645 + 0.044 = 0.689, or a 0.689 percentage point increase in the percentage of two-party votes. We have a similar interpretation of the effects of being the actual incumbent. The coefficient to INCUMBENT is shown as 4.290, implying that all else being equal, incumbents enjoy about a 4.3 percentage point increase in the percentage of two-party votes, as compared to nonincumbents. However, the *full effect* of being the incumbent also includes the interaction effect. Thus, we have 4.290 + 0.044(GROWTH). In this case, if the economy had grown by 1 percentage point and the incumbent party candidate is, in fact, the incumbent, then the expected gain from being the incumbent is 4.290 + 0.044(1) = 4.334 percentage points of the two-party vote. Finally, the interpretation of the coefficient to Inflation, shown as −0.484, is that all else being equal, the incumbent party candidate is expected to receive about 0.484 percentage points less of the two-party votes for every 1 percentage point increase in inflation. *But remember, these interpretations have little practical meaning because most of the estimated coefficients are not statistically different from zero at a reasonable significance level.*

5.4

a. Given the definition of the dummy variables, the base case (when all dummies have a zero value) is as follows: unmarried, non-black or Hispanic (e.g., white or Asian) males.

b. The Excel regression results are shown in Table D12.

Table D12

SUMMARY OUTPUT					
Regression Statistics					
Multiple R	0.637				
R Square	0.405				
Adjusted R Square	0.329				
Standard Error	4.637				
Observations	45				
ANOVA					
	df	SS	MS	F	Significance F
Regression	5	571.867	114.373	5.319	0.001
Residual	39	838.647	21.504		
Total	44	1410.514			
	Coefficients	Standard Error	t stat	P value	
Intercept	−5.999	4.484	−1.338	0.189	
EDUC	1.138	0.287	3.962	0.000	
EXPER	0.097	0.067	1.453	0.154	
FEMALE	−2.579	1.422	−1.813	0.078	
MARRIED	0.655	1.453	0.451	0.655	
BLK_HISP	−2.942	1.798	−1.636	0.110	

As we have seen before, the negative estimated coefficient for the intercept term has no meaningful interpretation. As for the estimated coefficient for *EDUC*, we have a value of about 1.14 with an associated *P* value of approximately 0.000. These results indicate that the coefficient is statistically different from zero at the 10% level of significance (i.e., 0.000 < 0.10), and the coefficient implies that for each added year of education, we expect the hourly wage to increase by about $1.14, all else being equal. *EXPER* has an estimated coefficient of about 0.10, implying that an additional year's worth of experience adds about 10 cents to the hourly wage, all else being equal. This interpretation is made with caution, however, as the *P* value indicates that the estimated coefficient is not statistically different from zero at the 10% level of significance (i.e., 0.154 > 0.10). The coefficient to *FEMALE* is approximately –2.58, indicating that females with the same education and experience as males tend to earn about $2.58 less per hour than males, all else being equal. This estimated coefficient is statistically different from zero at the 10% level, judging by the *P* value (i.e., 0.078 < 0.10). The coefficient to *MARRIED* is 0.65, indicating that married individuals tend to earn about 65 cents more than nonmarried individuals, all else being equal. But this coefficient is not statistically significant at the 10% level (i.e., 0.655 > 0.10). Finally, the coefficient to *BLK_HISP* is –2.94, implying that individuals who are black and/or Hispanic earn about $3 less than white (or Asian) individuals with the same education and experience. This result, however, is somewhat questionable given that the *P* value of about 0.11 is greater than 0.10, indicating that the coefficient is not statistically different from zero at the 10% level of significance.

5.5

a. The regression output from SPSS appears in Table D13.

We see that with *FEMALE*, the adjusted R^2 is 0.262, whereas without *FEMALE*, it is 0.245 (see Table D8); thus, based on adjusted R^2, adding *FEMALE* improves the model's performance. The "Sig." value for *FEMALE* is 0.000, so the coefficient is statistically different from zero at the 5% level of significance (i.e., 0.000 < 0.05).

b. The coefficient to *FEMALE* is 0.178, implying that, other things being equal, female students on average have a freshman GPA that is 0.178 GPA units greater than male students' GPA.

c. Adding the variable *ATHLETE* to the regression produces the results shown in Table D14.

Table D13

Model Summary

Model	R	R Square	Adjusted R Square	Std. Error of the Estimate
1	.514[a]	.264	.262	.566

a. Predictors: (Constant), *FEMALE, HSRANK,* SAT

ANOVA[b]

Model		Sum of Squares	df	Mean Square	F	Sig.
1	Regression	137.731	3	45.910	143.094	.000[a]
	Residual	383.725	1196	.321		
	Total	521.456	1199			

a. Predictors: (Constant), *FEMALE, HSRANK,* SAT

b. Dependent Variable: GPA

Coefficients[a]

Model		Unstandardized Coefficients		Standardized Coefficients	t	Sig.
		B	Std. Error	Beta		
1	(Constant)	.829	.133		6.242	.000
	SAT	.002	.000	.384	15.176	.000
	HSRANK	−.003	.000	−.273	−10.793	.000
	FEMALE	.178	.033	.135	5.342	.000

a. Dependent Variable: GPA

We see that the "Sig." value for *ATHLETE* is 0.347; thus, this variable does not seem to be important in explaining a student's freshman GPA, all else being equal. (This is also reflected in the adjusted R^2, which is approximately the same, 0.262, for both regressions.)

d. The output is shown in Table D15.

We see that the interaction term of *FEMALE* and *ATHLETE* is not statistically significant because the "Sig." value is 0.800; thus, there is no evidence that female athletes have statistically different GPAs from those who are not female athletes. If we interpret the coefficient for instructive purposes, it would mean that those students who are both female *and* athletes

Table D14

Model Summary

Model	R	R Square	Adjusted R Square	Std. Error of the Estimate
1	.514[a]	.265	.262	.566

a. Predictors: (Constant), *ATHLETE, FEMALE, HSRANK,* SAT

ANOVA[b]

Model		Sum of Squares	df	Mean Square	F	Sig.
1	Regression	138.015	4	34.504	107.532	.000[a]
	Residual	383.440	1195	.321		
	Total	521.456	1199			

a. Predictors: (Constant), *ATHLETE, FEMALE, HSRANK,* SAT

b. Dependent Variable: COLGPA

Coefficients[a]

Model		Unstandardized Coefficients		Standardized Coefficients	t	Sig.
		B	Std. Error	Beta		
1	(Constant)	.809	.135		6.015	.000
	sat	.002	.000	.387	15.154	.000
	hsrank	−.003	.000	−.276	−10.813	.000
	female	.181	.033	.137	5.403	.000
	athlete	.079	.083	.024	.942	.347

a. Dependent Variable: COLGPA

have a freshman GPA that is 0.046 GPA units higher than the GPA of those who are not female athletes.

Chapter 6

6.1

Estimating the regression using Excel gives us the results shown in Table D16.

Both the intercept and the coefficient to Time have *P* values, rounded to three decimal places, of 0.000, indicating that both are statistically different from zero at a very small significance level. The coefficient to Time is 0.092.

Table D15

Model Summary

Model	R	R Square	Adjusted R Square	Std. Error of the Estimate
1	.515[a]	.265	.262	.567

a. Predictors: (Constant), *FEMALExATHLETE,*
HSRANK, FEMALE, SAT, *ATHLETE*

ANOVA[b]

Model		Sum of Squares	df	Mean Square	F	Sig.
1	Regression	138.036	5	27.607	85.971	.000[a]
	Residual	383.420	1194	.321		
	Total	521.456	1199			

a. Predictors: (Constant), *FEMALExATHLETE, HSRANK, FEMALE,* SAT, *ATHLETE*
b. Dependent Variable: GPA

Coefficients[a]

Model		Unstandardized Coefficients		Standardized Coefficients	t	Sig.
		B	Std. Error	Beta		
1	(Constant)	.809	.135		6.013	.000
	SAT	.002	.000	.387	15.150	.000
	HSRANK	−.003	.000	−.276	−10.714	.000
	FEMALE	.179	.034	.136	5.278	.000
	ATHLETE	.065	.099	.020	.661	.509
	FEMALExATHLETE	.046	.182	.007	.253	.800

a. Dependent Variable: GPA

Given that we used the natural log of average MLB salary as our dependent variable, then multiplying the estimated coefficient to Time by 100 gives us $100 \times 0.092 = 9.20$. Thus, from one year to the next, average MLB wages tend to increase by approximately 9.2%.

6.2

Table D17 contains the regression results.

The adjusted R^2 without Time is 0.613 (see Table 5.3), whereas with Time it is 0.633; thus, the model with Time performs slightly better. The P value for Time, however, is 0.169 and thus is not statistically different from zero at a 10% level of significance (i.e., $0.169 > 0.10$).

Table D16

SUMMARY OUTPUT					
Regression Statistics					
Multiple R	0.987				
R Square	0.974				
Adjusted R Square	0.973				
Standard Error	0.169				
Observations	38				
ANOVA					
	df	SS	MS	F	Significance F
Regression	1	38.409	38.409	1341.902	0.000
Residual	36	1.030	0.029		
Total	37	39.440			
	Coefficients	Standard Error	t stat	P value	
Intercept	4.638	0.056	82.829	0.000	
Time	0.092	0.003	36.632	0.000	

6.3

Table D18 contains the regression results for reestimating Equation 6.5b but excluding the year dummies.

Comparing the results in Table D18 to those in Table 6.4, we see that the model with the year dummies has a higher adjusted R^2 (0.935) than the one without (0.914). In addition, we see that the estimated coefficients to UNEM, CARS, POLICE, and %pop15_24 have all changed. The coefficient to CARS is positive and now highly significant (with a Sig. value of 0.002). POLICE now has a much larger coefficient in absolute terms (–14.916 without year dummies, and –8.742 with them). And the coefficient to %pop15_24, which was insignificant in the regression with the year dummies, is now positive and strongly significant (with a Sig. value rounded to 0.000). The reason for these changes is that by excluding the year dummies, we do not control for year-specific events that may affect crime rates. As such, the remaining variables will tend to pick up some of the effects of these

Table D17

SUMMARY OUTPUT					
Regression Statistics					
Multiple R	0.836				
R Square	0.700				
Adjusted R Square	0.633				
Standard Error	4.132				
Observations	23				
ANOVA					
	df	SS	MS	F	Significance F
Regression	4	716.242	179.060	10.486	0.000
Residual	18	307.370	17.076		
Total	22	1023.612			
	Coefficients	Standard Error	t stat	P value	
Intercept	53.190	2.795	19.034	0.000	
GROWTH	0.731	0.194	3.769	0.001	
INFLATION	−0.527	0.302	−1.747	0.098	
INCUMBENT	4.163	1.818	2.289	0.034	
Time	−0.197	0.138	−1.433	0.169	

year-specific events if these remaining variables are correlated with the excluded year dummies. This is an example of the problem of "omitted variable bias" that can arise when a model does not include important explanatory variables and these excluded variables are correlated with the included variables. This topic is explored in greater detail in Chapter 7.

Chapter 7

7.1

Recall that high multicollinearity problems occur when two or more independent variables are almost perfectly linearly related. In this case, the inclusion of the independent variable GAMES, equal to the number of career

Table D18

Model Summary

Model	R	R Square	Adjusted R Square	Std. Error of the Estimate
1	.961[a]	.924	.914	6.9653080

a. Predictors: (Constant), pfa42, pfa41, pfa40, pfa39,
   pfa38, pfa37, pfa36, pfa35, pfa34, pfa33, pfa32,
   pfa31, pfa30, pfa29, pfa28, pfa27, pfa26, pfa25,
   pfa24, pfa23, pfa22, pfa21, pfa20, pfa19, pfa18,
   pfa17, pfa16, pfa15, pfa14, pfa13, pfa12, pfa11,
   pfa10, pfa9, pfa8, pfa7, pfa6, pfa5, pfa4, pfa2, pfa3,
   UNEM, CARS, %pop15_24, POLICE

Model Summary

Model	R	R Square	Adjusted R Square	Std. Error of the Estimate
1	.961[a]	.924	.914	6.9653080

a. Predictors: (Constant), pfa42, pfa41, pfa40, pfa39,
   pfa38, pfa37, pfa36, pfa35, pfa34, pfa33, pfa32,
   pfa31, pfa30, pfa29, pfa28, pfa27, pfa26, pfa25,
   pfa24, pfa23, pfa22, pfa21, pfa20, pfa19, pfa18,
   pfa17, pfa16, pfa15, pfa14, pfa13, pfa12, pfa11,
   pfa10, pfa9, pfa8, pfa7, pfa6, pfa5, pfa4, pfa2, pfa3,
   UNEM, CARS, %pop15_24, POLICE

(Continued)

games played, may be closely related to the independent variable *YEARS* (and perhaps to *YEARS SQUARED*). The reason for the close relationship is fairly straightforward: The more years a player plays in MLB, the more career games he will have played. It is not a perfect, linear relationship, as the number of games played each year is not likely to be exactly the same from one year to another for all players, but it may be close.

7.2

Table D19 reports the R^2 and Sig. F values for five auxiliary regressions.

As we can clearly see, all the auxiliary regressions have relatively high R^2 values and, based on the Sig. F values, are statistically significant regressions as a whole. Thus, we find clear evidence of high multicollinearity among these variables.

Table D18 (Continued)

Coefficients[a]

Model		Unstandardized Coefficients		Standardized Coefficients		
		B	Std. Error	Beta	t	Sig.
1	(Constant)	14.685	13.801		1.064	.288
	UNEM	1.972	.272	.192	7.261	.000
	CARS	.038	.012	.116	3.084	.002
	POLICE	-14.916	4.015	-.275	-3.715	.000
	%pop15_24	7.144	1.135	.295	6.292	.000
	pfa2	-11.838	3.347	-.076	-3.537	.000
	pfa3	-15.450	3.567	-.099	-4.331	.000
	pfa4	-23.676	3.713	-.152	-6.377	.000
	pfa5	20.997	4.100	.135	5.016	.000
	pfa6	-12.663	4.234	-.082	-2.991	.003
	pfa7	-13.111	3.508	-.084	-3.738	.000
	pfa8	-34.509	3.568	-.222	-9.671	.000
	pfa9	-21.501	3.898	-.138	-5.515	.000
	pfa10	-15.877	3.940	-.102	-4.029	.000
	pfa11	-53.831	3.474	-.347	-15.495	.000
	pfa12	-38.299	3.632	-.247	-10.544	.000
	pfa13	-4.848	3.758	-.031	-1.290	.198
	pfa14	37.213	4.325	.240	8.605	.000
	pfa15	-4.195	3.637	-.027	-1.153	.250
	pfa16	-26.855	3.389	-.173	-7.925	.000
	pfa17	-31.995	4.032	-.206	-7.935	.000
	pfa18	35.416	3.512	.228	10.083	.000
	pfa19	-19.489	3.477	-.125	-5.605	.000
	pfa20	-11.009	3.455	-.071	-3.186	.002
	pfa21	-18.071	3.591	-.116	-5.032	.000
	pfa22	-20.299	3.797	-.131	-5.346	.000
	pfa23	37.284	7.927	.240	4.703	.000
	pfa24	10.346	5.266	.067	1.965	.050
	pfa25	-23.309	3.802	-.150	-6.130	.000
	pfa26	-7.831	3.462	-.050	-2.262	.024
	pfa27	-.338	4.290	-.002	-.079	.937
	pfa28	29.317	3.524	.189	8.318	.000
	pfa29	-25.909	3.563	-.167	-7.272	.000
	pfa30	-23.700	3.579	-.153	-6.623	.000
	pfa31	-4.767	3.366	-.031	-1.416	.158
	pfa32	-34.700	3.815	-.223	-9.095	.000
	pfa33	-45.390	4.142	-.292	-10.959	.000
	pfa34	-11.270	3.832	-.073	-2.941	.003
	pfa35	-3.782	3.879	-.024	-.975	.330
	pfa36	5.548	3.770	.036	1.472	.142
	pfa37	-20.776	3.726	-.134	-5.576	.000
	pfa38	-18.247	3.805	-.117	-4.796	.000
	pfa39	-37.282	4.700	-.240	-7.933	.000
	pfa40	-24.283	3.710	-.156	-6.545	.000
	pfa41	10.518	4.641	.068	2.266	.024
	pfa42	20.736	3.756	.134	5.521	.000

a. Dependent Variable: CRIME

Table D 19

Auxiliary Equation	R^2	Sig. F
(1) HORSEPOWER = f(CARGO, MPG, SIZE, CYLINDERS)	0.664	0.000
(2) CARGO = f(MPG, SIZE, CYLINDERS, HORSEPOWER)	0.405	0.001
(3) MPG = f(CARGO, SIZE, CYLINDERS, HORSEPOWER)	0.758	0.000
(4) SIZE = f(CARGO, MPG, CYLINDERS, HORSEPOWER)	0.807	0.000
(5) CYLINDERS = f(CARGO, MPG, SIZE, HORSEPOWER)	0.820	0.000

7.3

Table D20 shows the SPSS output for the estimated model where the absolute values of the residuals from the original regression (see Equation 4.11) are used as the dependent variables in a Glejser test with *INCOME* as the explanatory variable.

The positive value for the estimated coefficient to *INCOME*, reported as 0.005, agrees with our graphical analysis of the residuals—namely, that the residuals tend to increase in absolute size as *INCOME* increases. The t statistic for *INCOME* is reported as 2.44 with an associated Sig. value of 0.018; thus, this indicates that the coefficient to *INCOME* is statistically different from zero at better than the 5% significance (95% confidence) level. In other words, there appears to be a positive, significant relationship between the absolute value of the residuals and *INCOME*, which is evidence of heteroscedasticity.

7.4

The plot of the residuals from the OLS estimation of Equation 5.10 is shown in Figure D2.

Although the plot exhibits somewhat of a wave pattern, we do not witness long strings of positive and negative errors, and thus there is no obvious autocorrelation problem in this model. (The Durbin-Watson test, mentioned in footnote 18 of Chapter 7, also confirms the conclusion that there is no evidence of autocorrelation.)

7.5

The two regressions, one including *EDUCATION* and one without it, are reported in Table D21.

Table D20

Model Summary

Model	R	R Square	Adjusted R Square	Std. Error of the Estimate
1	.332[a]	.110	.092	3.96716

a. Predictors: (Constant), *INCOME*

ANOVA[b]

Model		Sum of Squares	df	Mean Square	F	Sig.
1	Regression	93.713	1	93.713	5.954	.018[a]
	Residual	755.441	48	15.738		
	Total	849.154	49			

a. Predictors: (Constant), *INCOME*

b. Dependent Variable: ABSOLUTE RESIDUAL

Coefficients[a]

Model		Unstandardized Coefficients		Standardized Coefficients	t	Sig.
		B	Std. Error	Beta		
1	(Constant)	−4.099	3.916		−1.047	.300
	INCOME	.0005	.000	.332	2.440	.018

a. Dependent Variable: ABSOLUTE RESIDUAL

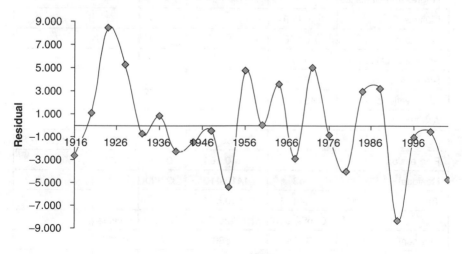

Figure D2

Table D21

SUMMARY OUTPUT: INCLUDING *EDUCATION*					
Regression Statistics					
Multiple *R*	0.553				
R Square	0.306				
Adjusted *R* Square	0.273				
Standard Error	4.828				
Observations	45				
ANOVA					
	df	SS	MS	F	Significance *F*
Regression	2	431.688	215.844	9.262	0.000
Residual	42	978.826	23.305		
Total	44	1410.514			
	Coefficients	Standard Error	*t* stat	*P* value	
Intercept	−9.399	4.386	−2.143	0.038	
EDUCATION	1.263	0.293	4.303	0.000	
EXPERIENCE	0.110	0.067	1.650	0.106	

SUMMARY OUTPUT: EXCLUDING *EDUCATION*					
Regression Statistics					
Multiple *R*	0.009				
R Square	0.000				
Adjusted *R* Square	−0.023				
Standard Error	5.727				
Observations	45				
ANOVA					
	df	SS	MS	F	Significance *F*
Regression	1	0.104	0.104	0.003	0.955
Residual	43	1410.410	32.800		
Total	44	1410.514			
	Coefficients	Standard Error	*t* stat	*P* value	
Intercept	8.579	1.586	5.410	0.000	
EXPERIENCE	0.004	0.073	0.056	0.955	

We can see that the models perform very differently overall. With *EDU-CATION*, the model produces a statistically significant regression (with a Sig. *F* of 0.000), but when *EDUCATION* is removed, the model is no longer significant. In terms of the coefficient to *EXPERIENCE*, it is 0.110 with *EDUCATION*, but 0.004 when *EDUCATION* is removed. The fact that the coefficient to *EDUCATION* fell so strongly is likely due to omitted variable bias. Table 7.6 can serve as our guide. First, letting X_1 be *EDUCATION* and X_2 be *EXPERIENCE*, and assuming that the coefficient to *EXPERIENCE* should be positive (i.e., wages increase with experience, all else being equal), then the question becomes, What kind of relationship would education and experience likely have? These two variables are likely to be negatively correlated. That is, the more time someone spends in school, then the less time they have to gain work experience. Indeed, the computed correlation between *EDUCATION* and *EXPERIENCE* is −0.369.[1] Thus, according to Table 7.6, the coefficient to *EXPERIENCE* should be biased downward when *EDUCATION* is excluded, which is what we found.

---

[1] The correlation was computed using Excel by choosing Tools from the main menu, then Data Analysis, and then Correlation.

Glossary

Adjusted R^2 The R^2 adjusted downward to take into account the number of independent variables included in a regression model. It can be used for comparing the goodness of fit of two regression models when they have the same dependent variable, but a different number of independent variables. (See R^2)

Alternative hypothesis Used in hypothesis testing, this hypothesis is offered as an alternative case to the "null" hypothesis, which is typically the focus of a hypothesis test. (See Null hypothesis)

ANOVA An acronym for "ANalysis Of VAriance," which is the breakdown of the total variation of the dependent variable into its two components: the variation explained by the regression and the variation that is unexplained (or the "residual" variation).

Autocorrelation Also known as "serial correlation," this is the case where the error term from one period in a regression is correlated with the error term from the previous period. If the relationship is a positive one, then this is the case of "positive autocorrelation"; if the errors are negatively correlated, then this is referred to as "negative autocorrelation."

Auxiliary regression Used to test for the presence of near-perfect multicollinearity. An independent variable that is suspected of being a nearly perfect function of one or more other independent variables is regressed against these independent variables. If the resulting regression is statistically significant (based on an F test), then this provides evidence of near-perfect multicollinearity.

Bivariate linear regression model (See Two-variable linear regression model)

BLUE An acronym for "Best Linear Unbiased Estimator." An estimator that is BLUE is the "best" in the sense that compared to all other linear, unbiased estimators, the one in question has the smallest variance for the estimated parameter(s).

Correlation coefficient A measure of the degree to which two variables are linearly associated. The coefficient ranges from -1 to $+1$, where a value of

−1 means that two variables are perfectly negatively correlated; a value of +1 means they are perfectly positively correlated. A value of 0 means that the two variables are not linearly associated. (See Covariance)

Covariance A statistical measure showing whether two variables tend to move together. A positive value for covariance indicates that if one variable increases, the other tends to increase, too. A negative value indicates that as one variable increases, the other tends to decrease. (Note: This measure is related to the correlation coefficient. The correlation coefficient, however, shows the *strength* of a linear association whereas covariance simply shows the *direction* of the relationship.)

Cross-sectional data set A set of data that is collected for one point in time. For example, stock prices on a selection of 100 stocks, for a given point in time. (See Time series data set; Pooled data set)

Degrees of freedom Equal to the number of observations in a sample minus the number of estimated parameters. The degrees of freedom represent the remaining amount of information in a sample of data that can be used for other purposes, such as hypothesis testing.

Dependent variable In a regression model, it is the variable that we are trying to explain. It is assumed that the dependent variable, sometimes referred to as the "Y" variable, is a function of the independent variable(s), which are often called the "X" variable(s).

Dummy variable Also called an "indicator" or "categorical" variable. These variables are created to indicate whether or not something is true. For example, if a sample of data contains observations on both male and female respondents, a dummy variable can be introduced taking the value of 1 if a respondent is female and 0 if the respondent is male. Note that if there are m separate categories, then only $m - 1$ dummy variables are needed to cover all categories.

Econometrics The literal translation is "economic measurement." Econometrics is a branch of study that uses regression analysis to test theoretical models in economics.

Error term The difference between the *actual* value of an observation minus the *predicted* value for that observation. The error term captures all factors, including purely random ones, that a regression model has failed to take into account. (See Residual)

F statistic A statistic used to perform an F test of significance.

F test of significance In a multiple regression model, the F test of significance tests the hypothesis that all coefficients to the independent (X) variables are simultaneously equal to zero. That is, the F test of significance tests for the statistical significance of the regression *as a whole*. (This test can also be performed for subsets of independent variables and for nonzero hypotheses.)

Fixed effects In a panel data set, the fixed effects refer to the unobserved, time-invariant factors associated with cross-sectional units that appear in the panel data set.

Forecast Using a sample regression model to predict the value of the dependent variable for a given value of the independent variable(s).

Gauss-Markov theorem A theorem that proves that if the linear regression model assumptions are satisfied (see Chapter 2), then the ordinary least-squares estimator has the least variance as compared to any other linear, unbiased estimator (i.e., OLS is BLUE).

Glejser test This is a test for nonconstant error variance. The first step involves performing an OLS regression and saving the residuals. The second step is to run another OLS regression where the absolute value of the errors from the first regression is the dependent variable and one of the original model's X variables (the one we suspect is the source of the nonconstant error variance) is the independent variable. If the coefficient to the X variable in this second regression is statistically different from zero, we have evidence of nonconstant error variance.

Heteroscedastic errors Also known as nonconstant error variance. The case where the variance of the error terms *is not* constant throughout the population regression line. (See Homoscedastic errors)

Homoscedastic errors The case where the variance of the error terms *is* constant throughout the population regression line. (See Heteroscedastic errors)

Independent variable(s) In a regression model, the variable(s) that determine, in part, the value of the dependent variable. Also known as "X" or "right-hand side" or "predictor" variables.

Interaction variable(s) These are independent variables that are created by multiplying two or more existing independent variables.

Linear A regression function is considered linear if all the coefficients (i.e., the βs of a population regression function) enter the equation with the power 1.

Model specification error The case where the regression model is improperly specified. Model misspecification can occur in a number of ways, such as omitting a variable from the model that theoretically should be included, including a variable that theoretically should not be included, or using the wrong functional form for the model.

Multicollinearity A problem where one of the independent variables is related to one or more of the other independent variables. The extreme case of *perfect multicollinearity* occurs when one of the independent variables is an exact, linear function of one or more of the independent variables.

In this extreme case, ordinary least-squares estimates of the regression model coefficients are not possible.

Multiple regression A regression model with more than one independent variable.

Nonconstant error variance (See Heteroscedastic errors)

Normality assumption In the context of regression models, it is the assumption that the stochastic error term, u_i, follows a normal probability distribution function.

Null hypothesis Used in hypothesis testing, this hypothesis is typically the focus of the test. It is tested against the "alternative" hypothesis. (See Alternative hypothesis)

Omitted variable bias The case when a relevant X variable is excluded from an OLS regression and, if it is correlated with included X variables(s), the resulting estimated coefficient(s) of the included X variable(s) is biased.

Ordinary least-squares (OLS) A method for estimating the coefficients of a sample regression model. The coefficients are chosen such that the sum of the squared residuals is minimized.

P value Used in hypothesis testing to test whether a sample estimate of a coefficient is statistically different from zero. It represents the probability of achieving the estimated coefficient for the sample at hand if the population's coefficient were zero. If the P value is less than the chosen level of significance, then the zero hypothesis is rejected.

Panel data set A data set in which the *same* cross section of data is pooled across time; for example, data collected for the 50 United States for a period of years.

Pooled data set A data set in which cross sections of data are pooled across time. The cross-sectional units may not be the same for each period. (See Cross-sectional data set; Time series data set)

Population regression function A functional relationship between the dependent and independent variable(s) for a population (as opposed to a sample) data set. (See Sample regression function)

Prais-Winsten estimation A method of estimating a regression model in the presence of autocorrelation. The procedure uses the residuals from the OLS regression estimation to discover the systematic component in the errors and then this information is used to refine the estimates of the coefficients.

R^2 (R Squared) Equal to the proportion of the variation in the dependent variable explained by a sample regression model. It is a measure of the overall goodness of fit for a sample regression function where values close to 1 represent a "good" fit and values close to 0 represent a "poor" fit.

Residual The difference between the *actual* value of an observation minus the *predicted* value for that observation in a sample regression. The residual (denoted with a lowercase "*e*" in this book) is similar to the error term (denoted with a lowercase "*u*") except the former is typically used for sample regression functions whereas the latter is used for the population regression function. (Note: In this book, both terms are used more or less interchangeably, where the context of the discussion determines whether they are population or sample regression function errors; See Error term)

Sample regression function The functional relationship between the dependent variable and one or more independent variables for a sample of data (as opposed to that of the population data). (See Population regression function)

Significance level (Sig; Same as *P* value.)

Significance *F* (Sig.) The Significance *F* (or Sig. for short) shows the probability of obtaining the estimated values of the X coefficients from a *sample* regression if it were true that all the *population's* X coefficients are simultaneously equal to zero. If the Significance F is less than our chosen level of significance, then we can conclude that the model *as a whole* is statistically significant in explaining the values of the dependent variable. (See *F* test of significance)

Spurious regression A problem where a regression of one time series variable (say, X_t) on another (say, Y_t) produces what appears to be a statistically significant regression when in fact the variables are not causally related.

Standard error Equal to the positive square root of variance. A measure of the typical difference between the value of a random variable and the random variable's mean. (See Variance)

Stochastic Variables or processes that are inherently random (i.e., not deterministic or exact).

***t* statistic (*t* stat)** A statistic that can be used to test hypotheses over estimated coefficients from a sample of data. Typically used to test the significance of separate estimated X coefficients. Generally, the larger the *t* value, the more likely it is that the estimated coefficient is statistically important. (See *P* value, *t* value)

***t* value** Used in conjunction with a *t* statistic to conduct tests of hypotheses for sample data results. Given a chosen level of significance, if the absolute value of the *t* statistic is greater than the given *t* value (obtained from a table of *t* values), then the hypothesis under consideration (i.e., the null hypothesis) can be rejected. (See *t* statistic)

Time index A variable created for use in estimating time trends. A time index assigns a number to each period's observation of a dependent variable.

The time index can then be used as an independent variable in a regression explaining the values of the dependent variable across time.

Time series data set A data set that records values of a variable across time; for example, monthly sales figures for a single firm. (See Cross-sectional data set; Pooled data set)

Trend An estimate of how a dependent variable tends to behave over time. A *positive* trend suggests that a dependent variable tends to increase over time, and a *negative* trend suggests that a dependent variable tends to decrease over time. Trends can be used in forecasting. (See Forecast)

Two-variable linear regression model A linear regression model that has an intercept term and one slope coefficient (i.e., only one independent variable). (See Multiple regression)

Unbiased In repeated sampling, if the mean value of a sample estimate is equal to a population's parameter, then the sample estimate is said to be an unbiased estimator of the population's parameter.

Variance A measure of the dispersion or spread of a random variable around its mean. For a sample of data, it is equal to the sum of squared deviations for a random variable from its mean, divided by the degrees of freedom.

Weighted least-squares A regression method used to correct for nonconstant error variance. The method first weights each observation on the dependent and independent variables according to their variance, then a least-squares estimation is performed on the weighted data. (See Nonconstant error variance)

References

Aldrich, J. H., & Nelson, F. D. (1984). *Linear probability, logit, and probit models.* Beverly Hills, CA: Sage.

Becker, G. (1968). Crime and punishment: An economics approach. *Journal of Political Economy, 76,* 175–209.

Berk, K. N., & Carey, P. (2000). *Data analysis with Microsoft Excel.* Pacific Grove, CA: Duxbury.

Berry, W. D. (1993). *Understanding regression assumptions.* Newbury Park, CA: Sage.

Bridgeman, B., McCamley, L., & Ervin, N. (2000). *Predictions of freshman grade point average from the revised and recentered SAT I: Reasoning test* (Research Report No. 2000–1). New York: The College Board.

Camara, W. J., & Echternacht, G. (2000). *The SAT I and high school grades: Utility in predicting success in college* (Research Notes RN-10). New York: The College Board, Office of Research and Development.

DeMaris, A. (1992). *Logit modeling: Practical applications.* Newbury Park, CA: Sage.

Diebold, F. X. (2004). *Elements of forecasting* (3rd ed.). Cincinnati, OH: South-Western College Publishing.

Donohue, J. J., III, & Levitt, S. D. (2001). The impact of legalized abortion on crime. *Quarterly Journal of Economics, 116*(2), 379–420.

Einspruch, E. L. (2005). *An introductory guide to SPSS® for Windows®* (2nd ed.). Thousand Oaks, CA: Sage.

Fair, R. C. (1996, Summer). Econometrics and presidential elections. *Journal of Economic Perspectives,* pp. 89–102.

Freeman, R. (1999). The economics of crime. In O. Ashenfelter & D. Card (Eds.), *Handbook of labor economics* (Vol. 3). Amsterdam: Elsevier North-Holland.

Geary, R. C. (1970). Relative efficiency of count of sign changes for assessing residual autoregression in least squares regression. *Biometrika, 57,* 123–127.

Glejser, H. (1969). A new test for heteroskedasticity. *Journal of the American Statistical Association, 64,* 316–323.

Greene, W. H. (2003). *Econometric analysis* (5th ed.). Upper Saddle River, NJ: Prentice Hall.

Gujarati, D. N. (2003). *Basic econometrics* (4th ed.). New York: McGraw-Hill-Irwin.

Hardy, M. A. (1993). *Regression with dummy variables.* Newbury Park, CA: Sage.

Judge, G., Hill, C., Griffiths, W., & Lee, T. (1985). *The theory and practice of econometrics*. New York: Wiley.

Kahane, L. H. (2000). Antiabortion activities and the market for abortion services: Protest as a disincentive. *American Journal of Economics and Sociology, 59,* 463–485.

Kahane, L. H. (2005). Abortion economics. In S. Bowmaker (Ed.), *Economics uncut: A complete guide to life, death and misadventure*. Cheltenham, UK: Edward Elgar.

Kramer, G. H. (1971). Short-term fluctuations in U.S. voting behavior, 1896–1964. *American Political Science Review, 65,* 131–143.

Liao, T. F. (1994). *Interpreting probability models: Logit, probit, and other generalized linear models*. Thousand Oaks, CA: Sage.

Medoff, M. H. (1988). An economic analysis of the demand for abortions. *Economic Inquiry, 26*(2), 353–359.

Menard, S. (1995a). *Applied logistic regression analysis*. Thousand Oaks, CA: Sage.

Menard, S. (1995b). *Longitudinal research*. Thousand Oaks, CA: Sage.

Prais, S. J., & Winsten, C. B. (1954). Trend estimators and serial correlation. *Cowles Commission Discussion Paper No. 383,* Chicago.

Rothstein, J. (2004). College performance predictions and the SAT. *Journal of Econometrics, 121,* 297–317.

Scully, G. W. (1974, December). Pay and performance in Major League Baseball. *American Economic Review,* pp. 915–930.

Stigler, G. J. (1973, May). General economic conditions and national elections. *American Economic Review,* pp. 160–167.

Thorn, J., & Palmer, P. (Eds.). (1997). *Total baseball: The official encyclopedia of Major League Baseball*. New York: Viking.

U.S. Bureau of the Census. (1993). *Statistical abstract of the United States*. Washington, DC: Author.

Witt, R., Clarke, A., & Fielding, N. (1999). Crime and economic activity: A panel data approach. *British Journal of Criminology, 39,* 391–400.

Wooldridge, J. M. (2002). *Econometric analysis of cross section and panel data*. Cambridge, MA: MIT Press.

Wooldridge, J. M. (2006). *Introductory econometrics: A modern approach* (3rd ed.). Mason, OH: Thomson/South-Western.

Zimbalist, A. (1992). Salaries and performance: Beyond the Scully model. In P. M. Sommers (Ed.), *Diamonds are forever: The business of baseball*. Washington, DC: The Brookings Institution.

Index

About the Author

Leo H. Kahane is a Professor of Economics at California State University, East Bay. He earned his BA degree in economics from the University of California, Berkeley, and his PhD in economics from Columbia University. He has authored numerous book chapters and published articles in economics journals. He is also the founder and editor of the *Journal of Sports Economics*. He and his wife, Cathy, live in Oakland, California, with their two sons, Jacob and Matthew Zoe.